4-29-81

S0-BSI-186

THE
BOATING
DICTIONARY
Sail and Power

THE
BOATING
DICTIONARY
Sail and Power

John V. Noel, Jr.,

Captain, U.S. Navy (Ret.)

LIBRARY
SEMINOLE COMMUNITY COLLEGE

REC. APR 21 1982

SANFORD, FLORIDA
32771

VAN NOSTRAND REINHOLD COMPANY
NEW YORK   CINCINNATI   ATLANTA   DALLAS   SAN FRANCISCO
LONDON   TORONTO   MELBOURNE

Van Nostrand Reinhold Company Regional Offices:
New York   Cincinnati   Atlanta   Dallas   San Francisco

Van Nostrand Reinhold Company International Offices:
London   Toronto   Melbourne

Copyright © 1981 by Litton Educational Publishing, Inc.

Library of Congress Catalog Card Number: 80-19804
ISBN: 0-442-26048-2

All rights reserved. No part of this work covered by the copyright hereon may
be reproduced or used in any form or by any means—graphic, electronic, or
mechanical, including photocopying, recording, taping, or information storage
and retrieval systems—without permission of the publisher.

Manufactured in the United States of America

Published by Van Nostrand Reinhold Company
135 West 50th Street, New York, N.Y. 10020

Published simultaneously in Canada by Van Nostrand Reinhold Ltd.

15 14 13 12 11 10 9 8 7 6 5 4 3 2 1

Library of Congress Cataloging in Publication Data

Noel, John Vavasour, 1912–
    The boating dictionary, sail and power.

    1. Boats and boating—Dictionaries. I Title.
GV775.N58   797.1'03   80–19804
ISBN 0-442-26048-2

To
my lovely seafaring daughter
Joy Noel McVay
who may finally decide to say:
"down below"
instead of: "downstairs."

Preface

The 3000 words selected here as being of interest to boat enthusiasts cover a wide range of maritime subjects. Most are directly related to powerboats and sailboats and reflect current usage, often different from their classic origins. Others relate to the more obvious features and characteristics of the ocean environment. Words relating to navigation, piloting, weather, ocean currents, tide, and common mammals, birds, and fish of the sea are included but not in great depth. Many sailors may never have the opportunity to cruise offshore but that adventurous world may intrigue them. Most amateur mariners spend months ashore for every month at sea or on a lake or river but all can share the experiences of others through reading their stories. This book should assist all in understanding the language of small-boat writers. For a general maritime reference book see the *VNR Dictionary of Ships and the Sea.*

For those who build boats or have one built for them there are included basic boat construction terms.

In view of the large number of electronic devices that now make even day cruising safer and more enjoyable there are included the basic words encountered. As fiberglass and stainless steel make boat maintenance much simpler such gadgets as depthfinders, radios, radars, relatively cheaper and more reliable every year, now demand a major share of an owner's attention.

This book is only a dictionary—it defines words but does not explain how. Standard words, like overhaul, are defined only in relation to their use in boating. Compound terms are usually listed under the noun unless the adjective is the distinctive word as it is in *apparent wind.* Nautical words used in definitions are defined themselves elsewhere in the book unless they can be found in a standard dictionary.

British terms are included or referred to only to avoid confusion or when the words seem to be heard on our side of the Atlantic. There is some evidence that both our language and that of our cousins abroad is becoming enriched by the adoption of nautical words of the other, including the Canadians and the Australians. The tremendous growth of class racing has undoubtedly been a major factor in developing a universal sailor's English. It has also resulted in a reduced emphasis on regional differences in the United States. Such differences do exist, however, and the reader's understanding is asked if the words he hears in his homeport do not always match those herein.

I acknowledge with appreciation the valuable assistance of Dr. John S. Letcher Jr. of Southwest Harbor, Maine, whose careful review of the manuscript has contributed so much. Thanks also to Bob Bavier of Yachting for his help with *boardboat*.

Comments and criticism will be received with appreciation through the publisher and will be a positive contribution to future editions.

John V. Noel, Jr.

A

aback. A sail is aback when sheeted to windward causing a braking effect on the ship's motion or when the wind strikes it on what has been the lee side. A ship is thus taken aback and may be forced astern. *See also* back.

abaft. Towards the stern; used by a seaman instead of aft of.

abaft the beam. Behind a horizontal line drawn at the center of and perpendicular to, the fore-and-aft axis of the ship.

abeam. The direction off to the side of a ship, midway between dead ahead and dead astern, that is at right angles to the middle of the ship.

able. Used in seaman's language it describes a ship as capable, seaworthy and well-equipped.

able bodied seaman (AB). An experienced deck hand, superior to an ordinary seaman: one who can "reef, hand, and steer." A rank in the Merchant Service.

aboard. In or on any ship or station. A sailor properly serves *in* a ship.

about. To go about or come about is to tack in a sailboat, i.e., to steer the bow into and then across or through the eye of the wind in order to have the wind blow against the other side of the sail.

abreast. By the side of. A ship may lie abreast, or alongside, another.

ABS. Acrylonitrile Butadiene Styrene, a plastic used to mold small boats. Also the American Bureau of Shipping.

absence flag or indicator. A flag or light that shows the absence of the ship's owner, master, or commanding officer; also called an absentee. In a yacht it is a small, blue, rectangular flag during the day, and a blue light at night.

absentee. *See* absence flag.

ABYC. American Boat & Yacht Council.

acceleration of the tide. *See* tide.

accomodation ladder. Portable steps from the gangway (access to the ship) to the water with platforms at the top and bottom. Sometimes called a gangway ladder but this term should never refer to a gangway. *See* gangway, ladder.

Act of God. An expression used in marine and other insurance and in chartering to indicate a misfortune or loss which could not have been prevented by taking reasonable precautions. Force majeure has a similar meaning.

adjustable pitch propeller. A propeller whose blades can be adjusted to increase, decrease, or reverse the angle at which they push the water. It permits the use of a constant-speed engine. *See* variable pitch propeller.

admiralty. The system of jurisprudence relating to both civil and criminal maritime law. Admiralty courts have jurisdiction over all matters relating to the sea. In the U.S. the Constitution grants such jurisdiction to all navigable waters, including the high seas, the Great Lakes, and navigable rivers. The U.S. jurisdiction covers all maritime contracts and other legal matters. In other countries such jurisdiction usually extends only to the sea below the low water mark in tidal waters.

adrift. Floating free upon the waters, neither moored nor anchored in any way, nor under any propulsive power. In Naval usage it means not properly stowed.

advance. Distance a ship continues to travel on its original course while turning; measured from the point at which the rudder was put over, to the point where the ship or boat has arrived at its new course.

advance staysail. A light 4-sided staysail set above the main staysail in a schooner-rigged boat. *See also* staysail.

advantage. A tackle is rigged or rove to advantage when the moving block holds the hauling part, thus giving maximum power. If the hauling part leads to the fixed block, there is less mechanical advantage and thus the tackle is rigged to disadvantage.

advection fog. Fog formed at sea by warm humid air over cold water.

adze. A hand wood-working tool with the cutting edge set at right angles to the handle in the horizontal plane. Used by boatwrights for trimming planks and timbers, it was the principal tool of the old-time builders of wooden ships.

A-frame. A triangular tubular metal frame sometimes used to support a lateensail in a catamaran. Also called bipod spars.

aft, after. At or towards the ship's stern or after part, as in: "go aft." After in the term "after engine room" is used as an adjective to describe the engine room nearest the stern. A seaman says: "abaft" not "aft of."

afterbody. The after part of a ship's hull, abaft the middle or midships, especially the underwater part.

after bow (quarter) spring. A mooring line at the bow (quarter) that leads aft from the boat to the pier. *See* mooring line.

afterguard. The officers in a ship who traditionally lived aft. Now a yachting word for the owner and his guests, or used to describe the officers of a yacht club.

afterguy. A line controlling the fore-and-aft trim of the spinnaker pole.

afterspring. *See* spring.

age of the moon. The period of time since the day of the last new moon, or of a change of moon.

age of the tide. The interval between the time of a new or full moon, and the maximum effect of these phases upon the range of tides or the speed of tidal currents.

agonic line. A line that joins points on the earth's surface where there is no magnetic variation.

aground. When a ship or boat is resting on the bottom it is aground. When put on the bottom deliberately she is said to take the ground. If done accidentally she is run aground. *See* grounding, strand, stranding.

Agulhas current. A strong branch of the South Indian Ocean current that flows south through the Mozambique Channel, along the east coast of Africa, and is deflected eastward by the Agulhas Bank.

ahead. The direction forward of the bow. Also, a ship may go *ahead* slowly, but when she backs, she goes *astern*. *See* astern.

Ahoy. A traditional nautical hail, still used in the U.S. Navy, but elsewhere usually replaced these days by "Hello" or "Hi There."

a-hull. A vessel that spreads no canvas, or uses no engines in very heavy weather is said to be lying a-hull as she drifts beam on to wind and sea; sometimes a sound tactic. Also called hulling. *See* heave to.

air, light or heavy. General terms for light wind conditions (roughly under 10 knots) or strong wind conditions (roughly over 20 knots).

Air Almanac. Similar to the Nautical Almanac and designed for celestial navigation by aircraft but popular with boatmen. Published by the Naval Observatory. *See* Nautical Almanac.

airboat. A shallow-draft boat driven by a propeller in the air, above the hull, instead of in the water. Useful in very shallow water or marshes.

airfoil. In the nautical sense, the curve of a sail over its whole area.

airlift. A suction pump used to draw up sand and debris from a wreck to recover artifacts, treasure, etc. Also a spray-tight opening or fitting on deck used for the escape of ventilating air in a ship.

airport. A round opening in a ship's or boat's side, also known as a porthole or port, fitted with a hinged glass cover (a portlight) and a metal cover, deadlight, or battleport (Navy). A ventilating deadlight as well as a windscoop may be inserted. British word is sidescuttle or scuttle.

airscoop. *See* windscoop.

Alaska current. The north-flowing branch of the Aleutian current which carries relatively warm water. It flows into the Gulf of Alaska where it circulates counterclockwise.

Albacore. A one-design centerboard sloop; LOA 15′, beam 5′, Designer: Uffa Fox.

Aldis lamp. A portable electric light, with a finger-operated shutter, used for signaling by ships, boats, and aircraft.

alee. On or toward the sheltered leeward side of a ship or boat, away from the wind. Except for the expression: "hard alee" used when tacking a sailboat, the word is seldom heard today. Common usage is "to leeward."

Aleutian current. The northern extension of the Japan current or Kuroshio, which flows east between 40 and 50 degrees north latitude. It divides into the Alaska current that flows north into the Gulf of Alaska, and a southward branch that becomes the California current.

algae. Marine plants ranging from very small (single-cell phytoplankton) to large kelp and other seaweed.

alidade. Aboard ship, a bearing circle equipped with a telescopic sight for taking bearings and azimuths. It is usually fitted over a pelorus or dumb compass with unobstructed vision. *See* pelorus, bearing circle.

All American. A one-design keel sloop. LOA 27½′, Beam 9′, Draft 4′. Designer: Thomas Colvin.

all hands. All those aboard ship except, under certain circumstances, those on watch. Also the name of a call made on a boatswain's pipe.

allowance. In a sailing race the time in seconds per nautical mile that a boat gives as a handicap to another boat.

all standing. Describes a ship or boat with all her sails set. She may run aground or jibe all standing—usually with catastrophic results. Men on duty but not actually on watch, for example the anchor watch, may turn in all standing which means fully dressed.

almanac. *See* Air Almanac, Nautical Almanac.

Almanac for Computers. An almanac that provides equations and numerical constants for use in celestial navigation calculations which can be done by computer or calculator; published by the Naval Observatory, first edition 1979.

aloft. Up above, topside—opposite of below or alow, usually in the rigging.

alternating current (A.C.). Electricity that flows through a wire alternately in opposite directions, in contrast to direct current (D.C.). Shoreside current in the U.S. is A.C.

altitude. In celestial navigation, the vertical angle between the horizon and the center of a celestial body, measured with a sextant. This observed altitude, when corrected for the sextant's index error, is *apparent* altitude, and when also corrected for dip and semidiameter (sun and moon) it becomes *rectified* or *corrected* altitude.

alto cumulus, altostratus. *See* clouds.

American Ephemeris. An astronomical almanac containing the coordinates of the sun, moon, planets, and certain stars as well as other data most useful to astronomers and sometimes to celestial navigators. Published by the Naval Observatory. *See* Nautical Almanac.

America's Cup. A trophy first won in England by the American schooner America and held since by the New York Yacht Club despite periodic challenges by foreign countries. Sailed today in 12-meter class yachts.

amidships or midships. In the center or middle of a vessel. "Rudder amidships" is an order to the helmsman to bring the rudder in line with the keel.

Amphibi-Con, Amphibi-Ette. One design centerboard sloops. LOA 25½' and 24', and beam about 8'. Designers: F. Butler and C. Hamlin.

amplitude. In celestial navigation, the angle at the zenith between the prime vertical and the vertical circle passing through the observed body.*

ampere. Amount of current flowing comparable to water flowing through a pipe.

anchor. A device that is lowered (dropped) to the sea bottom by means of a chain or rope. It holds a vessel in place. Old-fashioned or stock anchors have been largely replaced by stockless (patent) anchors that can be stowed in the hawsepipe. *See* Baldt, Bruce, Danforth, fisherman's, Herreshoff, kedge, Meon, mushroom, old-fashioned, plow, stockless and yachtsman's anchor.

anchorage. A place or area with good holding ground and protected from the sea where ships and boats may anchor.

anchor ball. A visual indicator that the vessel is at anchor. In inland U.S. waters it must be a black ball displayed aloft forward. 72 Colregs only require a ball displayed aloft where it can be best seen.

anchor buoy. A small float attached by a light line to the anchor which marks the location of the anchor on the bottom and is sometimes useful in retrieving it. Not to be confused with an anchorage buoy that marks the limits of an anchorage.

anchor cable, chain. *See* chain, rode.

anchor chock. A fitting near the bow of a boat to hold the anchor in place when it is stowed on deck.

anchor knot. *See* fisherman's bend.

anchor lights. *See* riding lights.

anchoring terms. To back an anchor is to make fast a second anchor or weight to its rode or cable to increase its holding power.
To break out an anchor is to dislodge it from its partially submerged position before hauling it up.

---

*In a radio wave it is the height of its crest from zero.

To bring home an anchor is to pull the ship up to it when heaving in.
To cast anchor is to drop it.
To fish an anchor is to bring an old-fashioned anchor aboard.
To house an anchor is to bring it up snugly into the hawsepipe.
To gimlet an anchor is to rotate it at the hawse.
To sight an anchor is to heave it in far enough to see whether it is foul or clear.
To shoe an anchor, *see* shoe.
To weigh anchor is to lift it off the bottom.

anchor knot. *See* fisherman's bend.

anchor lights. Lights required by 72 Colregs as well as the Inland Rules to be displayed aloft by a ship at anchor or moored. Also called riding lights.

anchor lining. Sheathing on the bows of a vessel to prevent damage when hauling the anchor aboard.

anchor ring. The ring fastened to the upper end of the shank of an anchor to which the chain or rode is shackled.

anchor shoe. A broad triangular piece of wood fastened to the fluke of an anchor to improve its holding power in a soft bottom.

anchor watch. A small group of men kept on duty to handle emergencies when the ship is anchored at night, or in heavy weather when the anchor may drag.

anemometer. An instrument that measures wind velocity and direction.

aneroid barometer. *See* barometer.

Annie Oakley. A sailboat spinnaker that is pierced with a number of small holes for better control or driving force.

annunciator. *See* engine order telegraph.

answering pennant. A red and white vertically striped pennant, one of the international signal code flags which, when hoisted singly at the dip (half way up the halyard) it means "your signal understood," and when two-blocked: "your signal read but not understood."

Antarctic Circle. The geographic parallel having a south latitude equal to the complement of the declination of the summer solstice (about 66 degrees and 33 minutes south).

Antarctic Circumpolar Current. The ocean current with the largest volume and highest velocity, flowing east around the Antarctic continent through all bordering oceans. Also known as the West Wind Drift.

antenna gain. Four times the ratio of the radiation intensity in one direction to the total power delivered to the antenna. A measure of the effectiveness of a receiving or a transmitting antenna.

anticyclone. A high-pressure weather mass around which the winds blow clockwise in the northern hemisphere and counterclockwise in the southern. Generally indicates fair weather. *See* cyclone.

antifouling paint. A special toxic composition applied to a ship's bottom to prevent marine growth such as barnacles.

Antilles Current. An ocean current (the northern branch of the North Equatorial Current) flowing northwest along the northern side of Cuba and Haiti. It eventually joins the Florida Current north of the Florida Straits, thus joining the Gulf Stream System.

anti-rolling fins. Long, shallow steel blades, hydrofoils, running fore-and-aft along the turn of the bilge to provide resistance to rolling. Sometimes actuated by gyroscope. Also called bilge keels.

anti-rolling tanks. Tanks fitted into each side of a ship into which water can be pumped and transferred to reduce rolling. *See* bilge keel.

anti-ventilation plate. A horizontal plate over the propeller of an outboard or I/O drive to keep air out of the propeller. Sometimes inaccurately called a cavitation plate.

Aphrodite 101. The American name for the International 101, a one-design racing and cruising keel sloop. LOA 33', beam 8', draft 5½'. The design is Danish.

apogee. The position of an earth satellite, such as the moon, when it is farthest in its orbit from the earth.

Apollo. A one-design centerboard sloop. LOA 15½', beam 6'.

apparent. In reference to celestial position means true or actual as opposed to mean. Since the earth moves in an elliptical orbit around the sun, its speed relative to the sun varies with its position in the orbit. Thus the time for a complete rotation of the earth varies and the length of the day varies. Therefore a mean or average sun is conceived about which the earth rotates in exactly 24 hours. Apparent noon sun, or time, for example, are real and true whereas mean describes the theoretical or average.

apparent wind. The wind felt by a person in a moving vessel. It is the vector sum of the true wind and the ship's course and speed. Also called relative wind. *See also* true wind.

appendage. Referring to a ship or boat, a fitting that extends beyond the main hull, such as struts, rudder, shafting, bilge keels, etc.

apple stern. Describes a round, convex stern of a boat or ship.

approach tack. Any tack in a sailing race that heads the boat towards a mark or other objective and that finishes at such a place.

Aqua-Cat. A one-design cat-rigged catamaran with daggerboards. LOA 12', beam 6'. Designer: American Fiberglass Corporation.

Aqua-Lung. Trade name for the first self-contained underwater breathing apparatus (SCUBA) of the demand or open-circuit type, permitting free dives to considerable depths. Invented by Cousteau and Gagnan.

archboard. A wooden piece connecting the hull planking and deck at the transom of a wooden boat.

arch knee. Curved timber fitted between the propeller post and the rudder post in a wooden boat.

Arctic Circle. The geographic parallel having a north latitude equal to the complement of the declination of the winter solstice, about 66 degrees and 33 minutes north.

Arctic Current. *See* Labrador Current.

ardent. Describes a sailboat that tends to come into the wind, thus requiring excessive weather helm. Contrary tendency is for a boat to fall away from the wind and to be slack. An ardent boat is said to show ardency.

argument. A numerical value with which the navigator enters a navigational table or formula.

arm. To fill the cavity at the bottom of a sounding lead with tallow or soap in order to bring up a sample of the bottom. Also the part of an old-fashioned anchor that branches out from the crown and becomes a palm or fluke. A timber knee is said to have two arms.

arm cleat. A cleat with one arm or horn. Also called a horn cleat.

Army Corps of Engineers Rules. *See* Inland Rules of the Road.

Arrow. A one-design centerboard sloop. LOA 18′, beam 6½′. Designer: A.M. Deering.

arse. The lower opening in a block opposite the swallow through which the rope or wire passes. Also called the breech.

ascension. The elevation of a celestial body above the celestial horizon. Right ascension is the arc along the celestial equator measured eastward from the vernal equinox to an hour circle passing through the celestial body. Right ascension is one of the coordinates for locating a celestial point.

ash breeze. Sailor's slang for rowing.

ashore. On the shore, land, or beach. A sailor goes ashore on liberty in the U.S. Navy and on shore leave in the Merchant Service.

aspect ratio. In nautical terms, the relationship between the height of a sail or rudder and its width or chord. A short boom and a high mast in a sailboat produce a high-aspect ratio rig.

astern. A direction, back, towards the stern or beyond; behind the ship.

astigmatizer. A simple optical device fitted to the telescope of a sextant that elongates the image of a star from a dot of light to a line, thus making easier an accurate measurement of altitude.

astro. Short for astro-navigation, the British word for celestial navigation.

Atalanta. A one-design centerboard sloop. LOA 26′, beam 7½′.

athwart, athwartships. Across, at right angles to the fore-and-aft axis of the boat; from side to side.

Atlantic. A one-design keel sloop. LOA 30½', beam 6½', draft 4½'. Designer: Burgess & Morgan.

Atlantic Ocean. Named by the Greeks as the sea beyond the Atlas mountains which are near the Straits of Gibralter.

atoll. A ring-shaped island or belt of islands formed by the skeletons of coral polyps which enclose a lagoon; common to the Pacific near the Equator.

at sea. Legally, for insurance purposes a vessel is at sea when it has cast off all lines from its berth or is underway at its anchorage.

audio frequency (AF). 20 to 20,000 cycles per second (Hertz). Sound we can hear is in this range.

Aurora. A luminous phenomenon appearing in high latitudes in the form of rays, bands, and arcs of light. Aurora Borealis is seen in the northern hemisphere, Aurora Australis in the southern. Also called Polar Aurora or northern lights.

automatic direction finder (ADF). One that automatically points out the station to which it is tuned without manual rotation of the loop antenna.

automatic pilot. *See* pilot, automatic.

avast. A command to stop or cease as in "avast heaving," which means stop pulling. Usage not recommended for those who are not old sailors.

awash. Just above sea level as a reef is awash. Also covered with water as the deck of a ship or boat may be awash.

aweigh. Said of an anchor when it has just broken ground when being hauled in. Not to be confused with a boat being underway. *See* weigh.

aye aye. The traditional nautical affirmative reply to a request, suggestion, or command.

azimuth. The direction of any place or object (such as the sun) from a given point, usually referred to as true north and expressed in degrees. Azimuth is generally used in regard to celestial bodies and bearing is used when terrestial objects are involved.

azimuth circle. A simple ring fitted with open sight vanes that fit over a compass bowl and by which azimuth or bearing may be read. It is fitted with a prism mirror in order to observe the sun. Without this mirror the instrument is called a bearing circle. *See* alidade.

B

baby stay. Another name for an inner forestay.

back. To cause a boat to go astern; to reverse engines. The wind backs when its direction shifts counterclockwise; it hauls or veers when the shift is clockwise. By international agreement, these definitions are true for both hemispheres. To back an anchor, *see* anchoring expressions. To back a sail is to hold it out to windward so that the wind will blow against the opposite side and thus slow or stop the sailboat. The back of a boat is its keel and keelson together. To back oars is to row backwards.

back and fill. An old expression describing the alternate backing and then the filling of the sails of a square-rigger working her way up a channel too narrow to permit tacking.

backbeach. Same as backshore.

backhanded. Said of a rope made by twisting each strand in the same direction as the yarns and then laying the strands left-handed. Also called backlaid rope. *See* plain-laid rope.

backhaul (rope). A rope used to haul something back into place.

back out. *See* walk out.

backrope. A small line on the hook of a block by which the tackle is swung out and hooked on. Also one of the stays leading from the lower end of the martingale of a sailboat.

backrush. The seaward return of water following the uprush of waves on a beach.

backshore. The part of a beach or shore that is usually dry when not reached by the highest tides. Also called backbeach.

backsplice. A method of finishing off the end of a rope by making a crown knot and then tucking the strands back 2 or 3 times each.

backstay. A supporting rope or wire that runs aft from aloft on a mast to the deck. A standing backstay is usually fixed on center-line aft. A shifting backstay is one that can be set taut or slack, depending on which tack the boat is one and thus which side of the mast is under tension. These backstays are led to both sides of the deck aft-port and starboard, and are tensioned or released by means of a Highfield lever; they are also called running backstays, runners or preventers.

backstaysail. A triangular sail hanked to the permanent backstay of a sloop, yawl, or ketch.

backstay stool. Planking or light plating projecting from the sides of a sailboat to which the ends of backstays can be made fast.

backwash. Water or waves thrown back by an obstruction such as a ship. breakwater, cliff, etc. Also called backrush.

backwater. Water resulting from an eddy, obstruction or opposing current remote from the main stream. An arm of the sea, usually parallel to the coast behind a narrow strip of land. To backwater (or back oars) is to row backwards.

backwind. Air flowing aft off one sail onto the lee side of another. The receiving sail is said to be backwinded and a sail may be said to backwind another.

badge. An insignia on the bow of a boat or a protective piece of wood on a boat's quarter where the side planking meets the transom.

baggywrinkle. Old bits and pieces of used line wrapped around a stay or shroud to prevent the sails from chafing.

baguio. Local name for a typhoon in the Philippines.

bail. To dip water from a boat. A bow-shaped fitting supporting an accommodation ladder over the side of a ship or the awnings in a boat. A spreader for holding the lines of a bridle apart. *See* bridle. The metal straps around a spar to which blocks or other gear are shackled are bails. Sometimes spelled bale.

bail shackle. The slip ring holding the hook down on a pelican hook. It is released by pulling out the bail pin.

balanced rudder. A rudder in which part of the blade is forward of the pivot point or axis, thus needing less energy to turn it.

balance lug. A lugsail whose boom and lug both project forward of the mast, thus providing a reasonably balanced sail. *See* lugsail.

balancing ring. A ring fitted to the shank of an anchor by which it can be hoisted by a crane.

baldheaded. Describes a schooner having no topmast.

Baldt anchor. Trade name for a modern ship's stockless anchor.

ballast. Any heavy material carried aboard a ship or boat to ensure her stability. Water is often used and is carried in ballast tanks which can be emptied or filled as needed. A merchant ship is in ballast when carrying no cargo; a yacht is always considered legally to be in ballast. *See* ballast keel.

ballast keel. The keel of a sailboat made and shaped from the iron or lead she needs for stability.

balloon sail. A large, light sail used by sailboats when reaching or running in light to moderate weather. May be a balloon jib, also called a reaching jib, a foresail, spinnaker, or topsail. Also called a ballooner or kite.

ball stopper. A plastic ball fastened to the end of a line such as a halyard to keep it from unreeving and going adrift.

balsa. A very light tropical wood used in liferafts and floats and as a core material in fiberglass boats. Also the name of a sea-going sailing raft found on the west coast of South America.

banana staysail. A thin, lofty, full headsail of 3/4-oz. nylon.

banca. General word for small craft of the Philippines.

bang plate. A strip of plastic, metal, or wood on a canoe to protect a wooden member, such as the stem or keel.

bank. A moderately flat-topped elevation of the ocean bottom, but with enough shallow water for safe navigation in fair weather.

bank cushion. The repelling force close to the bow of a ship or boat as it passes close to the bank of a river or canal, or to the side of a ship. It is caused by the bow wave striking the bank or other ship causing the bow to be pushed away.

bank effect. The lateral movement or deflection of the bow or stern of a moving ship or boat in a narrow waterway, or when close to another ship, as when going alongside another ship underway. The bow wave causes the bow to move away and the stern is attracted or pulled in. *See* bank suction.

bank suction. The attracting force upon the stern of a moving ship in a narrow waterway or when close to another ship. It is caused by the propeller current along which pressure is reduced.

Banshee. A one-design catboat with daggerboard. LOA 13′, beam 5′. Designer: R.L. Reid.

bar. A bank or shoal, usually at the mouth of a river which obstructs navigation and causes breaking, dangerous surf in heavy weather. Also a bar is a unit of atmospheric pressure (metric). *See* millibar.

barber. A severe cold storm at sea during which spray and snow freeze on deck and on the rigging.

barber haul. To attach a short line and a block to a headsail sheet to improve its angle of load and thus the efficiency of the sail. Used as both a noun and a verb. The control line is sometimes called a barber hauler and the block is the barber haul.

bareboat charter. *See* charter party.

bare poles. With no sails set on the masts a sailboat is said to be under bare poles; not uncommon in very heavy weather.

Barnegat Bay sneakbox. A small 13–14′ centerboard sloop that has raced in and near Barnegat Bay, N.J. for over 150 years.

barogram, barograph. *See* barometer.

barometer. An instrument for measuring atmospheric pressure. An aneroid barometer has a thin, metallic, partially air-exhausted, sealed chamber which senses pressure changes and records them by a dial pointer or a pen, on a moving cylinder of paper (barograph). The recording on paper is called a barogram. A mercurial barometer is a column of mercury set in a bowl of mercury whose height indicates atmospheric pressure. A marine version is designed to damp out the oscillations caused by ship movement.

bar port. A harbor that can be entered only at high tide when there is sufficient water to permit vessels to pass over the bar.

barracuda. A pikelike voracious, steel-colored, warm-water fish with prominent teeth that is sometimes dangerous to swimmers and grows to 6′. Edible in the Pacific, it can be poisonous in the Caribbean.

barrier reef. A coral reef that is separated from the shore by water too deep to have coral growth; distinct from the fringing reef which lies closer to shore.

bar warning sign. Usually a flashing light activated by the Coast Guard to warn mariners approaching from seaward that heavy seas are breaking over the bar and it should not be crossed.

basin. Any enclosed or sheltered area that protects ships and boats from tide and weather.

basking shark. *See* shark.

bass. Striped bass is a popular gamefish of up to 60 pounds found close to shore—also called rockfish, linesider, and squidhound. Channel bass are really drum. Sea bass is a common name for a small bottom food fish of our eastern coast that grows to 5 pounds and is locally known as blackfish, black perch, rockfish, and rock bass.

bare sailing. Sailing with the sheets hauled in too far, also called pinching the boat—a common beginners' error.

barge. In general, a heavy, flat-bottomed, often rectangular vessel used to carry cargo, usually in sheltered and inland waters but sometimes at sea. Usually pushed or towed by a tug. By U.S. government definition barges are any non-self-propelled vessels other than houseboats and dredges. The words lighter, barge, and scow are often used interchangeably in accordance with local usage, although in general barges make vogages while lighters are used locally. A barge is also a ceremonial boat used by officials and dignataries; in the Navy it is the Admiral's boat. To barge in a sailing race is to force your opponents to give you room to windward at the start or when rounding a mark.

bark. A sailing ship having as many as 5 masts, all of them square-rigged except the aftermost one which has fore-and-aft sails; once called a shipentine. British spelling is barque.

bar keel. A continuous, heavy steel bar, oblong in cross-section, extending along the bottom at the centerline. Also called a hanging keel since it is outside the hull.

barkentine. A 3- or 4-masted sailing ship having all masts fore-and-aft rigged except the foremast which is square-rigged. Also spelled barquentine.

barnacle. A salt-water crustacean of the order Cirripedia, enclosed in a shell permanently attached to some object—too often a ship's hull. There are 2 types—acorn and stalked barnacles (also known as gooseneck or goose barnacle).

barney post. A post in the cockpit of a sailboat on which jamcleats and fairleads are fitted to control sails and rigging.

bateau. In North America, one of the various small, scowlike craft that range from rowboats to Chesapeake Bay crabbing boats. *See* scow.

bathometer. Any instrument used to measure depth of water.

batten. A long, narrow, thin, flexible piece of wood or plastic used to stiffen the leech of a sail. It is inserted in a pocket on the leech.

batten down. To make secure, to fasten down in preparation for heavy weather.

battery charger. A device, also called a rectifier, to change A.C. to D.C. for charging a battery. Batteries always provide D.C.

bay. A wide indentation in the coast; smaller than a gulf and larger than a cove.

bayam. A violent squall with thunder and lightning that blows along the south coast of Cuba.

Bay Lady. A one-design keel sloop. LOA 20′, beam 6′, draft 3′. Designer: David Sheldon Jr.

bayou. A small, sluggish stream, generally tidal, that wanders through marsh and swamp. Most common in Lousiana, sometimes called a slough in other states.

BB II. A one-design keel sloop. LOA 20′, beam 6′, draft 3′. Designers: Borge & Bringsvaerd.

beach. The shore, including foreshore and backshore; a sand area from low water back to where vegetation starts. To run a boat ashore is to beach it. Beach is slang for the waterfront; a sailor going ashore hits the beach.

beachcomber. Literally a person who picks things up along the beach. Describes a man along the coast who does not seem to have a steady job. If he has quit the sea or has lost his job he may be said to be on the beach. *See also* comber.

beach gear. The varied equipment used by salvage crews in assisting a stranded vessel that includes anchors, wire rope, sheaves, and blocks.

beacon. Any structure marked by lights and/or distinctive shapes, placed ashore or in shallow water as an aid to navigation. Chart symbol is Bn.

beam. The width of a boat. Objects outside the boat may be reported as abeam if 90 degrees relative on either side or abaft the beam or forward of the beam.

beam ends. A boat is on her beam ends when she has rolled over 90 degrees. In more general terms it may describe a person in trouble.

bear. To lie in a certain direction. A distant object may be described as bearing just abaft the port beam. To bear off means to turn away; to bear down means to sail towards. To bear away or to bear up (luff) means to change course away from or towards the wind.

Bear. A one-design keel sloop. LOA 23′, beam 7′, draft 3½′. Designers: Nunes Brothers.

bear a hand. An expression meaning to hurry; as in "bear a hand and secure that line."

bearing. The direction or point of the compass in which an object is seen or sensed; expressed in general terms as: "off the port bow" or in points or in degrees true, magnetic, or relative. A danger bearing is a limiting one that indicates danger. Bearings are for terrestrial objects; azimuths are for celestial.

bearing circle. A ring fitted over a compass with which bearings can be taken by sighting through vanes fitted on the ring. If a reflecting device permits bearings, or azimuths of celestial bodies, it is an azimuth circle. If a telescope replaces the vanes it is an alidade.

beat. In a sailboat to advance against the wind by sailing close-hauled on alternate tacks; doing so can result in a long beat.

beat frequency. The intermediate frequency generated by two different frequencies being imposed on each other.

Beaufort Scale. A universally adopted wind-velocity scale.

Force		State of Sea	knots
0	calm	smooth	0–1
1	light airs	small wavelets	1–3
2	slight breeze	short waves, cresting	4–6
3	gentle breeze	small waves, breaking	7–10
4	moderate breeze	definite whitecaps	11–16
5	fresh breeze	moderate waves	17–21
6	strong breeze	larger waves	22–27
7	moderate gale	spindrift formed	28–33
8	fresh gale	much spindrift	34–40
9	strong gale	seas start to roll	41–47
10	whole gale	seas roll and break heavily	48–55
11	storm	surface all white, big seas	56–65
12	hurricane	enormous seas	above 65

becalmed. A sailing vessel unable to move for lack of wind.

becket. Any of various small ropes, lines, loops, or grommets common to sailing ships and named after their purpose. Most commonly a short line with a knot at one end and an eye at the other; used for temporarily holding ropes or small spars. Also a type of knot or bend. A becket oarlock is one formed by a piece of line made fast to a thole pin. Today a becket is an eye in the tail of a block.

becue. To rig an anchor for use on foul ground by bending the warp or rode to the crown instead of to the ring of the anchor. The rode is stopped to the ring with light line so that a normal pull on the shank is possible unless the anchor is caught on something. In that case the stops part and the anchor is hauled up crown first. This was also called scowing an anchor.

bee block. In the days of sail a block of wood or iron through which a stay's lower end was rove before it was set up and made fast. A modern bee block is used on the boom of a sailboat to bring the cringle down to its proper position for reefing.

bed. Short for seabed, the bottom of the ocean. Also the foundation for the engine in a boat.

bedding compound. Paste used under deck fittings before fixing them in position and in wooden boat construction as a sealant.

Beetle Cat. A one-design centerboard catboat. LOA 12′, beam 6′. Designer: John Beetle.

before the mast. Indicated service as a sailor. Sailors traditionally lived forward in a ship in contrast to the officers who lived aft.

belat. A strong northerly wind blowing along the south coast of Arabia between December and March.

belay. To make fast or secure a rope or line to a cleat or other fitting. Also to annul or cancel a command as in: "belay that last word."

belaying pin. In the days of sail a wooden or metal rod around which a line was made fast. Pins were usually fitted into fife rails around the masts or inside the bulwarks.

bell buoy. One fitted with a bell whose clappers are activated by the buoy's movement in a seaway; a common aid to navigation.

bellmouth. A ship's or boat's ventilating air supply intake terminal. Also called a cowl vent. *See* ventilator.

bell purchase. A tackle consisting of 2 fixed blocks and 2 movable ones.

bell rope. The piece of line, often braided, used to swing the clapper of a ship's bell.

bell, ship's. A bell which was struck every half-hour to mark the passage of time. *See* ship's time. Also used to sound fog signals when at anchor.

belly. The part of a sail that bulges out due to wind pressure.

belly guy. A rope or wire supporting the middle part of a sheer leg or spar. A belly strap is slung under a boat to carry out an anchor.

below. Nautical word for downstairs—one always goes below, never downstairs. Below decks is that part of the boat below the main deck.

belting. *See* guard rail.

bench hook. *See* sail hook.

bend, bending. To fasten or secure by means of a knot as in bending the rode to the anchor. A bend is a special form of knot used in the joining of 2 lines or in making fast a line to a ring, eye, spar, etc., that can be cast off easily.

bender. Old nautical word for a drinking party or celebration.

bending shackle. A U-shaped connecting link, with the curved end aft, connecting the anchor cable or rode to the anchor shackle. Sometimes called the end shackle.

Benguela Current. A strong northerly ocean current off the west coast of Africa. It is a continuation of the South Atlantic Current and turns west to join the South Equatorial Current.

bergy bit. Medium-sized piece of glacial ice afloat, less than 5 meters high, larger than a growler and a menace to navigation.

Bermuda or Bermudan rig. Triangular fore-and-aft sails having a foot, luff, and leech without a gaff. Also called a Marconi or jib-headed rig.

berth. Anchorage, mooring space, or the space alongside a pier assigned to a ship. Also a sleeping place for a man aboard ship; he is said to berth in that space. To give something a wide berth is to pass it at a distance.

Beverly Dinghy. A one-design centerboard cat-rigged dinghy. LOA 11½', beam 4½'. Designer: A.S.D. Herreshoff.

bias stretch. The elongation of sailcloth on a diagonal, usually caused by a distortion of the weave.

bib or bibb. Any piece of wood used as a support in boat construction.

bigboy. *See* blooper.

bight. The loop of a rope. The doubled over part of a rope when folded. Also a recess or indented area in a seacoast or ice edge. Caught in a bight is to be entrapped or snared.

bilge. The lower bottom of a boat or ship up to the point where the sides become vertical; thus the curve or turn of the bilge. Also where the bilge water collects, often requiring a bilge pump to pump the bilges. A sharply curved bilge is a sharp or hard bilge. If there is an angle instead of a curve it is called a chine. To bilge a boat is to damage its hull and cause it to leak. Also slang for rubbish or nonsense.

bilge block. A wooden piece used to support a ship in drydock.

bilgeboard (in a scow). A sort of centerboard projecting out and down from each bilge of an inland lake-racing sailboat or scow.

bilgeboard scow. *See* inland lake scow.

bilge keels. *See* anti-rolling fins.

bilge pump. Used in a boat to remove casual water or flooding due to holing, grounding, burst pipes, etc. An automatic pump that goes on when rising water activates a switch is an important safety device.

bilge well. *See* drain well.

bilge strake. Strake (planking or plating) along the turn of the bilge.

bill. Point of the flukes of an anchor; also called the pea.

billethead. *See* fiddlehead.

billfish. Any of the gamefish, such as the marlin, which have a long bill.

bill of health (B/H). A certificate needed by a ship/or boat entering port from a foreign country attesting either to the boat's freedom from disease or recent exposure to disease. It is the basis for granting pratique. *See* pratique.

bill of store. A license granted by the customs authorities to a ship or boat by which it is allowed to carry voyage stores and provisions duty free.

Bimini belt. A harness with a gimballed socket on a metal plate into which the butt of the fishing rod fits, as the angler, wearing the belt, plays a large game fish.

Bimini top. A light collapsible fabric sun protector rigged over the flying bridge or open cockpit of a boat. Also called a Navy top.

binder. In marine insurance, an agreement to insure; used before a final policy is written.

binnacle. The covered nonmagnetic lighted stand or receptacle for the magnetic compass.

bioluminescence. Light seen on the surface of the sea on a dark night, generated by living organisms, most commonly plankton. Also called seafire.

bipod spars. *See* A-frame.

bitter. Traditionally a turn of the hawser or cable around the bitts. The bitter end is the end of a line, rope, or cable that is on board; the last link of the anchor chain in the chain locker.

bitts. Short heavy steel posts, usually in pairs, located on deck and used for securing lines, ropes, etc. According to use and location there are towing bitts, mooring bitts, quarter bitts, etc. Bollards are corresponding fittings found on docks, piers, and wharfs.

blackfish. Common name for a number of dark fishes, large and small. Local name for sea bass. *See* bass. Also local name for tautog. A pilot whale is called a blackfish.

blackwall hitch. A knot used for fastening a line to a steel hook.

blade. The main flat portion of a rudder; also called the rudder body. *See* propeller.

blanket. In a sailing race, to pass between another boat and the wind.

blast. Signal on a ship's whistle: short 1 second, prolonged 4–6 seconds, and long over 6 seconds; as defined by 72 Colregs.

blind rollers. Long, high, sea swells that peak but do not break as they pass over shoal water. Also called blind seas or blinders.

blink. The reflected glare or light from sunlight shining on ice, snow, or white sand as seen in the sky above. Called ice, snow, or lagoon blink.

blinker. A blinker tube or gun is a hand-held light used to signal between vessels at sea. Now less common since all ships and most seagoing boats can communicate by voice radio.

block. A temporary support or shore such as a building block, used to support a ship's hull when under construction. Also a solid permanent piece of wood or metal used for any purpose in a ship or boat, such as a thrust block, sole block, etc.

block, pulley. A wooden, plastic, or metal shell in which one or more sheaves rotate. Rope or wire travels on these sheaves, either to gain mechanical advantage, especially with multiple blocks, or to have a fairlead. The sheaves of modern blocks rotate on plastic bearings or, for heavy loads, on steel bearings. The shell of the block is fitted with a hook or an eye at the top, and a line or becket at the other end. The space over the sheave nearest the hook is the swallow and the other end is the breech or arse.

blocks (for modern sailboats). *See* bullet, cheek, exit, fairlead, fiddle, foot block, jamming, fiddle, mainsheet swivel, ratchet, reacher, snatch, traveller, turning, tweaker, and twin-sheet lead.

block stopper. *See* stopper.

blocks, traditional. *See* bee, cat, cheek, clump, dasher, differential, fiddle, fly, gin, heel, jack, jewel, monkey, patent, purchase, rousebout, running, secret, shoulder, sister, standing, swivel, tackle, tail, telegraph, three-fold, thick-and-thin, and wrecking block.

blooper. A lightweight very full overlapping headsail set on racing sailboats opposite the spinnaker when running before the wind in winds over 10–12 knots. Also called a bigboy, a shooter, or a streaker.

blow. A gale or storm. To blow great guns describes very strong winds.

blowhole. A hole in shoreline rocks where the surge of the surf produces a jet of water.

Blue Bird. A one-design, cat-rigged, centerboard dinghy. LOA 7', beam 3½'.

bluefin tuna. Also known as horse mackerel. *See* tuna, mackerel.

Blue Jay. A one-design centerboard sloop. LOA 13½', beam 5'. Designer: Sparkman & Stephens.

Bluenose. A one-design keel sloop. LOA 23½', beam 6', draft 3½'. Designer: W.J. Rove.

blue peter. Slang term for the alphabet flag P, a blue rectangle with a white square in the center, traditionally hoisted at the foremast of a vessel on the day of her departure.

blue whale. The largest of the rorquals or baleen whales, up to 100' in length. Gentle and intelligent, it is nearly extinct due to relentless hunting.

board. To go on or into a vessel. Also a board is the distance covered in 1 tack when beating to windwared—same as a leg or tack.

boardboat. A small inexpensive sailboat such as a Windsurfer or Sailfish whose hulls resemble a surfboard. Also called a sailboard.

boardsailing. Same as windsurfing.

boarding ladder. Small lightweight portable steps hung over a boat's side to assist people coming aboard.

boat. A small craft, open or decked, propelled by oars, sail, or motor, and made of wood, fabric, metal, cement or plastic in various shapes. Generally any craft capable of being carried aboard ship, usually less than 65' LOA. A powerboat is one driven by engine alone; a sailboat uses sails but may have auxilliary power. A yacht is always referred to as a boat by her owner.

boat boom. A spar swung out from the side of a ship to which boats are hauled out.

boat box. Container in a boat for first aid and emergency gear.

boat deck. A partial deck above the main deck of a ship; usually where the boats are stowed.

boatel. Facilities for overnight lodging for people cruising in small boats. Usually part of a marina, also called a yachtel.

boat falls. The ropes by which a boat is lowered and hoisted in its davits.

boathook. A metal hook at the end of a pole used in a boat to fend off when going alongside or to pick up a mooring.

boathouse. A structure used to shelter one or more boats.

boatman. A person who frequently uses a boat as a means of livelihood or for pleasure.

boat nail. A cut nail, rectangular in cross-section with a thick head and a chisel point as well as an annular threaded bronze or monel nail used in wooden boat construction.

boat numbers. All motorboats of over 10 horsepower must by law display a number if operated in U.S. navigable waters. Numbering is regulated by state law and is not uniform.

boat painter. *See* painter.

boatswain. The petty or warrant officer aboard ship, known as Boats, responsible for deck seamanship and in charge of the deck hands, boats, anchors, etc. Pronounced bosun.

boatswain's chair. A wooden or metal seat used when sending a man aloft.

boatswain's locker. A space aboard a boat for stowing deck gear.

boatwell. A small, partly enclosed area used to moor boats.

boatyard. A waterfront facility for building, repairing, and storing boats.

bobbing a light. When a light is first seen on the horizon at sea, it will disappear if the observer moves his eyes down several feet, and it will reappear when the observer returns to his original position. This procedure will establish whether or not the light is really on the horizon and, if so, the approximate range to the light since the range to the horizon and the elevation of the light are known. Also called dipping a light.

bobstay. A rope, wire, chain, or rod that extends from the end of the bowsprit down to the stem, and counteracts the lifting strain of the forestay of a sailing ship.

boggin line. A length of chain secured to either side of the rudder as a safety device. Also called a rudder pennant.

bollards. Short, heavy steel posts, usually in pairs, on a dock, wharf, or pier for holding ship's mooring lines.

bolo. A light weighted line that can be twirled and propelled farther than a heaving line.

boltrope. A line or wire sewn around the edge to strengthen a sail awning or tarpaulin. Also called roping. *See* luffrope.

bonito. Any of several food and game fish of the mackerel family, 2 or 3 feet long, found worldwide. Also called skipjack.

bonnet. An additional strip of canvas fastened to a fore-and-aft sail, especially a jib, to increase its power in moderate weather. Also called a studsail. An additional piece of canvas was sometimes laced to the foot of a bonnet and was called a drabbler. Also any metal, canvas, or wooden cover such as that over the engine of an open boat.

booby hatch. A raised shelter over a ladder entrance or companionway leading below from a weather deck. Also called a companion or a doghouse.

boom. Any pole, spar, or timber that projects over the side, supports a sail, protects the ship's side when alongside a pier, etc. Most are described by their name, for example a boat boom, a cargo boom, etc. A wooden spar along the foot of a sail is a boom. Floating barriers rigged to contain oil spills are containment booms; log booms hold logs together into rafts. To lower the boom is slang for punish.

boom crutch. The support for a mainsail boom when the sail is lowered, or for a cargo boom when it is down and secured. Also called boom rest, boom saddle, boom cradle, boom crotch, or boom gallows.

boom guy. Same as lazy jack or lazy guy.

boom horse. A semicircular iron bar at the end of a sailboat boom for the sheet block to move on. Also called a boom traveler. Also a metal fitting on top of the boom used as a clew outhaul.

boom jack. Same as boom vang.

boom out. To extend the corner of a sail with a spar, boathook, etc.

boom plug. The fitting at the forward end of the mainsail boom that engages the gooseneck.

boom shears. A boom crutch in the shape of shears.

boom traveler. *See* boom horse.

boom vang. A line used in a sailboat to steady the boom. Also called boom jack.

boot topping. The surface of the hull of a boat along the waterline, a narrow stripe of contrasting paint.

bora. A cold, strong, very gusty northeast wind blowing off the coast of Yugoslavia in the Adriatic Sea; similar to a williwaw.

bordereau. A marine insurance word meaning list or schedule.

bore. A steep, moving wall of water, a wave, caused by the piling up of the advancing flood tidal wave as it is constricted in the mouth of a river or narrow bay. The current of the river increases the steepness and thus the danger of the bore. Also called an eagre, mascarat, or pororoca.

bottle paper. A printed U.S. government form on which latitude, longitude, and date are entered by the recording ship before sealing in a bottle which is thrown overboard. Those recovering the bottles are asked to report place and date; thus information is gathered on ocean currents.

bottlescrew. Same as turnbuckle or rigging screw. Bottlescrew and rigging screw are common British usage; turnbuckle is more common in the U.S. *See* turnbuckle.

bottom. The floor of the sea or the bottom of a ship. A ship may be referred to as a bottom. She has moved on her own bottom if she sailed rather than being shipped.

bound. A ship may be bound for a certain port, be homeward bound, or fogbound.

bouse. To pull strongly on a tackle, to tighten standing rigging or a lashing by passing a line or swifter around it; as in "bouse down the shrouds." Also spelled bowse.

bow. The forward part of the ship. Archaic word was prow. Stem is the most forward structural part of the bow. *See* stem, bow shapes.

bow cushion. *See* bank cushion.

bower anchor. Traditionally a principal anchor, either the port or starboard bower. If unequal in size, not usual today, the larger is the best bower, the other the small bower. The word bower is not used in the Navy and seldom in the Merchant Service.

bowhead whale. The Greenland right whale or polar whale, a baleen whale of moderate size, endangered and completely protected except for a small quota for certain Alaska natives who still depend on the bowhead for food.

bowline. A line attached to the leech of a squaresail, leading forward, to steady it. A particular knot forming a loop that cannot slip. A bowline on a bight is a special knot used to support a man sent aloft. Pronounced bolin.

bowman. The man in the crew of a sailboat who handles headsails and thus works forward, on the bow.

bowse. Same as bouse.

bow shapes. A plumb bow is straight and vertical; a raked bow slants forward; a spoon bow has a convex curve; a clipper bow is in the shape of a concave curve, and a Meirform or bulbous bow has a bulbous shape below the waterline. Some may have flare or overhang, others a projecting underwater stem or ram.

bowsprit. A built-in spar projecting forward and slightly up from the bow of a sailing vessel. It extends the headsails and supports the masts because of the headstays that are fastened to it.

bow wave. The moving bulge or mass of water pushed forward of and around the bow by a vessel underway; the cause of bank cushion.

box the compass. To name all the 32 points of the compass from north through east and around back to north, starting N, N by E, NNE, NE by N, NE, NE by E, ENE, E by N, E, etc.

brace. A rope or line used in a square-rigger to control the horizontal movement of the sails and yards. To brace up is to bring the yard closer to the centerline by hauling on the lee braces, thus sailing closer to the wind.

braid. Modern fiber line made by braiding instead of twisting. Braided filament lines, called braid-on-braid, are the latest and most expensive.

Braidline. Trade name for a special type of flexible rope for boats. It has a braided sheath over a core.

brails. The lines or ropes by which sails are gathered to the mast or yards for furling and stowing. To brail up is to haul in by means of the brails.

brash ice. Small fragments of floating ice, not more than 2 meters across.

brave west winds. A sailor's term for the strong and persistent westerly winds over the ocean in the middle latitudes—35 to 65; strongest in the Roaring Forties—40 S to 50 S.

Brazil Current. That portion of the westerly South Atlantic Equatorial Current that turns south along the coast of Brazil then turns east near the Rio de la Plata.

breach. A whale or dolphin breaches when it leaps out of the sea. Waves or surf breaking over something, a rupture or hole in a boat's side.

break. To break a flag is to unfurl it suddenly when it is two-blocked by a smart pull on the halyard that parts the light line with which it has been stopped. An anchor breaks ground when it starts away from where it has dug in. A man breaks out stores from a storeroom; a line never breaks for a seaman, it parts.

breakdown light. *See* not-under-command.

breaker. A small cask or barrel, traditionally of wood, containing water for a boat. A container for emergency food in a boat, not a cask, is called a bread breaker.

breaker (wave). A wave or swell breaking on shore and forming surf. May curl over and break suddenly with a crash (plunging breaker) or crest and break slowly over a considerable distance, (spilling breaker) or peak up without breaking (surging breaker). This behavior is a result of different contours and gradients on the bottom.

breast. To breast a ship or boat in or out is to move it laterally towards or away from the pier or dock or another ship or boat. A breast line is one perpendicular to the ship, usually rigged amid-ships. Also called a breast fast or breast rope.

breeze. A light, moderate or strong wind, up to 27 knots; short of a gale. *See* Beaufort Scale. Land and sea breezes, also known as solar winds, are caused by the difference between land and sea warming to the sun as well as retaining the sun's heat. In the morning the land heats faster, warm air rises and the sea breeze moves in over the land to replace the rising warm air. The reverse happens at night when the land breeze blows towards the sea, which retains the sun's heat at night longer than the land. To shoot the breeze is to have a talk; an ash breeze is the act of rowing.

bridge. A ship or boat's structure or station topside containing the controls and instruments for directing the vessel. *See* flybridge, command bridge.

bridge deck. In a sailboat the structure between the cockpit and the cabin which is decked over to prevent water from going below. Also called a booby hatch.

bridle. Any span of rope, wire, or chain with both ends made fast and the strain taken in the middle, used in towing, moving cargo, mooring, etc.

brigantine. A 2-masted sailing vessel with square sails on the foremast and fore-and-aft sails on the mainmast.

brightwork. Unpainted brass, copper, chromium, or stainless steel kept clean and shining. Unpainted wood such as teak is referred to as bright. It may be oiled or varnished. The British limit the use of bright to wood.

bring. When combined with another word or phrase means to accomplish something. A rope is brought to a winch; a ship is brought up all standing by sudden anchoring or stranding. A line is brought up with a round turn when its motion is stopped by passing it around a cleat. A sailboat is brought about on the opposite tack. A boom being rigged in is said to be brought home.

broach. A boat when running before a heavy sea may accidentally swing parallel to the sea and broach which may include dismasting, a knockdown, rolling over, and capsizing.

broad on the bow (quarter). A relative bearing midway between the beam of a boat and dead ahead (astern), either port or starboard. Broad on the port quarter is the same as 225 relative.

broad reach. *See* reach.

broad strake. One of the 3 rows of planking or plating next to the garboard strake.

brogan. A decked version of the Chesapeake sailing log canoe.

broken water. An area of disturbed moving water or breaking waves in an otherwise calmer sea.

broker, yacht. A person who handles the sale and charter of yachts.

brow. A ramp or long, wide plank sometimes fitted with rollers, used for passage between ships moored alongside or between a ship and a pier. It may rest aboard ship on a platform called a brow landing, or on a brow truck fitted with wheels. Sometimes a brow is called a gangplank or a gangboard and, quite incorrectly, a gangway. *See* gangway.

Bruce anchor. A modern British-designed anchor with 3 curved flukes or palms extending from a single arm.

Brummel hook. A patented connector in the form of interlocking C-shaped clips used to connect 2 lines, or a line to a sail.

brushing. Testing a racing sailboat while being tuned by racing it against a similar boat that maintains her sails under constant trim.

Buccaneer. A one-design centerboard sloop. LOA 18′, beam 6′. Designer: J. R. MacAlpine-Downie.

buckeye. A distinctive Chesapeake Bay centerboard schooner up to 80′ long with sharply raked masts, once used as a market and fishing boat; now built or converted as a yacht. Also called a bugeye.

buckler. A general term for a device that prevents the leakage of water through hawse holes, chain pipes, etc.

bugeye. *See* buckeye.

bulb keel. *See* fin keel.

bulkhead. The proper nautical word for a wall in a boat, usually a transverse partition. Also a seawall or a wood or stone quay.

bullboat. A hide or skin boat with a willow frame once used by American Indians.

bulldog clip. A shackle or clamp, closed with several bolts, used to join 2 pieces of wire together in a bulldog splice. Several clips are used for 1 splice. British term is bulldog grip.

bull earing. An earing or ring for hauling the edge of an awning out taut.

bullet block. A block with aluminum sheaves to use with wire for heavy loads such as vangs, outhauls, and halyards on large sailboats.

bullnose. A closed chock, usually centered at the bow, used as a fairlead for the anchor rode. British word is bullring.

bull rail. A large timber set along the edge of a wharf or pier. Also see guard rail.

bullrope. A line led to the mooring buoy from the bowsprit of a small boat to keep it from touching the buoy.

bullseye. Same as deadlight, a fixed piece of heavy glass set into a deck, bulkhead, or door to admit light.

Bullseye. A one-design keel sloop. LOA 15½', beam 6', draft 2½'. Designer: Nathaniel Herreshoff.

bullseye squall. One that forms in fair weather, particularly off South Africa. Identified by the small isolated cloud that forms the center of the invisible vortex of the storm.

bulwark port. Same as a freeing port.

bulwarks. The raised wooden fence or steel plating along the side of a ship or boat above the deck.

bumboat. Any small harbor craft selling goods or services to ships.

bumkin. The short outrigger or spar projecting aft over the stern of a sailboat to which backstays or vane gear are made fast. Also spelled boomkin.

bumper. New but acceptable word for fender.

bung. The wooden plug set flush in a wooden deck or joiner work over a bolt or screw head.

bungee. Same as elastic shock cord.

bunk. Nautical word for bed. Bunkboard is a wooden board used to protect the sleeper from a sweaty steel hull or to keep him in his bunk when the ship rolls.

bunt. The belly or middle part of a sail. A buntline is a rope used in furling a squaresail. In modern sailboats that part of the sail between the reef points and the foot after tack and clew cringles are made fast when reefing a sail.

bunting. Signal flags.

buoy. A floating, anchored, unmanned device used to mark a channel, a danger, an obstruction, etc.; may be nun, spar, can, lighted, bell, whistle, or other buoy. An anchor buoy marks the location of an anchor; an anchorage buoy marks an anchorage. A mooring buoy provides something for a ship or boat to moor to. A sea buoy is the one farthest towards the sea. There are many special-purpose buoys whose names reveal their use.

buoyage. A system of floating markers of distinctive shape, color and numbering that mark navigable channels to ensure a safe passage for vessels. The U.S. and Canada use the lateral system; other countries, including those in Europe, use the cardinal system. Progress is being made by the International Association of Lighthouse Authorities to agree on 2 universal standards. *See* system A,B.

buoy raft. An inflatable emergency life raft that can be ballasted with water after launching to improve stability.

burdened vessel. *See* give-way vessel.

burgee. A swallow-tailed pennant used as a distinguishing flag by yachts and some merchant ships.

burton. A small, common, general-purpose tackle or purchase, usually formed by 2 blocks with a hook block in the bight of the running part.

bush. The mass of spray or dense water vapor marking the base of a waterspout.

buster. A violent southerly squall encountered on the south coast of Australia.

bustle. An underwater bulge in the after part of the hull of a sailboat.

Butterball. A one-design, cat-rigged centerboard boat. LOA 9½', beam 5½'. Designer: R.T. Miller.

button. The projecting ring above the leather on an oar to keep it from sliding through the oarlock.

by. In nautical terminology means near, toward, or in position, as in NE by N (one point north of northeast). Down by the bow or stern describes a ship whose draft is greater at the bow or stern. If a mast goes by the board, it goes overboard. A ship sailing by the wind is sailing close hauled; a ship sailing by the lee is sailing free or down wind. By and large (an adverb) describes the ability of a sailing ship to sail efficiently on a wide range of courses close hauled as well as large (free); thus by and large has come to its present general meaning. By the run describes a line or tackle that is fully released and allowed to run free.

C

cabin. The nautical word for a room in a ship or boat where people live. In small boats it is the major space below decks.

cabin top. A built-on structure over a boat's cabin which provides more headroom. Also called a coach roof or a trunk.

cable. Any heavy rope, wire, or chain used for anchoring, towing, salvage, or for transmitting electricity. Most anchor cables are steel link chains, unless used in boats, when they may be of rope or chain and are called rodes.

cable-laid rope. Three or 4 plain-laid, 3-stranded ropes twisted together in the opposite direction to the twists of the individual ropes. Also known as water-laid rope it was superior to plain-laid rope when used as an anchor cable.

cable stopper. *See* pelican hook.

caique. A small, originally Turkish coasting/sailing vessel of the eastern Mediterranean, used for commerce and fishing. Its simple design and seaworthiness have appealed to yachtsmen who copy it.

calderata. A brisk hot wind off the mountains of the north coast of Venezuela.

caisson. Any watertight structure, usually under air pressure, used in underwater repair and construction.

Cal 20, 21, 23, etc. One-design centerboard sloops of different sizes. Designer: C.W. Lapworth.

calashee watch. Old sailing term for all hands on deck to handle sail.

calender. A device of 2 rollers that applies heat and pressure to sailcloth as part of the finishing process after weaving. The process is known as calendering.

California Current. An ocean current flowing south along the west coast of North America to about latitude 23 N, where it moves westward to join the North Equatorial Current. It originates as the southern branch of the Aleutian Current between 40 and 50 N.

calm. A state of sea and weather marked by little or no wind.

calving. The breaking away of ice from a berg, shelf, or glacier into the sea. The resultant piece of ice is a calf.

camber. The convex curve of a ship's deck athwartships, higher in the center than at the sides. Also the curvature of a sail fore-and-aft, sometimes called flow or draft.

cam cleat. A quick-release fitting for holding a line or sheet of a sailboat between the teeth of two adjacent cams.

cam stopper. A holding device built into modern blocks by which the line passing through the block may be stopped from running and held.

camel. A heavy spar or timber used to hold a ship or boat away from a pier or from another vessel.

Canary Current. An ocean current of the North Atlantic clockwise circulation that flows southwest past Portugal and the northwest coast of Africa, from the Canary Islands to the Cape Verde Islands. There it divides to move west with the North Equatorial Current as well as southeast and then east to become the Guinea Current.

can buoy. A cylindrical, flat-topped navigational buoy usually black in U.S. waters. It carries odd numbers and is left to port when entering port from seaward. *See* nun buoy.

candela. The International Standard Candle—the unit of light or candle power used to express the power of navigational lights.

canoe. A general word for a narrow, usually double-ended open boat propelled by paddles or sail. The sea-going canoes of the Polynesians had outriggers for stability and made very long voyages of colonization and exploration.

Canoe, International. A one-design centerboard sloop. LOA 17′, beam 3½′, Designer: Peter Nethercott.

canoe stern. A sharp stern of a boat, much like a spoon bow.

canopy. A metal or fabric cover or hood for protection from the weather for the people or machinery of a boat.

cant. A piece of wood (cant timber) laid on deck to support something under construction. To cant something is to place it at an angle. Cant frames are those not perpendicular to the keel. A cant spar is one suitable as a boom.

cantline. The groove between strands on the outside of a rope.

canvas. Classically a double warp, single weft fabric made of hemp used for sails, awnings, tarpaulins, etc. Classified as to thickness and strength by numbers 0–12, 0 being the strongest. Modern canvas is made of cotton, synthetic fibers, or a combination. Canvas is also used as a collective term for sails.

cap. A metal band or collar at the end of a spar. The center piece or fitting on a compass card supported by the pivot. A piece of leather over the end of a rope. A cap stay is one between the tops of adjacent masts; sometimes called a triatic stay or signal stay. The top of a mast is sometimes called the cap.

capacitor. A device that stores electric charges. Also called a condenser.

cap block. One of the pieces of wood used at times in a building dock or drydock as a leveling device under a ship's keel.

cape. An area of land projecting into the sea; more prominent than a point. Cape Stiff is sailor's slang for Cape Horn. Cape Flyaway in old sailing days was sailor's slang for imagined, falsely reported land.

Cape Ann oar. An oar with a square loom or shaft.

Cape Cod Mercury. A one-design keel or centerboard sloop. LOA 15′, beam 5½′, draft 2½′ (3½′ with centerboard). Designer: Sparkman & Stephens.

Cape Cod Knockabout. A one-design centerboard sloop. LOA 18', beam 6'. Designer: R.S. Fox.

Cape Dory 10. A one-design centerboard catboat. LOA 10½', beam 4'. Designer: Andrew Vavolitis.

Cape Dory Typhoon. A one-design keel sloop. LOA 18½', beam 6', draft 2½'. Designer: Carl Alberg.

capel. An end connection for wire rope made with a metal cap instead of an eye splice.

cap log. The major horizontal timber on a quay or pier, designed to take the impact of a ship coming alongside. Also called a cap wale.

capping. A strip of wood fitted to the top of the gunwale of a wooden boat to strengthen it.

Capri. A one-design keel sloop. LOA 14', beam 6', draft 2½'.

cap scuttle. A small hatchway closed by a cap or lid fitted over the outside of the coaming.

capstan. Originally a vertical, revolving, concave barrel usually ridged with whelps and powered by men turning wooden capstan bars set into pigeon holes in the capstanhead, drumhead, or trundlehead. In modern ships it is called an anchor windlass or winch; both of which may have vertical or horizontal drums. *See* winch.

captain. Technically and nautically a grade or rank in the Navy, Coast Guard, and other U.S. government services. Also a title by which a ship's master or anyone having master's papers not serving under a master, or the commanding officer of any rank of a government ship should be addressed. *See* master, commanding officer. The chief of the paid hands of a yacht is the captain; the owner or other amateur in charge is the skipper. In naval ships the man in charge of the washrooms and toilets is known as the Captain of the Head.

car. Same as slide.

caravel. A small Mediterranean trading vessel of the 14th through 17th centuries. Originally lateen-rigged on two masts it came to be square-rigged on two and lateen-rigged on the third, the mizzen. The ships of Columbus were caravels.

cardinal point. The four principal points of the compass—north, south, east, and west.

cardinal system of buoyage. A system using buoys and other marks to indicate the mark's direction from the danger being avoided. Since the mark tells the navigator the direction of the danger, he can steer accordingly. *See* buoyage.

careen. To move or turn a boat over on its side; afloat or on a soft beach for cleaning the bottom and for repairs. Careening gear or tackle leading ashore is sometimes used, and the procedure may also be called heaving down.

cargo boat. *See* tramp.

cargo cluster. Lights used aboard ship when working cargo at night.

cargo hook. A special steel hook fitted with a swivel at the end of a cargo whip used for lifting cargo. Also the handheld steel (hand-hook, box hook or cotton hook) used by stevedores.

cargo ship. A merchant ship carrying cargo or freight; may be a liner (scheduled) or a tramp (unscheduled).

Caribbean Current. An ocean current flowing westward into the Caribbean through the Yucatan Channel and then north past Florida as the beginning of the Gulf Stream System.

Carinita. A one-design keel sloop. LOA 20', beam 7', draft 3½'. Designer: Al Mason.

Carley float. A ship-carried life raft made of an oval buoyant ring enclosing a wooden grid. Has been largely replaced by rubber life rafts.

carling. A short fore-and-aft timber or steel beam placed under a deck to strengthen it where deck fittings impose an extra load. Also spelled carlin or carline.

carpenter's stopper. A device used in salvage work to hold fast rope and wire under heavy strain.

carriage. A sliding fitting on a track or traveler to which a sheet block or vang block is attached.

carrick bend. A knot used mostly in fastening two hawsers or large ropes together. Also called a sailor's or anchor knot.

carrier. Radio frequency signal generated in a transmitter, modulated in frequency (FM) or in amplitude (AM) or left as continuous wave (cw).

carry away. To break, part, give way, or wash overboard.

car-top. Any pleasure or work boat that can be carried on top of an auto.

carvel. A type of boat construction using wooden planks meeting flush, in contrast to clinker in which the planks overlap.

cask. A barrel, hogshead, pipe butt, tun, or keg, normally made of wood to carry liquids.

cast. Heaving the lead to measure the depth of water is to cast the lead. To move a ship's bow; to cast to starboard is to swing the ship to the right upon getting underway from an anchorage. To cast off means to throw off, as a mooring line is cast off a bollard.

castaway. Someone put ashore on a lonely island or coast. To cast away a ship means to wreck her, usually intentionally.

cast off. A command given in a ship or boat when leaving from alongside, meaning to throw off all lines, or the one indicated.

catamaran. A twin-hulled ship or boat, most commonly a racing or cruising sailboat, often called cat for short.

cat block. Block used in hoisting aboard an old-fashioned anchor.

catboat. An east coast pleasure sailboat having a single unstayed mast stepped forward with no headsail. It is very beamy and stable, has a centerboard and is often called a cat for short. A cat-sloop is one with a bowsprit and thus a headsail; a cat yawl, ketch, or schooner is one with no headsail.

catch a crab. Said of an oarsman when, on his recovery stroke, he strikes the water accidentally, thus breaking the rhythm of the rowing.

Cathode Ray Tube (CRT). Picture tube in a radar or TV.

catenary. The dip or curve in a rope, wire, cable, chain or fishing line. It often provides an important spring effect when anchoring, mooring to a buoy, or when towing.

cat ketch. *See* catboat.

cat-rig. A boat rigged without headsails. Also called una-rig.

cat schooner. *See* catboat.

catskin. *See* catspaw.

cat sloop. *See* catboat.

catspaw. A light passing breeze as well as the ruffled surface of the water that results (which is also called a catskin). *See* flaw. Also a twisting hitch made in the bight of a line, forming two eyes through which the hook of a tackle can be passed.

catting. Hoisting aboard and securing an old-fashioned anchor.

Catyak. A one-design lateen-rigged centerboard boat. LOA 9½', beam 5'. Designer: Fred Ford, Jr.

cat yawl. *See* catboat.

caulk. To seal a joint between steel plates or wooden planks. For the latter various materials such as oakum are used, hammered in with caulking tools. Also spelled calk.

caulk off. Slang meaning to nap, doze, or sleep. Spoken: "cork off."

cavil. *See* kevel.

cavitation. A damaging phenomenon around rotating propeller blades and struts involving the sudden collapse of transient vapor bubbles associated with the flow of water. It produces corrosion and reduces efficiency.

cavitation plate. *See* antiventilation plate.

cay. A low insular bank of coral and sand; a small, low island. Also spelled key.

cedarstrip. Describes a small boat or canoe made of narrow thin strips of cedar, usually over an oak frame.

ceiling. The inside planking, sheathing or plating of a ship, including the flooring of a ship's cargo hold. It is not the same as ceiling as used ashore. *See* deckhead, overhead.

Celebrity. A one-design keel or centerboard sloop. LOA 19½', beam 6½', fixed draft 2½'. Designer: P. Evanson & Son.

celestial. Pertaining to the heavens. Celestial navigation uses the observation of the sun, moon, stars, and planets to fix a vessel's position.

centerboard. A hinged metal or wooden fin that can be raised and lowered beneath a sailboat to improve her resistance to lateral pressure of the wind. It is housed in a centerboard trunk or case. Also called a centerkeel, centerplate, or sliding keel, and, if very heavy, a drop keel. *See* daggerboard.

centerkeel. *See* centerboard.

centerplate. *See* centerboard.

centerplate keel. Similar to a bar keel but built up by fitting a center, vertical member below the ship's bottom, and stiffening it by continuous narrow steel plates called keel slabs on each side. Also called a side keel.

centerplate rudder. A rudder made of a plate pivoted on the rudder stock so that it can kick up over an obstruction.

center of buoyancy. A point through which passes the result of all upward hydrostatic forces by which a floating ship is supported; the center of a ship's immersed volume.

center of effort. In a sailboat the theoretical point at which the resultant of the wind forces on all sails may be calculated to act, usually taken as the center of area of the sails.

center of gravity. The theoretical point at which all components that comprise a ship's weight may be considered as concentrated: where the sum of all moments of weight is zero. In surface ships the center of gravity is usually above the center of buoyancy.

centipede. A strong rope running below the bowsprit of a large sailing vessel, fitted every 3 or 4 feet with small loops to assist the crew in handling headsails.

certificate of protection. One granted by the U.S. government to a foreign-built yacht bought by a U.S. citizen giving the boat the protection of the U.S. flag.

certificate of registry. A document issued by the government establishing the nationality and ownership of a vessel, often abbreviated to registry.

chafing gear. Any material or device used to prevent or reduce wear of ropes, cable, canvas, etc. May be chafing mats, battens, chain, strips of leather, plastic, canvas, or baggywrinkle.

chafing plate. One that is rounded to minimize wear on lines, as at a hatch coaming.

chain. Connected iron or steel links used principally as anchor and mooring cable. Often fitted with cross-pieces or studs for increased strength and to prevent kinking. An anchor cable for boats is a rode.

chain grab. *See* wildcat.

chain hoist. Lifting gear using an endless chain, several blocks and certain gears for lifting heavy weights aboard ship, especially in the machinery spaces, or in dry-dock.

chain hook. A heavy steel hook attached to a short handle used by men in handling anchor chain, as in putting on a stopper.

chain locker. Compartment below decks where anchor chain is stowed aboard ship as it falls down the chain pipe.

chain pipe. A heavy vertical steel tube just forward of the anchor windlass or wildcat through which the anchor chain falls down into the locker below. Also called a chain locker pipe, chain taker pipe, spurling, spilling or spill pipe, deck pipe, or monkey pipe. British term is naval pipe.

chain plate. A flat strip of metal bolted to the side of a sailboat to which the lower ends of a shroud is made fast.

chains. The platform or station, traditionally located near the chain plates from which the leadsman heaves his lead while taking soundings.

chain stopper. A device for holding an anchor chain on deck using a short length of chain (one end made fast to the deck), a turnbuckle for adjusting tension, and a pelican hook for holding and releasing the cable. Also called a dog or cable stopper.

Challenger 15. A one-design centerboard sloop. LOA 15′, beam 5′. Designer: F.S. Ford, Jr.

Champion. A one-design keel sloop. LOA 21′, beam 7½′, draft 3¼′.

chandler. A merchant, a maritime retailer. A ship or yacht chandler sells all the gear and supplies needed to outfit a boat for sea.

channel. The deeper, navigable, and usually marked and buoyed part of a bay, harbor, river or other body of water. A large strait, as the English Channel. Also a radio frequency.

chantey. A sailor's song, traditionally sung in unison to expedite some heavy hauling chore such as hoisting the anchor. British spelling is shantey.

Charlie Noble. Slang for the smokestack or visible exhaust funnel of the ship's galley.

chart. Nautical word for map, showing the coast line with its major geographic features, aids to navigation, depths of water, nature of bottom, etc. Charts for U.S. waters are produced by the National Ocean Survey, and for the rest of the world by the Defense Mapping Agency Hydrographic Center and by various foreign hydrographic offices. Standard charts are made for ships, and special folding ones for boats. *See* Marine Weather Services charts, pilot chart.

chart datum. The plane of reference to which all depths of water are referred, including tide tables. In the U.S., it is mean lower low water or mean low water. In the U.K. it is the lowest water predictable—the lowest astronomical tide.

charter party (c/p). A formal agreement to hire, rent, or lease a boat. A bareboat or demise charter requires the charterer to provide crew, equipment, stores, fuel, etc. A time charter is for a fixed period; a voyage charter is for a specified voyage.

chart house. The compartment near the bridge where charts are stowed and where the navigation is done. Also called a chart room.

chartlet correction. A paste-over as a partial chart correction, provided in Notices to Mariners.

cheater. Another word for a spinnaker staysail.

check. To slack or ease a rope, maintaining tension but not parting the line. Snub is a stronger word for a line or wire that is held just short of parting.

checking bollard. A bollard used when pulling vessels through the entrance to a drydock.

Checkmate A. One-design centerboard sloop. LOA 13½', beam 5'. Designer: K.R. Watt.

check the rudder or helm. When changing course an order to the helmsman to slow the swing of the ship and not pass the desired heading. Often said: "check her."

check valve. One that permits a fluid to pass through only in one direction. Those used for overboard discharge are also called clack or clapper valves.

cheek. 1. One of the projections on the lower mast of a wooden ship that supports the trestle trees and framing. Also called the mast cheek, and in steel construction, cheek plates. The cheeks on the upper masts are called hounds. 2. One of the sides of a block, or of the jaw of a gaff. 3. The curve or turn of the bilge of a ship or boat.

cheek block. One used for sheets and halyards; usually a fixed block attached to a convenient boom, deck, cabin top, or coaming. Sometimes called a clamp, and by the British a bee block.

cheek knee. One of the side knee pieces by which the cutwater was secured to the bow of a wooden ship.

cheese. British word for a coil of line which has been coiled or flemished down or, according to the British, cheesed down. *See* coil, fake.

Chesapeake log canoe. A double-ended sailboat made from two or more large hollowed logs, developed and still raced in Maryland and Virginia waters.

chine. The line of intersection between the sides and the bottom of a flat or V-bottom hull. *See* bilge. Also the bottom edge of the stern transon of an outboard motorboat.

chine boat. Any boat whose sides and bottom meet at an angle.

chinse. To caulk lightly or temporarily.

chip log. An old method of measuring a ship's speed by using a measured and marked line attached to a chip or piece of wood. When cast overboard and timed the amount of line run out was a measure of speed. *See* log.

chipping. Removing rust and old paint by using a hammer or a scraper.

chock. Heavy metal fitting through which rope, wire, or chain has a fairlead on the deck of a ship or on a pier or dock. May be an open or a closed chock and may be fitted with a roller to reduce friction (a roller chock). British word is fairlead. Also any piece of wood or metal used to prevent anything aboard ship from moving in a seaway. To chock is to secure something. A boom chock is a fitting shaped to receive the end of a boom when lowered.

chock-a-block. Two blocks close together; full, or no room to go further, or no more room for storage of cargo. *See* two-blocked.

choke. To foul or jam, as the hauling part of a tackle is thrust into the block in order to stop movement. This is also called choking the luff.

chop. A short sea in a moderate wind, a choppy sea. Chop chop is nautical slang for hurry.

chow. Slang for food. Chow line in the Navy is the mess line and chow down means its ready.

Christ disturber. A light sail carried aloft in a square-rigger. *See* kites.

chronometer. An accurate clock or watch used for celestial navigation. Very accurate, cheap, modern watches, with or without radio time ticks, now serve many small boatmen as accurate navigational timepieces. Chronometer error is the difference from Greenwich Mean Time.

Chubasco. A violent wind and rain squall met in the rainy season along the west coast of Central America and Mexico.

chuck. A narrow passage or strait swept by tidal currents. Also the current itself.

chum. Odoriferous and sometimes ground bait thrown overboard to attract fish. The procedure is called chumming or tolling.

chute. Slang for spinnaker.

ciguatera. Food poisoning from eating various tropical reef and inshore fish such as grouper, barracuda, jack, etc. which become poisonous at times. Serious but not always fatal.

cirro-cumulus or stratus. *See* cloud.

cirrus. In general cirrus clouds are above 20,000'; often thin wisps or a thin haze producing a halo around the moon. This accompanies good weather. *See* cloud. Also one of the appendages of a barnacle.

clack valve. *See* check valve.

clam. An edible bivalve mollusk that lives mostly just submerged in mud and sand off the coast. More popular in the U.S. than abroad, clams are important as food and bait, and are harvested by hand or by powered clam dredges.

clam, giant. *See* giant clam.

clamp. In wooden boats, a timber fastened to the inside of the frame timbers to support the shelves and the ends of the deck beams. A cheek block. Any device used to hold something together.

clamp down. To sprinkle a deck with water and then dry it with a swab. Not the same as swabbing which involves the use of a wet swab periodically rinsed and wrung out.

clapper valve. *See* check valve.

clap on. To take hold and haul as: "clap on the halyard." To clap on a stopper means to put one on and use it. To clap on sail means to set more canvas.

clapotis. Waves reflected from a seawall, bulkhead, or steep beach.

clasp hook. Same as sister hook.

class. A one-design group of boats that compete on equal terms, such as Star boats. Also a Coast Guard subdivision of boats according to size that determines the equipment they must carry.

classification. In its maritime sense means placing a vessel in a certain category as regards size, material condition, strength of construction, equipment, etc., as specified by a government or private organization, mostly for insurance purposes.

classification society. The private or public organization that establishes standards of safety and sound construction for ships. There are 13 throughout the major maritime countries, patterned after Lloyd's Register of Shipping in the U.K. The American Bureau of Shipping is the U.S. society.

claw off. Said of a sailing ship when close hauled in a gale trying to sail away from a lee shore.

cleading. The wooden or metal casing along the inside of a lifeboat behind which buoyancy tanks are fitted. Plastic foam is now used instead of tanks.

clean. Sharp, neat, as in the clean lines of a ship. Free of obstruction, as in a clean anchorage; opposed to foul. Also means free of any unfavorable or qualifying clause as in a clean bill of health or bill of lading. A clean charter is one free of commission or of agency fees. Clean full (also called rap full) refers to sails kept drawing steadily. A clean run describes the fine afterbody of a ship that causes little disturbance of the water or wake when underway, in contrast to a full run.

clear. To free from entanglement, as in clearing a tackle. A clear anchor is one that is not foul. A line free to run is clear. To clear the forecastle is to remove all people, promptly. Clearing the harbor, a cape, or other obstruction, means departing and passing safely.

clearance. Official permission, often in writing, for a vessel to enter or leave port in regard to customs, immigration, health, etc.

clearing iron. A caulking tool, same as a ripping iron.

clear-view screen. A circular revolving glass disc set into a bridge or cabin window to ensure a clear view through rain, snow, and spray.

cleat. 1. Any piece of wood or metal designed to hold rope, wire, or to provide fairleads, usually anvil-shaped and fastened to bulwarks, decks, or spars. Modern sailboats use a variety of mechanical cleats, some with hinged wedges or teeth designed to hold a line and release it quickly if necessary; these include jam cleat, clam cleat, and cam cleat. 2. A transverse piece of wood or metal used to prevent slipping on an inclined plank or brow. 3. Metal clips on a ship's frame that hold cargo battens. 4. To cleat a line is to make it fast on a cleat. *See* kevel.

clevis. Same as shackle but not a word as commonly used at sea.

clevis pin. A short metal rod or pin used to close a shackle, clevis, turnbuckle end, etc.

clew. The after lower corner of a fore-and-aft sail, and one of the two lower corners of a squaresail or spinnaker. To clew up is to haul a squaresail up to its yard; to clew down means to haul on the clew lines and thus force the sail down.

clew cringle. A loop or eye formed in the boltrope at the clew of the sail. A clew jigger is a light tackle used in clewing up. There are also clew ropes, patches, rings, and traveling rings, all associated with the clews of sails and their handling.

clinch. A method of securing a heavy rope to a ring by seizing the rope after taking several turns around the ring.

clinker built. A method of boat construction in which the lower edges of each plank overlap the upper edges of the plank below. Also called lapstrake construction. *See* carvel.

clinometer. An instrument for measuring the roll of a vessel, same as inclinometer. May use a pendulum or a bubble.

clip. *See* slide.

clip hook. *See* sister hook.

clipper. The American built, very fast sailing ships of the 19th century. Initially schooner-rigged and later square-rigged, their importance declined rapidly with the advent of steam and the opening of the Suez Canal. The clipper bow remains with its distinctive concave curve. *See* bow shapes.

close. A boat closes the range when the range markers or day beacons marking the channel seem to draw together as the boat nears the center of the channel; the range opens when the markers seem to separate as the boat strays from midchannel.

close hauled. Sailing on the wind, as near to the wind as possible. *See* reach.

close reefed. Describes a sail or a sailboat with all reefs taken in.

close up. Describes a signal flag or group of flags hoisted all the way up. Same as two-blocked which is no longer correct in the Navy.

cloth. According to sailmaker's usage, a length of canvas or material sewn up with others to make a sail. *See* miter.

clothes stops. Short pieces of cord used to hang up washed clothes.

cloud. Visible moisture and/or ice in the sky. Cirrus clouds are high and feathery and indicate fair weather; cirro-cumulus, a mackerel sky indicating possible foul weather, and cirro-stratus, thin, hazy and halo-producing. Intermediate clouds are altostratus, dark and usually containing rain and snow; and altocumulus, layers, rolls or castles. Cumulus are low clouds, puffs of wool that indicate fair weather; cumulus-stratus are low and dark (if low enough they are fog), and cumulonimbus are thunderheads full of storm which sometimes extend quite high. Nimbus and nimbo-stratus are low dark rain clouds which, when broken up in stormy weather become fractonimbus and scud.

cloud tickler. A light sail carried aloft in a square-rigger. *See* kites.

clove hitch. One consisting of two half hitches in the same directions put around a rope, spar, etc.

clove hook. *See* sister hook.

club. Any spar that extends along the foot of a fore-and-aft head-sail, *see* club-footed jib.

club burgee. One that carries a yacht club insignia.

club foot. Describes a ship's bow in which most of the displacement is at the forefoot, near the keel, as in a bulbous bow.

club-footed jib. One with a boom along its foot that can be rigged to a traveler thus not requiring handling when the boat is tacked.

clump. A heavy mass usually of cement that anchors a mooring buoy.

clump block. A strong, thick, single block of various sizes with a wide sheave and swallow.

clutter. Radar reflections of waves, snow, rain, etc., that interfere with a clear radar picture. Also called sea return.

coach roof. *See* cabin top.

coachwhipping. Nautical decorative fancy work done with cord on stanchions, bellropes, etc., and on the end of manropes. Similar to coxscombing in purpose but not in design.

coak. A small piece of hardwood used as additional security in scarfing two pieces of wood together.

coaming. The raised borders around hatches and doors afloat and around open cockpits of boats to prevent the easy entry of water.

coast. The land that borders the sea.

Coast and Geodetic Survey. Now the National Ocean Survey.

coaster. A ship or a person engaged in maritime business along a coast.

Coast Guard. In general terms a governmental, paramilitary organization charged with enforcing the laws regarding safety at sea, customs regulations, and other laws that apply to mariners. It provides welcome and important assistance to mariners in distress. The U.S. Coast Guard is under the Department of Transportation in peacetime and the Navy in wartime.

Coast Guard Auxilliary. The valuable, volunteer civilian arm of the Coast Guard concerned with small boat safety and assisting the Coast Guard. It has nearly 50,000 members. It is over 40-years-old.

Coast Pilot. A publication issued by the National Ocean Survey giving detailed information concerning the nature of the U.S. Coast and inland waters, particularly the hazards and the aids to navigation and other local data useful to mariners. *See* Sailing Directions.

Coast 13. A one-design centerboard sloop. LOA 13½', beam 5'. Designer: Daniel Naughton.

coat. Traditionally a piece of tarred or painted canvas or leather fitted around a mast, rudder casing, etc., to prevent the entry of water below decks. Now usually replaced by modern sealing devices and techniques. Also called a collar.

cobia. A worldwide migratory, schooling gamefish that grows to 100 pounds. In Australia called a black kingfish, in the Caribbean a lemonfish or ling, and in Chesapeake Bay a crab-eater, coalfish, or sergeant fish.

coble. A small, open, clinker-built fishing boat, once common on the east coast of England.

cock. A valve, faucet, or tap used in controlling the flow of liquid or gas. May be a draincock, indicator cock, oilcock, petcock, or steamcock. *See* seacock.

cocked hat. The Biritish term for the triangle often resulting from plotting three lines of position or bearings that fail to meet at the ideal point.

cockpit. The well or sunken space for the crew in the after part of a boat.

cod, codfish. Any one of several bottom-dwelling food fish of the family Gadidae. For centuries an important commercial fish, especially for the Europeans, now suffering from overfishing.

code. In the maritime sense an international system of ship-to-ship and ship-to-shore communications by flag, flashing light or radio, involving a code book and various code flags.

code pennant. A signal flown at a yacht club to indicate that members are using their own code instead of the international system.

coffee grinder. Slang for the expensive hand-cranked deck winches used in large racing sailboats. Often the handle is on a pedestal. Also grinder.

cofferdam. The empty space between compartments aboard ship. Also the watertight wall built around a damaged area of the hull; same as caisson.

coil. Rope made up in a series of adjacent rings, usually 200 fathoms long. To coil a line is to lay it down in a circular pattern on deck, one loop roughly on top of another. If a line is to be used (run out) it should be faked down in long bights or loops so that it will not kink. *See* fake, flemish.

coir. A weak, elastic, and buoyant natural fiber from coconut husks used for rope and mats.

collar. The eye or loop at the end of a stay or shroud that goes over the masthead and holds the mast. Also same as coat.

collier. Any ship used to carry coal.

collier's patch. The result of the old-fashioned practice of tarring a worn place in a sail.

collision bulkhead. One that is watertight, athwartships and usually near the bow to limit flooding in the event of a collision.

collision mat. Mat made of canvas thrummed with rope yarns close together; used over the side to slow the entrance of water if the ship is holed. Boatmen call it a fothering blanket.

colors. The national flag or ensign. *See* ensign.

Colregs 72. The International Regulations for Preventing Collisions at Sea, 1972.

comb cleat. A piece of hardwood with holes bored through to serve as fairleads for various parts of the running rigging of old sailing ships.

comber. Short for beachcomber—a long curling wave that breaks on the beach. Also a deep-water wave whose crest is pushed over by the wind, much larger than a whitecap.

combination buoy. A buoy fitted with both light and sound signals.

combination lantern. A lantern having both red and green sections; used as sidelights in a small boat.

combination rope. Fiber rope that incorporates some wire strands.

come about. To tack a sailboat; that is, to bring the wind on the other side of the sails by causing the bow to pass through the wind. Also come round or come around is often used in the same sense.

come home. Said of an anchor when it drags or when it is heaved in. Anything that is brought to its normal stowage position is brought home.

Comet. A one-design centerboard sloop LOA 16', beam 5'. Designer: C.L. Johnson.

come up behind. Command to slack or ease a line being hauled in so that it can be belayed; usually shortened to up behind.

command bridge. In a multi-bridge cabin cruiser or sport fisherman the bridge on which controls, such as the wheel, are being used.

Commodore. The president of a yacht club.

companion. Usually a structure such as a booby hatch or dog house, built over a companionway (ladder). Sometimes the ladder itself is called a companion.

companionway. Usually a ladder or staircase aboard ship. Sometimes companion for short and thus confused with the structure built over the companion as a protection against weather. A companion hatchway is an opening in the deck.

company. The crew of a ship or boat. Boats sailing together are said to be in company.

compass. An instrument that indicates direction on the earth's surface. Originally it was magnetic, and a floating magnet pointed towards the earth's magnetic pole. Most ships and many boats now use a gyroscopic or gyro compass in which a rapidly spinning wheel seeks to align itself with the earth's axis and thus points to the true north. A radio compass provides the bearing of a radio signal. Also a compass is the name of a simple drafting tool used to describe a circle.

compass card. The circular card on which directions are marked attached to the magnetic needles of a magnetic compass.

compass error. The algebraic sum of deviation and variation—essentially the difference between the magnetic course or bearing and the true.

compass range. A pair of markers, beacons, or other seamarks that, when placed in line by directing the boat indicate a true compass direction against which the boat's compass can be compared. British word is transit.

compass rose. Outer and inner graduated concentric circles on a nautical chart used for laying out courses and bearings. The outer circle marks the true direction, the inner one indicates magnetic. The difference is the variation in that vicinity.

composite sailing. A combination of great circle courses and a latitude line that meets great circles tangentially.

compressor. A device for holding anchor chain cable from running out by jamming it against the chain pipe. Also the brake band on an anchor windlass for checking and temporarily holding the anchor chain.

computer, navigation. *See* navigation computor.

conch. A large gastropod mollusk or marine snail found mostly in tropical waters, it has a brightly colored shell and edible flesh. Also known as a whelk, periwinkle, or winkle depending on local usage, although the latter terms generally refer to smaller animals found farther north. Sometimes pronounced conk.

concluding line. A small rope down the middle of a side ladder, made fast to each step.

condenser. A device that stores electric charges. Also called a capacitor.

cone. A fabric or metal shape used as a gale warning when hoisted ashore and either singly or in pairs end to end as dayshapes under Colregs 72.

cone shell. A cone shaped, tropical marine snail, that can inject venom through small teeth at the sharp end. Has been known to kill people.

conger eel. A large (up to 10′) varacious salt-water eel, related to the moray eel, and found off Europe and North America.

conn. The control of a ship or boat underway—a person is conning the ship when he is directing her course and speed. British spelling is con.

connecting shackle. One used in joining lengths or shots of anchor chain. Also called a joiner shackle or Kenter shackle, or chain shackle.

Consul. An officer of the U.S. Foreign Service, or that of any country, who in a foreign port protects the interests of his country and its nationals, and who performs the necessary legal, commercial, and humanitarian services.

containership. A ship converted or designed to carry cargo containers below and above decks. British word is vanship.

Contender. A one-design cat-rigged centerboard sloop. LOA 16′, beam 4½′. Designer: Bob Miller.

continental shelf. The ocean zone extending from the line of permanent immersion on the coast to depths of 120 meters. From there to the bottom of the sea is the continental slope.

continuous wave (cw). Unmodulated radio waves transmitted at constant frequency and amplitude. Used for Morse code (dot-dash).

contline. The space between the strands of a rope that is filled with worming.

contraguide rudder. A rudder having an upper and a lower section somewhat offset to improve the thrust and the efficiency of the propeller.

contra preferentum. The principle that holds that any ambiguity in a marine or other insurance policy must be construed against the party who drafted it.

contrapropeller. The arrangement of vertical or horizontal pieces of steel plate attached to the rudder post or struts of a ship to divert the propeller stream into a more efficient shape and thus improve propeller thrust.

controller. Same as chain stopper, also called cable or bow stopper. *See* stopper.

copper fastened. Said of a wooden ship or boat whose hull was fastened together with copper or bronze nails, screws, or bolts.

coral. A colony of sea animals known as polyps, their jellylike bodies are enclosed in a shell of calcium carbonate. One type forms the red jewelry coral of the Mediterranean; another forms tropic reefs. Fire coral is a smooth, dull, yellow, plantlike organism in the shape of moose horns whose stinging cells inflict painful welts and rash upon contact. Coral is also called madrepores. A coral head is a massive mushroom or pillar underwater made up of coral. *See* reef, geographical. Also the unfertilized eggs of lobsters.

corange lines. Lines on a chart passing through all points having the same tidal range.

cordage. The collective word for rope, line, cord, etc.

Corinthian. A yachting word for an amateur sailor as distinct from a paid crew member or one who makes his living by yachting.

Coriolis Force. The effect of the earth's rotation on all moving bodies particularly on air and water masses. It is the force that deflects the trade winds from a south or north direction.

cormorant. A large fish-eating, diving bird; some, as those in the Galapagos, cannot fly. They are a major source of guano.

corner reflector. *See* radar reflector.

Coronado 15. A one-design centerboard sloop. LOA 15½', beam 5½'. Designer: Frank Butler.

corrected time. In sailboat racing, a boat's elapse time less her time allowance.

corposant. Ball or streak of light or flame sometimes seen on the rigging of a ship at sea, caused by atmospheric electrical discharge. Also called St. Elmo's Fire or Light.

cotidal. Pertaining to the same high water level at various places. Indicated by cotidal lines, the basis for a cotidal chart, connecting all the points that have high tide at the same time.

Cottontail. A one-design centerboard sloop or cat-rigged boat. LOA 11', beam 5'.

Cougar Mk. III. A one-design centerboard sloop-rigged catamaran. LOA 18½', beam 8'. Designer: Prout Bros.

counter. The aftermost part of the stern of a boat that overhangs the rudder above the waterline. Also called the fantail which in the Navy is the space on deck all the way aft.

counter current. One running in the opposite direction, either below or adjacent to the principal current.

course. The direction in which a boat is steered, measured in most cases from north (000) clockwise in a circle of 360. Also the lowest sail on each mast of a square-rigger.

course made good. The single resultant direction from one point to another of a boat underway steering a number of different courses.

course over the ground. The actual path of a ship with respect to the earth.

cover. A standard tactic in sail racing when leading is to tack as your opponent does astern of you, keeping between him and the mark or the wind. Thus you cover him.

cover board. The outermost piece of decking, cut to follow a boat's sheer, it covers the upper ends of the ribs. Also covering board.

cove stripe. A decorative stripe painted on a boat, running fore and aft on the hull topside just below the rail.

cow hitch. Same as a lark's head. Also a term for any unusual or ineffective knot.

cowry. A tropical marine mollusk with a colorful, glossy shell, highly prized by collectors and sometimes used as money in the south Pacific. Also spelled cowrie.

cow's tail. Nautical term for the unsightly, frayed end of a rope.

coxcombing. Decorative lashing or winding usually done with white cord around boathook shafts, tillers, etc. Similar to coachwhipping in purpose but not design.

coxswain. The man who steers and is in charge of a boat. Spoken coxun.

c/p. Charter party.

CPA. In piloting, the closest point of approach to a hazard, buoy, point of land, etc.

CQR anchor. A patented anchor shaped like a plow. Also called a plow anchor or spade anchor, and in the U.K., a ploughshare anchor.

crabbing. Moving sideways in a sailboat because of wind pressure; making leeway.

cracking the sheet. Easing the sheet of a sail so that the boom or the foot of the sail can move outboard.

cradle. The framework upon which a boat rests in a marine railway, storage yard or in launching ways. The support for a boat or other cargo carried on deck. Also called a crib. *See* launching cradle, skids.

craft. A collective term for small boats, lighters, barges, etc.

crank. A vessel with low stability that is easily inclined, and that has a long slow roll, is said to be crank. Opposite of crank is stiff. A crank ship may also be called tender or cranky. *See* stiff.

cranse. An iron hoop or band with eyes, fitted to a spar or mast to which shrouds, stays, blocks, etc., are fastened. The band securing the jibboom to the bowsprit is known as a cranse iron. Also spelled crance.

crawdad. *See* crayfish.

crawfish. *See* crayfish.

crayfish. A freshwater crustacean locally called crawfish or crawdad, resembling a lobster but much smaller. A popular but inaccurate name for the ocean spiny lobster. *See* spiny lobster.

creek. A small stream, sometimes tidal. By British usage, it is a narrow sheltered inlet, deeper than a cove.

crew. The men and women who man a boat and form its complement.

crib. A structure filled with stones or rubble forming part of a temporary breakwater, harbor blockage, bridge support, etc. Also a cradle.

cribbing. A cribbing ram is a battering ram used to knock away the wooden supports called blocking or cribbing under a ship or boat about to be launched. *See* block.

cringle. Formerly limited to a rope eye or a metal ring in the edge of a sail, but now a word used almost interchangeably with grommet.

Cromwell Current. An easterly flowing subsurface current moving along the Equator in the Pacific. In other oceans similar subsurface countercurrents exist and are called Equatorial undercurrents.

Crosby rig. A method of arranging the sheet of a mainsail using several blocks instead of a traveler. Used on Lightnings in particular.

cross-cut. Describes a headsail when all the panels of canvas are roughly horizontal.

cross-hawse. When, in a boat moored with two anchors, the rodes lie across each other just forward of the bow.

crossing the line. A traditional ceremony afloat involving the initiation of all who have not previously crossed the Equator. These pollywogs are made shellbacks after suffering various indignities under the supervision of King Neptune.

crossjack. The squaresail extending below the lowest yard on the mizzenmast of a square-rigger. Pronounced: krojek.

crosspointing. Line or strips of leather or canvas braided around a stanchion, boathook handle, etc., for decoration. Originally it was a way of finishing off the end of a rope by cutting away the inner yarns and braiding the outer ones.

crosstree. An athwartships wood or steel spreader on the mast over which the shrouds are led down in a sailboat. Crosstrees are one continuous piece whereas spreaders may be fittings on one side of the mast only. *See* spreader.

crowfoot. One of the small lines rove through the euphroe or led to a single rope to support an awning. *See* euphroe.

crown. The part of an old-fashioned stock anchor where the arms and the shank join. In stockless anchors the part between the arms where they pivot on the shank.

crowning. *See* becue.

crow's nest. A lookout station aloft in a boat or ship.

CRP. A Controllable Reversible Propeller. *See* pitch.

CRT. Cathrode Ray Tube.

cruise. To boatmen a cruise means more than 1 day underway not racing.

cruiser. Any pleasure boat capable of feeding and sleeping its crew.

crustacean. Pertains to the large, important, class of hard-skinned aquatic animals such as lobster, crab, shrimp, barnacle, etc. All breathe by means of gills or similar organs.

crutch. Any forked device for supporting a spar, boom, steering oar, etc.

cuckhold's knot. A hitch securing a line to a spar. The two parts of the line cross each other and are seized together.

cuddy. A small room or cabin below decks; a locker forward in a small open boat, too small to be a cabin but providing some shelter.

cucumber, sea. An echinoderm that lies on the bottom—its soft round body sometimes ejects its intestines in defense. The Chinese consider it a food and an aphrodisiac.

cumshaw. A gift or a tip, often in return for work or services performed.

cumulonimbus. A massive, towering cloud with vertical development; its summits rise in towers and mountainous shapes. Also called a thundercloud or thunderhead. *See* cloud.

cumulus. A cloud with the appearance of a mass of cotton wool billowing up into the sky. *See* cloud.

cunningham hole or eye. An opening in a sail for a loop of line by which the sail can be flattened or eased. The line is often called a cunningham. There may be one to flatten the foot and another called a luff-puller for the luff.

curl. Excessive curvature in the luff or leech of a spinnaker, or in the leech of a mainsail or jib, or in the foot of a jib.

current. A moving horizontal stream of water as in nearshore, tidal, and ocean currents. A current's velocity is its drift, and the direction towards which the current flows is its set.

Current Charts. The usual short name for the Tidal Current Charts issued by the National Ocean Survey on which tidal current data are shown graphically for a number of important places such as San Francisco Bay. Tidal Current Chart Diagrams are published monthly by NOS to be used with the Charts.

Current Tables. Usual short name for the Tidal Current Tables published by the National Ocean Survey that give daily predictions for the times and drift of the currents.

cusp. Sand or mud deposited along the shore by wave action in the form of points or bars pointing seaward.

cut. Appearance, style, as in "cut of her jib." Cut and run for a sailing ship meant to cut one's anchor hawser and perhaps the ropeyarn with which the sails were lightly furled and sail away quickly.

Cutlass. A one-design keel or centerboard sloop. LOA 23½', beam 7', fixed draft, keel 4', centerboard 3'. Designer: R.D. Carlson.

cut splice. Two lines spliced together so as to form a slit or an eye.

cutter. In modern American usage, a Coast Guard patrol ship, a square-stern pulling boat, or a single-masted sailboat whose mast is set further aft than that of a sloop. A cutter is similar to a sloop but has more than one headsail.

cuttlefish. An edible, oval, invertebrate sea animal, a mollusk and a decapod equipped with suction disks. Closely related to the squid, it lives in shallow coastal waters, moves by jet propulsion and feeds mostly on shrimp. It ejects a dark ink when pursued and grows to 3 feet in length.

cuttyhunk. A traditional tough, braided linen fishing line, now largely replaced by the synthetic fiber lines that resist rot.

cutwater. Originally a strengthening and protective timber bolted to the outside of the stem; now describes the leading edge of the stem near the waterline or the stem itself.

cw. *See* continuous wave.

cyclone. A closed atmospheric circulation, rotating counterclockwise in the northern hemisphere (clockwise in the southern); also called a low. If it is of tropical origin with a warm center and strong winds to 64 knots, it becomes a tropical storm. If winds are higher it becomes a very violent and destructive hurricane or, in the Indian Ocean a cyclone, and in the western Pacific a typhoon or baguio. *See* anticyclone.

D

D International signal code alphabet flag. When hoisted singly means: keep clear am maneuvering with difficulty. Spoken: delta.

Dacron. Trade name for a modern synthetic polyester fiber used for sails and cordage.

Dagger. A one-design centerboard catboat. LOA 14½′, beam 5′. Designer: J.R. MacAlpine-Downie.

daggerboard. A sliding keel moving vertically in a trunk but not hinged as is a centerboard. It has the same purpose.

Daily Memoranda. Provide a synopsis of the latest information on navigational aids as well as dangers to mariners and advance information on the more important items that will be published in Notices to Mariners; issued by the Defense Mapping Agency Hydrographic Center.

dan buoy. A small floating device used to mark temporarily obstructions or dangers to navigation, such as fishing gear. Also used to mark schools of fish.

Danforth anchor. A popular boat anchor with two triangular flukes close to the shank, and a rod stock passed perpendicularly to the flukes and to the shank at their juncture. This prevents the flukes from rolling out of the ground and at the same time permits the anchor to be housed in a hawsepipe. Also known as a lightweight or LWT anchor.

danger angle or bearing. In coastal piloting, that angle or bearing marking a hazard; one that establishes a limit for safe navigation.

danger buoy. One that marks a shoal, rock, or other hazard to navigation. In U.S. waters it has red and black stripes; in Europe it is usually green.

dangerous semicircle. Area in the direction of advance of a hurricane or typhoon subject to winds of greater velocity than those in the opposite or navigable semicircle. Also called the dangerous quadrant.

danger signal. Under the Rules of the Road, the five or more short and rapid blasts on a ship's whistle required when failing to understand or approve of the movements of another vessel. Also called a signal of doubt.

dasher block. A small block rigged at the end of the spar or gaff for a flag halyard.

date line. That meridian of longitude separating east and west; generally follows 180 degrees but by international agreement it shifts to include all the islands of a group. When eastward bound, add a day; when westward bound drop a day. Also called the international date line.

datum. A level or plane of reference from which the height of the tide is measured. Usually in the U.S. it is the level of low water or lower low water. Now marked on most navigational charts in meters and called the chart datum.

Davidson Current. An ocean current flowing north along the west coast of North America as a countercurrent to the California Current. It is normally detectable only in November-January when the upwelling along the coast has stopped.

davit. A small derrick or crane, often used in pairs, for handling boats, ladders, stores, etc. The most common boat davits are: gravity, crescent, quadrental, and radial. The davit head is the top part on which the boat falls, or to which span wires are attached. Mechanical davits, other than the simple radial or gravity types are known to the British as luffing davits.

Davy Jones. Traditionally among sailors the spirit of the sea, usually considered evil. Davy Jones' Locker is the ocean bottom and is thus overboard.

Davy Jones' wheel inspector. In the north Pacific, a boatsman's name for a deadhead or floating log.

daybeacon. A large, brightly painted sign; may be lighted or numbered. In U.S. waters usually has a triangular or rectangular shape outlined by reflecting material; used to mark a channel and, when in pairs, to mark the line or range of the center of the channel. It is set on posts driven into the bottom, or on small structures ashore. Also called a daymark or leading mark.

dayboat. *See* day sailor.

daymark. *See* daybeacon, dayshape.

day, nautical. From noon to noon, using mean civil time.

day sailor. A small sailboat, usually open but may have a cuddy forward, used for short sails or racing. British word is dayboat which also applies to a small powerboat if not used for racing or overnight cruising.

dayshape. The black ball, cone, or diamond required to be shown by a ship towing, being towed, fishing, not under command, etc. Also somewhat inaccurately called a daymark, or a day signal.

day tank. An additional fuel tank in large diesel-powered boats located above the highest part of the fuel injection system to ensure gravity flow to the engine at all times.

day's work. Twenty-four hours of navigation from noon to noon, including sun lines and morning and evening stars sights.

DC–14. A one-design lateen-rigged catamaran with daggerboards. LOA 14½', beam 6½'.

dead. Absolute, as dead calm, dead low water, dead ahead.

deadeye. A disk of wood pierced with holes once used instead of turnbuckles to tighten shrouds and stays.

deadhead. 1. A floating log, most of which is submerged; sometimes called a sleeper. 2. Any heavy post on a pier or dock used for making lines fast. *See* checking bollard. 3. A block of wood or a log used as an anchor or as a mooring buoy. A boat sailing with a minimum crew to meet the owner or the charter group is deadheading.

dead in the water. Said of a ship that has no way on.

deadlight. A hinged metal cover for an airport; also called a battle-port in the Navy. A ventilating deadlight is one that admits air but not light. A heavy, fixed, usually round glass set into the deck or a bulkhead or door, synonomous with bullseye and decklight.

dead reckoning (DR). The ancient but still important method of estimating a ship's position by using as input the courses steered and the speed made good. Now also done mechanically by a dead reckoning tracer or an inertial system.

deadrise. 1. The vertical distance between a ship's keel and the turn of the bilge. Also expressed in terms of the angle that the underbody makes with the horizontal in an athwartships section. 2. The name of a small (30–40') powerboat with a V bottom, low freeboard, engine aft, and a cuddy forward, used on the east coast of the U.S. as a workboat, especially in Chesapeake Bay for crabbing and oystering. The deadrise launch of North Carolina waters has a round stern.

dead rope. One that does not pass through a block or fairlead.

dead water. Relatively still water downstream from an obstruction or water drawn along behind a moving ship by separation of the boundary layer. Also a phenomenon reported by sailing ships and slow steamers, especially where a layer of fresh water is above the salt water. At the boundary the energy of the forward motion of the ship may be partially absorbed by the generation of internal waves, thus causing the ship to be slowed. This is known as the boundary layer phenomenon. *See* internal wave.

deadweight. The deadweight tonnage is the difference between a ship loaded and her light displacement. Total deadweight is the carrying capacity of a ship; for computing cargo deadweight tonnage subtract fuel, water, stores, etc.

deadwood. The structure between the keel line and the stern post of a ship or boat.

Decca. Medium frequency hyperbolic continuous wave radio navigation system of relatively short range but accurate and used in coastal waters of the U.S. and Europe.

decibel (DB). Strength of communication signals or of sound. Expressed logarithmically.

deck. The floor of a ship. Boats normally have a cabin sole and a deck topside which should not be called the floor. Decks aboard ship are numbered and named according to use; as boat deck, berth deck, mess deck. *See* floor, sole.

deck cleat. *See* sampson post.

deckhead. The ceiling (as the word is used ashore) of a compartment. This is also called the overhead. *See* ceiling, overhead.

deckhorse. A bar placed athwartships on deck on which the sheet block of a fore-and-aft sail can travel.

deck iron. A wood-caulking tool with a broad straight edge; also called a dumb iron.

decklight. A heavy piece of glass fixed in a deck to provide light. Also called a bullseye or deadlight.

deck pillar. *See* stanchion.

deck pipe. *See* chain pipe.

deck stopper. *See* stopper.

deck stringer. The strake or line of deck plating that runs along the outboard edge of a ship's deck, adjacent to the hull plating.

decksweeper. *See* jib.

declination. The angular distance of a heavenly body from the celestial equator measured on the hour circle of the body, north or south of the equinoctial. Magnetic declination was an old term for variation.

deep. An indicator of fathoms on a leadline. "By the deep six" sung out by the leadsman indicates a depth of 6 fathoms. On either side are the marks 5 and 7 reported in a similar fashion: "by the mark 5," by the mark 7."

deep scattering layer. A layer of tiny ocean animals such as jellyfish, copepods, etc., who rise near to the surface at night and sink during the day.

deep six. To give something the deep six is to throw it overboard or deep six it.

Defense Mapping Agency Hydrographic Center (DMAHC). Current name for the Naval Oceanographic Office, formerly the Navy Hydrographic Office that produces charts and publications relating to navigation and hydrography. Works with the National Ocean Survey (NOS) which is under the National Oceanic and Atmospheric Administration (NOAA) of the Department of Commerce.

demersal fish. *See* flatfish, groundfish.

departure. Position on a chart (such as the sea buoy) from which a ship leaves an anchorage or a port when setting out on a voyage. Also the distance a ship makes good east or west along a parallel, expressed in nautical miles.

depth. The vertical distance amidships from a ship's keel to her upper or main deck, or to the deck to which it is referred.

depth finder. Same as echo sounder or depth sounder.

depth recorder. An instrument that shows and records the depth of water as measured by echo sounding.

depth sounder. Same as depth finder or echo sounder.

derelict. Goods, cargo, or a ship abandoned by the owner at sea and large enough to be a menace to navigation.

derrick. A fixed structure or fitting on a ship, barge, drilling platform, etc., used to handle material.

detachable link. A link of anchor cable (chain) that can be taken apart, opened and reassembled.

development class. A one-design class of boats without rigid uniform specifications permitting variations in building and rigging.

deviation. A magnetic compass error (the angle between the compass needle and the magnetic meridian) caused by the magnetic properties of the ship. Together with variation, a terrestrial force, it makes up magnetic compass error, the difference between what the magnetic compass reads and true north. Semicircular deviation varies as the ship changes course. Also a marine insurance word meaning the departure of a merchant ship from her scheduled route without lawful reason.

deviation table. A record of magnetic compass deviation kept handy to the navigator where deviation can be combined with variation as shown on the chart to obtain compass error and thus a true course.

devil fish. *See* manta ray.

devil's claw. A very strong steel hook used to hold a link of anchor chain.

dhow. An Arabic and African small trading vessel, originally lateen-rigged and now often diesel powered which has been trading in the Red Sea, Persian Gulf, Indian Ocean, and on the African coast from the dawn of history.

dew point. *See* point.

diamond shape. When required to be displayed by Colregs, a shape consisting of two cones having a common base. *See* shape.

diamond stays. A pair of stays, one on each side of a mast, held out by spreaders, forming a diamond shape. They start and finish together on the mast at some distance apart, providing lateral rigidity and strength. A long diamond stay is sometimes called a diamond shroud.

diaphone. A sound signal device used as a coastal aid to navigation in low visibility (fog), usually powered by compressed air and giving a low-pitched strong blast ending in a sharply descending note called a grunt. *See* nautiphone.

die lock chain. Modern anchor chain in which the links are made in two sections forged together.

differential block. One fitted with two or more sheaves of different diameters. *See* chain hoist.

digital. Describes instrument presentation in numbers rather than by pointer indication.

ding. Boatman's and surfer's word for a hole or fracture in a boat or surfboard.

dinghy. A small square stern boat used with oars or with sail for racing or general utility, or as a yacht tender.

dinette. A small eating place in the cabin of a boat—a table flanked by seats which usually convert into a berth.

dink. Short and popular word for dinghy.

dinky. An auxiliary diesel generator aboard a vessel.

dinoflagellates. Highly developed, very small, mobile organisms, mostly single-cell, that form a major part of the plant plankton that are the basis for the ocean food chain. *See* red tide.

diode. Semiconductor or vacuum tube that passes current in one direction only.

dip. Short for dip of the horizon or height of eye correction of a sextant measurement of altitude of a heavenly body. The moon or sun is said to have dipped when its lower limb or bottom of observed curvature touches the horizon. Magnetic dip is that of a compass needle due to the attraction of the earth's magnetic field.

dip, at the. A signal flag or the colors are at the dip when hoisted half way. All the way up is two-blocked or close up.

dip colors. As a salute merchant ships dip their colors to a warship when underway, and the warship returns the salute.

dipper. The Big Dipper or Ursa Major, a constellation in the northern hemisphere, is important to mariners because the two end stars of the container point to Polaris, the north star.

dipping a light. Same as bobbing a light.

dipping lug. *See* lugsail.

dip the eye. To arrange two loops or eyes or mooring lines on the same bollard so that either can be cast off without disturbing the other.

displacement. Weight of a ship in tons equal to the weight of water she displaces.

displacement hull. In a powerboat, as distinct from a sailboat, a hull that is relatively narrow, round-bottomed and easily driven at moderate speeds. It has a built-in maximum, or hull speed, beyond which no practical increase in power will increase the speed. A displacement boat is one wholly supported by the volume of water she displaces in contrast to a planing hull. *See* hull.

distance made good. Number of miles along her intended course that a ship or boat travels.

distress signal. To a mariner, any recognized action that indicates an emergency and requests assistance. It may be a gun fired at intervals of a minute, a continuous sounding of a fog signal, rockets or shells showing red stars, SOS or Mayday by any method, the international code signal NC by flag or light, flames as from a burning barrel of oil, the national flag flown upside down, flying a square flag having above or below it anything resembling a ball, a smoke signal giving off orange-colored smoke, a person slowly and repeatedly raising and lowering his/her outstretched arms, or the bright flashing of a strobe light.

ditty bag or box. A small container for a sailor's personal gear.

diurnal. Daily, happening every day as a diurnal tide occurs once a day, with one high water and one low. British term is single-day tide.

diurnal inequality. The difference in height and/or time of the two high waters or of the two low waters of the tide each day. Also the difference in velocity of either the flood or ebb currents each day.

diurnal range. The difference in height between mean higher high water and mean lower low water where the tides are mainly diurnal.

dividers. A pair of small, sharp, hand-held metal rods hinged at one end, used to measure and step off distances on a chart.

DMAHC. Defense Mapping Agency Hydrographic Center, the government office that produces charts of the world except those of the U.S. which are published by NOS.

dock. A large basin, either permanently filled with water, a wet dock, or one that can be filled and drained, a dry dock. The word is often used interchangeably with pier and wharf. To dock a ship is to put her alongside or in a dock.

dockage. The charges against a ship for docking or wharf facilities.

docking keel. Doubling strips of steel attached to a ship's bottom parallel to the keel and about halfway up to the turn of the bilge to assist the hull to withstand the stress of docking. Also called a bilge keel.

documentation. A marine document of ownership, issued by the U.S. Coast Guard. Permitted but not required for pleasure boats of 5 net tons or over. Documentation marks a boat as a U.S. vessel with the consequent protection under international law. Other countries have similar regulations.

dockyard. A ship or boat repair facility.

dodger. A weather cloth on the bridge, in the cockpit of a boat over the companionway or elsewhere, rigged as protection from the weather. Not quite the same as a Bimini or Navy top which are rigged mostly for sun protection.

dodging. A word used by powerboat sailors when they encounter heavy seas and maneuver at minimum speed to avoid damage.

dog. Any one of the many simple devices or handles used for closing a door, hatch or port, also called a snib or staple. A dog or dog iron is a bar bent at a 90° angle at both ends which is used to fasten large timbers together.

dog curtain. A flap on a canvas binnacle cover.

dogging. To whip together adjoining strands of a fiber rope when splicing.

doghouse. The short deckhouse, usually over the main hatchway, which is raised above the level of the cabin top of a boat. Also called a booby hatch or companion.

dog shores. Short timbers used for holding a ship in a launching way and preventing her from launching when the keel blocks are removed. British term is dog shapes.

dog watch. One of the 2-hour watches into which the time 1600–2000 is divided. The first dog watch is 1600–1800, the second dog is 1800–2000. In a 3-section watch this permits each section to share the different watches in a 24-hour period.

doldrums. An ocean area, the equatorial trough, of calm or very light winds near the equator between the trade winds of the two hemispheres. Also called the intertropic convergence zone, it is here that tropical storms generate.

dollie, dolly. 1. A small bollard to fasten line on a dock wall from barges and other craft. 2. A strong frame on small wheels used for moving heavy weights. Any heavy bar or tool used for moving weights is a dolly bar. 3. A steel bar that supports a rivet being hammered closed.

dolly winch. A small hand-powered winch used on sailboats.

dolphin. 1. A cluster of piles, piling or a single pile. Also called a rack. *See* pile. 2. A heavy mooring post on a dock or pier. 3. A pudding fender. 4. An ocean mammal of the family Delphinidae. *See* porpoise.

Dolphin. A one-design keel or centerboard sloop. LOA 21', beam 7½'. Designer: Sparkman & Stephens.

dolphin fish. A brightly colored food and game fish of tropical waters that lives in schools, weighs up to 60 pounds and is also known as dorado, mahimahi, or coryphene, and should not be confused with the mammal dolphin.

dolphin striker. A short spar hanging down from the bowsprit of a sailboat to spread the martingale stays. Also called a martingale boom.

DOMES. Deep Ocean Mining Environmental Study.

donkey. An upright stick inserted in the gunwale of a racing sailboat. It is supported by a wire to the centerboard trunk and is used to assist a crew member when hiking out.

donkey engine. Any small auxiliary power source used at sea or on a dock or pier.

donkey's breakfast. Traditional slang for a sailor's straw mattress.

Doppler navigation system. One using the Doppler principle that a change in the frequency of sound or radio waves is a result of motion. By measuring the frequency shift the speed can be calculated and the distance recorded.

dorade ventilator. A specially designed windscoop or ventilator on the deck of a boat through which air passes but on which spray and rain are trapped and drain off.

dorado. A prized food and game fish. *See* dolphin fish.

dory. A small double-ended fishing and pleasure boat, originally of wood and used for hand-lining of bottom fish, or for setting out trawls when carried by large fishing vessels. Thwarts of working dories could be removed so that the dories could be nested on deck.

double-banked. A rowing boat in which two opposite oars are pulled by two rowers on the same seat. If only one man pulls both oars the boat is single-banked.

double-ended. Describes craft such as canoes whose sterns come to a point as their bows do.

double-head rig. Any combination of two sails in the fore triangle of a sailboat, usually a headsail with a high clue and one with a low clue, set as far aft as the genoa overlap point, used for close reaching.

double luff. A tackle in which the blocks have two different sheaves each. *See* double purchase.

double purchase. A tackle consisting of two single-sheave blocks; the standing part being fastened to one of them. Also called a double whip and a gun tackle.

Douglas Scale. A series of numbers, 0–9, denoting sea state from calm through rough to confused. Now replaced by the World Meteorological Organization Code 75. Not to be confused with the Beaufort Scale of wind force.

douse. To put out or pull down as in "douse that light" or "douse the jib." To cease or to quit, and to drench with water. Also dowse.

down below. Means downstairs aboard ship, just as upstairs in proper nautical language is topside. The word stairs is not used afloat.

down by the head or stern. Describes a ship or boat that lies deeper in the water than normal, forward or aft. Down by the bow is the same as down by the head. Trimmed by the head or stern is also used.

downhaul. Any line afloat, usually on a sailboat, that is used to haul something down, such as a sail. *See* inhaul, outhaul.

DR. Dead Reckoning.

DRA. Dead Reckoning Analyzer.

drabler. *See* bonnet.

dracone. A large flexible container or bag for transporting certain liquids by water. It is usually towed by a tug.

draft. The depth to which a freely floating ship or boat is submerged as indicated by the draft marks at bow and stern in feet. A sailmaker's word for the curve or belly sewn into a sail. A single sling or pallet of cargo is a draft. British spelling is draught.

draft control. Hoisting, setting, and adjusting tension on a sail to ensure optimum curvature or draft under different wind conditions.

drafting. A sailboat riding the stern wave on the quarter of another boat that may be larger and faster. The boat astern tries to ride the slope of the second wave created by the moving stern of the boat ahead.

drafting machine. Mechanical parallel rulers used in navigation and piloting to lay down courses, bearings, etc.

drag. The force opposing the forward motion of a ship or boat caused by skin friction, wave generation, rudder action, a protruberance from the hull, the effect of shallow water etc., often referred to as resistance. Also the amount that a ship's draft aft is greater than that forward is her drag. A ship or boat, as well as their anchors are said to drag when the anchor is no longer holding. Also any device that impedes or reduces movement such as a sea anchor or a drogue may be called a drag.

drag sail. *See* sea anchor.

Dragon. A one-design keel sloop. LOA 29', beam 6½', draft 3½'. Designer: Johan Anker.

draincock. *See* seacock.

drain well. A small tank projecting down from the inner bottom of a ship into the double bottom to permit pumping out the bilges if necessary. Also called the bilge well.

draw. In describing a ship's draft the ship or boat is said to draw so many feet, forward and aft. A well-filled and trimmed sail is said to draw well.

dredge. Any device used to remove and bring up sand, mud, etc., to deepen a channel or an anchorage. It may be grab, bucket, or suction dredge. To operate a dredger is to dredge.

dredging. Using an anchor at short stay, dragged over the bottom, to hold the bow of a ship up against the wind while bringing a ship alongside a pier.

dress. A ship or boat may be dressed on festive occasions by showing flags and pennants on the standing rigging.

drift. 1. The speed of a current or of moving ice in knots or in miles per day. 2. The movement of anything on the surface of the sea due to wind and current. 3. A length of rope or chain roused out on deck. 4. The difference in diameter between any pin, spar, or fitting, and the hole into which it is fitted. 5. A pin or long bolt used in riveting or bolting. 6. Leeway or set in a sailboat being moved sideways by the wind. 7. To a naval architect drift is any break in the sheer line.

driftbolt. A metal rod used as a fastener in wooden boat construction.

drift current. Any broad, shallow, slow ocean current in which only Coriolis force and wind friction are significant as generating factors. Also called wind drift or just drift. *See* ocean current.

drifter. The lightest possible headsail of a sailboat used for racing in very light airs. Also called a ghoster and a windseeker.

drift lead. A weight fastened to a line and dropped over the side of an anchored boat and tended to detect possible dragging of the anchor.

drift sail. A sea anchor.

driver. The fifth or sixth mast from forward on a multimasted schooner.

drogue. A prepared device, an improvised contraption, or even a long hawser or warp streamed astern by a boat in very heavy weather to help avoid being pooped by slowing the speed of the boat through the water. A drogue such as a canvas cone towed by its open end may be used as a sea anchor to hold a boat's head to the sea in bad weather, but the two words are not synonymous. Sometimes spelled drag. *See* sea anchor.

drop. For a boat to drop astern or drop aft means that it goes or passes astern. Also the depth of a sail from head to foot, measured in the middle.

drop keel. A heavy ballast keel rigged so that it can be raised and lowered. Sometimes inaccurately used instead of centerboard.

dropping moor. A method of anchoring in which a ship drops one anchor while moving slowly ahead to drop a second anchor. Anchor cable scope to both anchors is then equalized and the ship lies to two anchors. Sometimes called a flying moor.

DRT. Dead reckoning tracer.

drum. A revolving steel cylinder on a windlass or capstan and used for handling rope or wire. Sometimes called a capstan head, drumhead, or trundlehead. Also the name of a fish.

drumhead. The round top of an old-fashioned sailing ship capstan, fitted with pigeon holes into which the capstan bars were fitted. Men pushed on these bars to move the drumhead to haul in a line or cable. Also called capstan and trundlehead.

drydock. A structure into which a ship can be floated—blocks and shores having been laid down to receive her—the dock emptied, and repair work done. A large gate opens and closes to enable the ship to pass out and in. Also called a graving dock.

dry out. To strand a boat deliberately at high tide in order to work on the hull at low tide.

dryrot. A fungus that attacks and consumes moist wood, common and destructive in wooden boats.

D shackle. One shaped like the letter D, having a screw pin to close the straight side.

DSL. Deep Scattering Layer.

dub. To cut and smooth a wooden timber by hand.

duck. A light cotton material, finer than canvas, traditionally used for sailors' clothes but now replaced by synthetic fiber mixtures.

duckboat. A small, open, flat-bottom boat used to carry hunters through shallow water.

ducktail stern. One that slants forward.

duct. A layer in the atmosphere or in the ocean whose characteristics are different in regard to temperature, density, etc. Thus sound in water and electromagnetic transmission in air may be refracted, distorted, or channeled. The phenomenon is known as ducting and can produce extraordinary radio, radar, and sound reception.

duct keel. *See* box keel.

dugong. An aquatic mammal related to the manatee, found in the south Pacific. Lives on vegetation along the coast and in rivers. *See* sea cow.

dugout. A native canoe or boat made from a single log hollowed out by tools or fire.

dumb. Having no means of propulsion as a dumb barge. A dumb sheave is a groove for a rope in the end of a spar, or as part of a bulwark, etc.

dumb chalder. A metal cleat or block bolted to the after side of the wooden sternpost of a boat for the end of the rudder pintle to rest upon.

dumb iron. A type of caulking iron used in wooden boat building.

dummy gantline. *See* gantline.

dump, fastening. A bolt used in fastening wood that does not pass all the way through at one end.

dungarees. Blue cotton work clothing (denim) traditionally worn by sailors.

dunnage. A sailor's personal gear or baggage.

Dunn's anchor. Trade name for a modern ship's stockless or patent anchor.

Duster. A one-design cat-rigged centerboard boat. LOA 14', beam 4½'. Designer: O.P. Merrill.

dutchman. A piece of wood, metal, or plastic used to fill a void, as a spacer piece in a ventilating duct used to replace a heater unit. A patch of any kind, or a piece of steel fitted or driven into an opening, often to conceal poor workmanship.

dutchman's log. A chip log.

DWT. Deadweight tonnage.

Dyer Dhow. A one-design cat-rigged centerboard dinghy. LOA 9', beam 4½'. Designer: W.J.H. Dyer.

Dyersin Dink. A one-design cat-rigged centerboard dinghy. LOA 10', beam 4½'. Designer: P.L. Rhodes.

E

eagre. Same as bore. Also spelled eager.

earing. A short line secured to the cringle, ring, or grommet in a sail or awning to pull it into place.

ease. To take the pressure off. To ease the rudder is to reduce the amount of rudder angle. To ease a line is to slack it, to reduce tension.

easing-out line. Any line used to slack off something or ease it out, as on a mooring chain, collision mat, etc.

East Australian Current. A south Pacific ocean current setting southward along the east coast of Australia.

East Greenland Current. A north Atlantic ocean current setting south and then southwest along the east coast of Greenland.

easting. The distance a ship makes good towards the east.

easy. Carefully, comfortably, without strain; as in: "lower that draft easy."

eat to windward. Means to take advantage of every puff and flaw to gain distance to windward.

ebb. The falling tide ebbs and is called the ebb. The rising tide floods. There is an ebb current and an ebb stream.

echograph. A fish finder that uses the echoes from sound waves to delineate schools of fish underwater. Also called a fishfinder.

echo ranging. *See* SONAR.

echo sounder. An electronic device afloat that generates sound waves and measures the time it takes for them to be reflected from the bottom. This interval is translated into depth of water since the velocity of sound in water is known and thus depth is recorded. A depth alarm can be set to ring at any preset depth. Also called a depth finder, Fathometer (a trade name) or sonic depth finder.

ecliptic. The great circle on the celestial sphere that the sun seems to describe in 1 year around the earth from east to west as the earth revolves around the sun. It is the plane of the earths orbit around the sun.

economy vent. Boatmen's name for a gooseneck ventilator.

ED. On a chart it means existence doubtful.

eddy. A circular movement of water or air usually formed where currents pass obstructions, or between adjacent currents flowing in opposite directions, or along the boundary of a permanent current. Mesoscale eddies are large slow patterns of oceanic rotation that are the chief mechanism for the storage and transport of midocean energy. They are being studied by a U.S.- Russian project known as Polymode.

edge cut. A method of cutting sails to provide draft by putting extra cloth on the edge of the luff and the foot.

Edo. Trade name for a popular echo sounder.

eel. A snakelike fish that includes the saltwater moray and conger as well as the freshwater eels. The latter are highly prized as food by many non-Americans. The moray and conger can reach 13 feet in length and can be dangerous to unwary swimmers. All eels breed in saltwater—those of both Europe and north America spawn in or near the Sargasso Sea. Their larva are known as elvers or glass eels.

eelgrass. An important saltwater weed that provides food for water-fowl and marine life.

Eell's anchor. A patented stockless anchor with long flukes used in salvage work.

electromagnetic log. A log that uses a retractable rodmeter fitted with an induction device to produce voltage that varies with the speed of the boat.

elephanta. A southerly gale that blows along the coast of Malabar in September and October marking the end of the southwest monsoon.

elliott eye. An eye worked over a thimble in the end of a hawser.

El Niño. A warm ocean current setting south off the coast of Ecuador. In some years this current extends south to the coast of Peru where the normal upwelling of cold and nutritious deeper water is interrupted. This has a disastrous effect on the fish and consequently the seabird life, resulting in an economic crisis as anchovy and guano diminish.

ELT. An Emergency Locator Transmitter (see below) for aircraft.

Emergency Position Indicating Radio Beacon (EPIRB). A small battery-powered radio transmitter automatically started by water immersion, that floats on the surface and sends distress messages on frequencies normally guarded by ocean-crossing commercial aircraft and by the U.S. Coast Guard. Now carried by many prudent deep-water boatmen, fishermen, etc. Aircraft carry an ELT (see above). The class C EPIRB for coastal waters and the Great Lakes broadcasts on VHF channels 15 and 16 alternately.

end for end. To reverse the ends of a line, such as boat falls, in order to equalize wear.

engine order telegraph. Instrument for sending orders to the engineroom from the bridge. Also called an annunciator.

ensign. The national flag or colors of a country, flown from a gaff on a mast underway and from a flagstaff on the stern in port. *See* colors.

Ensign. A one-design keel sloop. LOA 22½', beam 7', draft 3'. Designer: C.A. Alberg.

Enterprise. A one-design centerboard sloop. LOA 13', beam 5'. Designer: Jack Holt.

entrance. That part of a boat's immersed hull forward of amidships. Also known as the forebody.

entry. The shape of a boat's hull at the stem, usually described as fine or sharp, or full and rounded.

EP. Estimated Position.

Ephemeris. *See* American Ephemeris.

EPIRB. Emergency Position Indicating Radio Beacon.

equation of time. The difference between mean or average time and apparent or sundial time. Can be found for each day in the Nautical Almanac.

equator. An imaginary circle around the earth, equidistant from the north and south poles, that separates the north and the south hemispheres, and from which the latitude of any place is measured, either north or south.

Equatorial Counter Current. An easterly flow along the equator between, and opposite in direction to the North and the South Equatorial Currents.

Equatorial Undercurrent. An easterly flowing subsurface stream that is thin, relatively narrow and fast. It follows the equator and in the Pacific it is called the Cromwell Current.

equator, oceanographic. The zone of maximum sea water temperature lying generally along the geographic equator; that area where the surface water is over 28° Celsius.

equinoctial. The celestial equator; pertains to the equator.

equinox. The time at which days and nights are the same length; March 21st and September 21st when the sun's apparent path intersects the equinoctial equator.

Ericson 27. A one-design keel sloop. LOA 27', beam 9', draft 4'. Designer: Bruce King.

establishment of a port. *See* lunitidal interval. Also known as high-water full and change.

estuary. The mouth of a river where the tide meets the stream and where sea water and fresh water have mutual influence in regard to movement, salinity, temperature, etc. The adjective is estuarine.

ETA, ETD. Estimated Time of Arrival, Estimated Time of Departure.

Etchells 22. A one-design keel sloop. LOA 30½', beam 7', draft 4½'. Designer: Skip Etchells.

etesian winds. The northerly winds of considerable strength that blow across the eastern Mediterranean in summer.

euphroe. A type of deadeye, a block of wood or metal with multiple holes used to hold the many lines of a crowfoot for spreading an awning, or to hold the many parts of the main sheet of a fully battened junk. Also spelled uphroe.

even keel. Describes a boat or ship having no list, either to port or to starboard, and no uneven trim, not down by the bow or by the stern.

exit block. One designed for internal halyards, those inside a mast, and for the control lines that pass through a bulkhead. Called an exit plate if there is no sheave.

exposure suit. *See* survival suit.

Explorer. A one-design centerboard sloop. LOA 17'. beam 6½'. Designer: Sailstar Co.

eye. Traditionally the loop in a shroud or stay that fits over the top of the mast.

eye, anchor. The hole at the end of the shank of an anchor through which the anchor ring or shackle is passed.

eye block. A rope-strapped block with a thimble secured to the strap.

eyebrow. Elliptical metal ridge over an airport or porthole for shedding water; known in the U.K. as a rigol, often spelled wriggle.

eye of a storm (typhoon). The center of relative calm about which the storm revolves.

eye of the wind. The exact direction from which the wind blows.

eyes of the ship. That part of the ship's bows near the hawse, topside and all the way forward; the usual station for the lookout there (fog lookout).

eye splice. A loop spliced into the end of a rope. A metal oval or thimble is normally inserted—if not it is a soft splice.

F

face. The after, driving surface, or side of a propeller blade, also called the thrust surface or driving face.

fag end. The untidy loose end of a rope that has become untwisted, or an unraveled edge of a piece of canvas. The process of becoming untwisted is fagging. *See* cow's tail.

fair. Favorable, as a fair wind; or smooth and matching, as in fairing in a timber in wooden boat construction or a line in hull design. Free and unhindered, as a line may be said to have a fair lead aft.

fairlead. A ringbolt, eye, loop, chock, or any device with holes used to guide a line easily in the required direction. Also called a fairleader. Fairlead means chock in the U.K.

fairlead block. One used to provide a clear and easy lead for genoa sheets and halyards, for example, usually mounted on a slide.

fairwater. Any plating, casting, or other device used to reduce water resistance on the hull or exterior fittings of a boat, such as a strut.

fairway. The navigable and thus safe part of a harbor, river, etc., including the main ship channel. A fairway buoy marks a fairway or channel.

fake. One of the windings of a rope or line as it lies in a coil. To fake down is to lay out a line in long bights or loops so that it can run out without twisting, an impossibility from a circular coil. Also flake. *See* coil, flemish.

Falkland Current. An ocean current flowing northward along the coast of Argentina. Originating as part of the westwind drift, it joins the Brazil Current at about 35°S, where both turn east across the Atlantic.

fall(s). A line passed through one or more blocks used as a hoisting tackle, as in boat falls. The fixed end is the standing part and the movable end is the hauling part. To move or go as in fall astern or fall in with. To fall afoul is to collide with and, more generally, to have a dispute with another vessel. A sailboat falls off (away) from the wind or from a desired heading.

false keel. In wooden boats the shoe or planking sometimes fastened under the keel to provide protection when grounding. Also called a false keel shoe.

fancy work. Decorative knots and pieces of canvas; includes cross-pointing, McNamara lace, and whiplashing.

fanning. Describes a sailboat making little headway in light air. A more modern word is ghosting.

fantail. The aftermost deck area on the weather deck of a Naval ship. On a merchant ship, the overhanging stern section or counter.

Farallone Clipper. A one-design racing and cruising keel sloop. LOA 38', beam 9½', draft 5½'. Designer: Stephens Marine.

faro. A small atoll-shaped reef or coral knob with shallow lagoons, part of a barrier or atoll rim.

fashion board. British term for splash board.

fast. Tight, secure as a line is made fast to a cleat. Old name for mooring line still used in stern fast, the line used to secure the stern of a boat while the bow painter secures the bow.

Fata Morgana. A mirage commonly observed in the Straits of Messina, marked by multiple distortions, generally in a vertical plane.

fathom. Traditional nautical measure of depth or of length—6 feet. Charts are marked in fathoms, feet, and meters—it is important to know which—meters are used on all new charts. A cable is 100 fathoms but is rarely used now. A fathom is 1.83 meters.

Fathometer. A trade name for an echo sounder.

fay. To fit together, as two planks. The meeting surfaces are faying surfaces.

feather. The curve in the blade of an oar. To feather oars when rowing is to turn or rotate them 90° on the return stroke. A feathering propeller is one whose blades can be turned to a neutral or feathering position, thus reducing drag when a sailboat is under sail alone. To feather a sail is to allow some of the wind to spill out. To feather a boat is to keep her as upright as possible (on her feet) by luffing up sharply in puffs of wind. Also a bit of spray is called a feather.

feaze. To unwind strands at a rope's end to produce feazing, a ragged end.

felloe. The outer edge of a boat's wooden steering wheel.

felucca. The ancient lateen-rigged, twin-masted trading and fishing vessel of the Mediterranean. Now rare except on the Nile.

fend off. To push away or hold off, as the bowman of a boat coming alongside fends off to avoid sudden contact.

fender. Any device of wood, wicker, or plastic used between boats moored alongside, or between a boat and the pier, as a bumper or buffer to prevent chafing and damage. A common boating synonym is bumper—not approved by some purists.

fender board. A plank rigged outboard of several fenders.

fender rail. A timber bolted horizontally along a boat's side above the waterline to act as a fender. Also called a fender guard, a guard rail, or a sheer rail.

fenger drogue. A drogue made of two planks fastened together along their lengths at an angle to each other and streamed by means of a bridle.

ferrite antenna. One made up of a coil of wire around a core of high-frequency magnetic material called ferrite.

ferrocement. A boat and small ship construction method using steel frames, wire-mesh, and cement.

fetch. The distance a wind blows over the sea without appreciable interference from land; an important factor in the size of the waves thus generated. Other uses of the word are now rarely heard: such as fetch (reach) the harbor, or fetch up on the port tack, or fetch (set) a compass course, fetch up with a round turn, or fetch up all standing. To fetch the mark means to reach it without another tack. A point of sailing between close hauled and a reach was sometimes known as a fetch.

fetch line. A sailboat pointed at and fetching a mark is on her fetch or layline. *See* layline.

fiber-clad rope. A combination of wire and fiber in which each strand of wire is wrapped in fiber. Also called marline-clad rope.

fiberglass. A composite material made up of glass fibers set in plastic, usually a synthetic polyester resin, used widely for boat hulls up to about 100 feet in length. A fiberglass mat is a felted matrix of chopped fibers loosely held together with a plastic binder. Fiberglas is a trade name, the British term is GRP or glass reinforced plastic.

fiber rope. Made up of fibers, yarns, and strands in that order; traditionally of natural fibers such as manila, hemp, and cotton, but now usually made of synthetic fibers such as Dacron and nylon that are more elastic, much stronger, and more durable. Fiber rope over 5 inches in circumference is a hawser. Synthetic fiber rope is often prestretched to reduce elasticity.

fid. 1. A round, tapered, pointed, and traditionally wooden hand tool for opening strands of rope for splicing. A very large fid was called a commander. 2. A fixed sailmaker's tool for making eyes and cringles in canvas, thus called a cringle fid. *See* marline spike. 3. A square, wedge-shaped piece of wood or iron once used to support a topmast.

fiddle. Portable fence around a ship's table or galley range top put up in rough weather when the ship is rolling. Also called a rack.

fiddle block. One having two or more sheaves of different diameters arranged one above the other in the same plane similar to a sister block. Used in sailboats, most commonly with mainsheet rigs and boom vangs.

fiddlehead. Instead of a figure head a carved wooden scroll at the upper end or top of the stem with the carving turned outward from the ship. If the carving of the scroll turns inboard it is a billethead.

fife rail. A rail traditionally arranged in a semicircle around the foot of a sailing ship's mast, fitted with holes in which the belaying pins were inserted. Also called a pin rail.

figure-eight fake. Coiling rope to produce a series of overlapping figure eights which advance one or two rope diameters with each turn.

fin. A vertical metal plate under a boat's hull to provide resistance to lateral movement.

fine. Long and sharp, as in the fine lines of a boat. Also means close or near as in: "fine on the bow" which means nearly dead ahead.

finger pier or slip. A pier or floating structure projecting at right angles to a large pier or float to provide dockspace or berthing space for ships or boats.

fin keel. A deep short ballast keel sometimes with a fatter, cylindrical bottom that constitutes most of the ballast. Also called a bulb keel.

Finn. A one-design centerboard planing catboat. LOA 15′, beam 5′. Designer: Richard Sarby.

fins, antirolling. *See* antirolling fins.

Fireball. A one-design centerboard dinghy. LOA 16′, beam 4½′. Designer: Peter Milne.

fireboat. A harbor vessel, usually a tug, fitted with high-pressure pumps, hoses, nozzles, etc., to fight fires afloat and on the waterfront.

fire bulkhead. A flame resistant transverse bulkhead required by law to be built into ships and large boats at specified intervals from bow to stern.

Firefly. A one-design centerboard sloop. LOA 12′, beam 4½′. Designer: Uffa Fox.

fire point. Temperature at which a material if ignited will continue to burn. *See* flash point.

fire warp. A flexible wire rope led from a ship to a point on the pier alongside, or to a buoy or anchor so that in case of fire, ashore or on board, the ship could be swung away from its berth.

fishhook stroke. *See* J-stroke.

fisherman's anchor. A small one-piece boat anchor similar to a mushroom anchor. Also the British term for an old-fashioned stock anchor.

fisherman's bend. The most common version is two half hitches or two round turns around the anchor ring. Also called an anchor knot.

fisherman's paravane. Same as a flopper stopper.

fisherman's staysail. A sail set between the masts of a schooner, now used mostly in yachts.

fishfinder. Same as echograph.

fishhook. A small broken strand of wire on wire rigging that lacerates unwary hands, same as a meathook.

fitting. A general word for any part, piece of machinery, or equipment, not having a more specific name.

Five-o-Five (505). A one-design centerboard sloop. LOA 16½', beam 6'. Designer: John Westell.

Five-point-Five Meter (5.5). An international racing sloop built to a development rule. LOA 32', beam 6', draft 4¼'.

fix. A boat's position as determined by any means of piloting or navigation.

fixed light. A navigational aid that shows a constant light.

flag. A piece of cloth, usually rectangular but sometimes a burgee or a pennant, used to show nationality, to signal with, to show an affiliation such as a yacht club, or to show rank. Flags are flown anywhere on halyards and often on flagstaffs. Yachts may fly yacht ensigns, national colors, a yacht club burgee, or personal and organization flags or pennants. *See* luff.

flag of convenience. A flag under which shipping companies worldwide register and operate their ships to avoid taxes and the regulations of their own countries. Panama and Liberia are popular for this purpose.

flag officer. In the Navy an admiral. In yachting circles an officer of a yacht club, for example: commodore, vice-commodore, rear-commodore, or flag captain—each of whom may fly a personal flag on his own yacht.

flagstaff. The small spar on which the national flag is shown when afloat.

flake. Same as fake. Also a small stage or platform rigged over the side. To flake a sail is to lower it and stow it in layers as it comes down rather than to furl or wrap it.

flake out. Sailor's slang for to lie down, to take a rest, or to take an equal strain on all parts.

flam. *See* flare.

flanker. A light headsail used in modern racing sailboats.

flapper valve. One that permits flow in one direction only, closing a swinging hinged plate if the liquid starts to flow in the wrong direction.

flare. A pyrotechnic device used to attract attention, usually in an emergency at sea. In naval architecture the flare of a boat's side is the spreading outward from the waterline to the main deck, a concave curve, the opposite of tumblehome. Flam refers particularly to the upper part of the flare, and is useful in keeping spray off the deck.

flare-up light. An intermittent white light with a maximum interval of 15 minutes required by the Inland Rules of the Road to be shown by a pilot vessel underway.

flasher. A headsail for a sailboat, commonly used when running before the wind, similar to a spinnaker but without a pole.

flashing light. Communications by means of code sent by blinker or searchlight between ships. Also a navigational aid, a light whose period of light is less than its period of darkness. A flashing light aboard ship as required by Colregs has at least 120 flashes per minute. *See* lights, navigational, light, occulting, quick-flashing light.

flash point. The temperature at which fuel or other volatile liquids gives off explosive vapors—seldom the same as the fire point.

flat. Area of shallow non-navigable water. Short for flatboat.

flatboat. A scow, barge or lighter with square ends and flat bottom.

flatfish. Any flounder, fluke, sole, or halibut; fish that lie and swim on one side instead of upright. Also referred to as ground fish since they live on the bottom.

flattie. A small flat-bottom rowing or sailboat with straight sides and a pointed bow.

flaw. A sudden violent gust of wind, a temporary increase in wind strength. *See* catspaw, squall.

flemish. To flemish or flemish down is to coil a line on deck in concentric circles, each loop lying flat on the deck. *See* fake, coil.

flemish down. *See* coil down.

flemish eye. One made at the end of a line or halyard, usually to prevent the line from passing through a block and going adrift.

Fleur Bleue. A one-design keel sloop. LOA 25', beam 7', draft 4½'. Designer: A. Yokoyama.

flexible rope. Wire rope with a fiber core or composed of many fine wires making it easier to use for mooring lines and other uses requiring flexibility.

flinders bar. A bundle of soft iron bars placed in the binnacle of a magnetic compass to compensate for deviation caused by the ship's vertical magnetic field.

floating star (floater). A light headsail used in modern racing sailboats.

flood. The inflow of tide, in contrast to the ebb which is the outflow. The flood tide forms flood currents and a general rise in the water level.

floodgate. The door of a drydock or tidal basin that controls the entrance of water.

floor. In a boat floor refers to the structure supporting the sole and connecting the ribs or timbers from side to side. Removable sections of the sole may be called floorboards.

floorboard. A removable part of the sole.

flopper-stopper. An antirolling system used by some powerboats when fishing offshore. Delta-shaped metal plates are suspended under water, parallel to the surface, on each quarter, held out by booms.

Florida Current. Part of the Gulf Stream System that passes through the Florida Straits and along the coast as far as Cape Hatteras. *See* Gulf Stream System.

flotation gear. Anything designed to keep something afloat as, for example, the air tanks in a lifeboat.

flotsam. *See* jettison.

flounder. Any of several large flat groundfish that swim on their side and have both eyes on the same side. An excellent food fish that grows to 200 pounds.

flow. Flood or rise of the tide. To ease or slack the sheet of a sail, an eased sheet is a flowing sheet (rare). Flow is the same as camber, the fore-and-aft curvature in a sail.

fluke. 1. The palm or flat part of an anchor that goes into the ground when an anchor is dropped and set. 2. A type of flatfish, similar to a flounder. 3. The barb on the end of a harpoon. 4. The lobe of a whale's tail.

fly. *n* 1. The length of a flag measured from its hoist near the staff to the end that flutters in the wind (that end is also called the fly). 2. A small pennant set at the top of a mast to indicate wind direction. *vb.* 1. A sailing ship may fly up into the wind which means to turn quickly to windward. 2. To let fly is to let go quickly.

fly block. The moving block in a Spanish burton purchase that supports the hauling part of the fall.

flybridge. Same as flying bridge; a commercial term not always acceptable to old salts.

flying. A sail set flying is one supported only by its corners, not hanked to a stay, for example, a spinnaker or blooper.

flying a hull. What a catamaran does when she lifts a hull clear of the water when sailing.

flying block. A movable block once used aloft in square-riggers.

flying bridge. The topmost bridge of a boat.

flying fish. Any one of several small edible tropical fish that launch themselves into the air and glide to escape their enemies. A flying fish sailor is one who delights in calm seas and mild weather.

flying foresail. A square foresail sometimes used on sailboats when running before the trade winds.

flying jib. The sail set on the fore topgallant royal stay in square-riggers. Now the headsail set forward of the jib of a sailboat.

Flying Junior. A one-design centerboard sloop. LOA 13½', beam 5'. Designer: Uffa Van Essen.

flying moor. To anchor or moor with two anchors, dropping them in succession a short distance apart while underway and then adjusting scope of cable to rest between them. Same as a dropping moor.

Flying Scot. A one-design centerboard sloop. LOA 19', beam 6½'. Designer: G.K. Douglass.

Flying Tern. A one-design centerboard sloop. LOA 14', beam 5'. Designer: E.G. Van deStadt.

FM. *See* frequency modulation.

foam. A chemically produced smothering suds or foam blanket used to fight oil and electric fires, especially in the engineroom.

foehn wind. A warm dry wind blowing offshore, such as the southeasters of Cape Town or the Santa Ana of the coast of southern California.

fog. A cloud touching the sea, a mass of tiny water droplets causing a reduction of visibility to below 1000 meters. *See* mist. When mixed with polluted air it is smog. A ship delayed because of fog is said to be fogbound, a common happening before radar.

fog bow. A rainbow seen in the fog or in a cloud.

fog eye. A spot of sunlight showing through fog.

fog lookouts. Special lookouts required by Colregs to be stationed either in the eyes of a ship or aloft if the fog only exists near the water. They must report ships, boats, buoys, etc.

fog nozzle. A fire fighting device that produces a fine, smothering mist or spray of water.

fog signal. Any horn, whistle, bell, gun, diaphone, nautiphone, or other device used to produce warning signals when in low visibility.

foil. *See* headfoil.

foot. The bottom or lower edge of any sail. A sailboat is said to foot well when she makes good progress to windward.

folboat. A popular small folding boat with a fabric-covered folding frame, used mostly on lakes and rivers.

footband. The strengthening band of canvas along the foot of a squaresail on the after side.

foot block. Similar to a cheek block but one incorporating bails to which tackles or other blocks may be made fast.

footing. Fore-and-aft fixed strips of wood on the bottom of a small boat. A sailboat is footing when it is sailing fast, close hauled or close reaching.

foot locks. Wood or metal strips on a brow or gangplank for better footing.

foot well. A depression or cockpit in a small sailboat in which the helmsman can place his feet.

Force 5. A one-design daggerboard catboat. LOA 14', beam 5'. Designer: Fred Scott.

force majeure. A marine and other insurance term meaning an act of God; something that cannot be foreseen or prevented.

fore-and-aft. Lengthways in a boat, from bow to stern as opposed to athwartships. A fore-and-aft sail is one rigged in line with the keel in contrast to a squaresail that is perpendicular to the keel.

fore. Short for foremast.

forebody. The forward part of the hull or body of a boat, especially underwater.

forecastle. In modern usage the forward part of the main deck of a ship, called the foredeck in a boat. Pronounced: fohksul.

foredeck. The forward part of the deck of a sailboat where the headsails are handled.

forefoot. The foreward, outboard end of a boat's stem where it meets the keel.

foreguy. The line that holds the spinnaker pole down rigged from the outboard end of the pole back to a fitting on deck. In some gaff-rigged boats it is a line leading from the end of the main boom to control the boom when running before the wind.

forehand. To take a strain on a piece of gear near the moving block so that the line can be belayed, is to forehand it (rare).

foremast. The foreward mast of a sailboat, except in a yawl or ketch in which the forward mast is much larger and is known as the mainmast. The after mast is then the mizzenmast or jigger.

forereach. The movement ahead or into the wind that a sailboat makes when tacking or luffing or when hove to.

foresail. A general word for any sail set forward of the most forward mast such as a jib, genoa, staysail, spinnaker, or a reaching foresail. Also a sail set abaft the foremast of a schooner.

foresheets. Old term for the bow, the forward part of a boat in contrast to the after part, still called the stern sheets.

foreshore. Part of a beach or shore that lies between high and low water at normal tides. *See* backshore.

forestay. The wire running from near the top of the foremast forward to the stem or bowsprit; often same as the headstay. An inner forestay may be rigged from slightly lower on the mast to the same position on deck and is used to support another headsail.

forestay sail. A headsail set on the forestay.

foretriangle. The area between the most forward mast of a sailboat and the forestay.

fother. An old word meaning to stop a leak in a boat's hull by covering the hole with canvas or other handy material or by using a collision mat or fothering blanket.

foreward. Towards the bow-up front.

foul. Jammed, tangled, not clear for running; covered with sea growth.

foul bottom. Unsafe for mooring or anchoring, as a foul berth or foul ground; to entangle, confuse, or obstruct. To foul up is to perform badly or to get into trouble. A foul anchor is one that is entangled in its own cable or has picked up something off the bottom or cannot be hauled in. Foul weather is bad, stormy weather.

found. Equipped with stores and provisions. All or fully found describes a boat having all necessities aboard; well found describes a vessel thoroughly and well equipped for a voyage.

fourfold purchase. A tackle made up of two blocks with two sheaves in each block.

Four Seventy (470). An Olympic one-design class centerboard sloop. LOA 15½′, beam 5½′. Designer: André Cornu.

Four Twenty (420). A one-design centerboard sloop. LOA 13½′, beam 5½′. Designer: Christian Maury.

foxtail. A short-handled brush used for sweeping. Also a short line attached to a jackstay.

fractional rig. One in which the sails of a sloop do not reach the masthead but extend part way. A ¾ rig is an example.

frame. One of the transverse girders of a ship's hull, from the keel to the highest continuous deck.

franchise. In marine and other insurance, the percentage or amount of insured value to be borne by the insured in case of loss.

frap. To wrap something with line or small stuff, called frapping gear.

frapping lines. Those used to steady a boat when it is being raised or lowered from a ship. They are passed around the boat falls of the davit and are tended on deck.

Franklin buoy. A ring-shaped lifebuoy fitted with a light that is lit when the buoy is thrown overboard to assist someone in the water at night.

free. Loose, adrift, not made fast as in free for running. A boat sails or runs free with the wind near or abaft the beam in contrast to close-hauled. Free pratique means a clean bill of health.

freeboard. Vertical distance from the waterline of a boat to the deck.

freeing port. An opening in a bulwark to permit the escape of water. Also called a freeing scuttle, a bulwark port or a wash port.

freer. *See* lift.

frees. The wind frees when it shifts away from the bow of a boat sailing close hauled. This is a freer or lift—opposite to a header. *See* head, lift.

free wave. One that persists after the wind has died down. Same as swell.

French bowline. One having two loops, handy for putting a man over the side. Same as a double bowline or a bowline on a bight.

frequency, electronic. Number of cycles repeated in one second. *See* Hertz.

frequency modulation (FM). A method of transmitting voice or music by varying or modulating the frequency of a radio wave rather than its amplitude.

fresh breeze. A wind of 17–21 knots; 5 on the Beaufort Scale.

freshen. To shift the position of a rope, line, chain, or wire that is exposed to friction and wear at one spot. The spot where there may be wear is the nip and the expression may be to freshen the nip. The wind freshens when its velocity increases.

fresh gale. A strong wind of 34–40 knots, 8 on the Beaufort Scale.

friendship sloop. Originally a fishing boat designed and built in Friendship, Maine. Its seaworthiness and comfort led to pleasure boats being built in the same style.

frigate bird. The sailor's man-o'-war bird—very fast, aggressive, and predatory with a long forked tail, 4 to 7-foot wingspread, whitish below, dark above, and found in tropic waters.

Frisco Flyer. A one-design keel sloop. LOA 25', beam 7', draft 4'. Designer: Tor Holm.

frog's leg. The foot of a spinnaker when made up in stops to which the spinnaker sheet is made fast.

front. The boundary between two atmospheric air masses.

frostbiters. Those who race small, frostbite dinghies in the winter —a sport known as frostbiting.

FRP. Fiberglass Reinforced Plastic. *See* fiberglass.

fry. A general term for the young of fish and other sea life.

full and by. A sailboat with all sails set and full of wind, sailing close-hauled, but not being pinched.

full and change. In reference to the tides, the times of the full and the new moon.

full rigged ship. A fully square-rigged vessel with three or more masts. The sails on each mast from bottom up are: courses, lower topsails, upper topsails, lower topgallants (t'gallants), upper t'gallants, royals, and skysails. Also called a square-rigger, a square-rigged ship, or just a ship.

funnel. The smokestack or chimney of a power boat. The galley funnel is known as Charlie Noble.

furl. To take in or wrap up a sail to its yard or boom and fasten it there with a gasket. Furling in the bunt describes the usual way a squaresail is furled at sea.

futtocks. Curved pieces of wood that make up part of the ship's frames.

futtock shrouds. The chains or rods that are downward extensions of the topmast shrouds. They stiffen the top as well as take the stress of the topmast rigging.

FWG. Foul weather gear.

G

gaff. A spar for supporting the top of a four-sided fore-and-aft gaffsail as in the old-fashioned, gaff-rigged sailboat. A storm trysail using a small gaff is a gaff trysail, usually set abaft the lower foremast of a schooner. A steel hook attached to a pole or a handle is a gaff when used to boat a hooked gamefish.

gaff-headed. A four-sided fore-and-aft sail rig with a gaff at the head or top of the sail. Now largely replaced in modern sailboats by the triangular jib-headed or Bermuda rig.

gaff jaws. A fitting that attaches a gaff to the mast. *See* throat.

gage. *See* gauge.

gain. Increase in power, as through an amplifier, expressed in decibels.

gale. A strong wind; moderate, fresh, strong, or whole gale, ranging from 28 to 55 knots. *See* Beaufort Scale.

gale warning. A weather forecast predicting winds of 34 knots or higher, issued by the National Weather Service. *See* Small Craft Advisory, storm warning.

gall. To chafe or wear. Also a wind dog, supposed to signify the onset of a strong wind.

galley. Nautical word for kitchen. Classic Mediterranean rowing and sailing vessel in use between 3000 B.C. and the 18th Century A.D., having one or more banks of oars and a square or lateen sail.

gam. A herd, pod, or school of whales. Also an offshore conversation between 2 vessels.

gamefish. Those aggressive, sight-feeding fish or sharks that will take a bait or artificial lure and will resist capture.

gangboard. An old word for brow or gangplank.

ganger. Any short length of chain or rope used to haul a heavy cable into position.

gangplank. Same as brow in modern usage. Also a plank running from the stem of a boat to the first thwart. Old word was gangboard.

gangway. The opening in a ship's rail or bulwark for the passage of people or cargo by means of a brow, gangplank, or accommodation ladder. When spoken as a command or request gangway means make way, let me through.

Gannet. A one-design centerboard sloop. LOA 14', beam 5½'. Designer: Fox & O'Day.

gantline. A line rove through a fixed single block, a whip, used to send something or someone aloft, as a man up a stack.

gantry. Any overhanging or spanning structure or framework containing a crane that rolls on tracks; used in shipyards and on piers and may be called a gantry crane. A similar stationary frame, with or without a crane is found on container ships and on large fishing vessels.

garbage scow. *See* honey barge.

garboard strake. Row of planks or steel plates nearest to the keel and extending fore-and-aft. Also called a sand strake.

garua. A heavy fog common to the coastal areas of Chile, Peru, and Ecuador; similar to the inversion fog of coastal California.

garvey. A small boat used for hunting or fishing.

gasket. 1. Traditionally a small line or strip of canvas used to fasten a sail when furled to its boom or gaff. Some boatmen call them tiers (tie-ers) or ties. 2. The seals on machinery and on watertight doors and ports.

gat. A natural or artificial channel or passage through shoals, banks, or extending inland; often marked by current. Also spelled gut.

gate. Door to a drydock or canal lock.

gate valve. A common fluid control device using a wedge-shaped block; the gate to move across and close off the opening.

gather. To take in, as gather in the jib. A boat gathers way as she gets underway.

gauge. A measuring device. A position of a sailboat relative to another boat and the wind. If upwind of another a sailboat is said to have the weather gauge; downwind she has the lee gauge. Also gage.

gear. A common collective nautical word for equipment, supplies, baggage, or anything that has no more specific designation. A sailor's baggage is always his gear, carried aboard in his seabag.

Geary 18. A one-design centerboard sloop. LOA 18′, beam 5′, Designer: L.E. Geary.

gelcoat. The finish coat of polyester resin on a fiberglass boat, applied to the inside of the female mold as the first step in lamination.

gencon. A standard charter party form. *See* charter party.

gennaker. A sail that is a cross between a genoa and a spinnaker. It is set flying like a spinnaker but is cut more like a ballooner or a reaching jib.

general inference. A description of the general weather pattern and pressure distribution together with the weather forecast.

General Prudential Rule. Same as the Rule of Special Circumstance. *See* Special Circumstance.

genoa jib. A triangular headsail much larger than a normal jib, used by sailboats when reaching and beating. It overlaps the mainsail and is also called the jenny. *See* ghoster, yankee. Modern boats often have several genoas; the largest can be more than twice the size of the mainsail in area and is thus the major driving sail.

gentle breeze. A wind of 7–10 knots; #3 on the Beaufort Scale.

geo-navigation. As distinct from celestial navigation it means fixing one's position by observing terrestrial objects, land or the bottom. More commonly known as piloting.

georef. A geographic reference system used internationally at sea in reporting a ship's position or for search and rescue operations.

ghoster. A very light headsail similar to a genoa and a yankee but with its luff extending to the top of the forestay. Used only in very light airs—also sometimes called a drifter or a wind-finder.

ghosting. Sailing with little or no apparent wind. Once called fanning.

giant clam. The largest of the bivalve mollusks, up to 5 feet across, that lives fixed in a coral reef. Its normally open, fluted shell closes quickly to trap an intruder. There is no record of a diver having been so trapped. Also called tridacna.

giant squid. A large cephalopod, the major food of the sperm whale. With a body up to 4 meters long and tentacles to 15 meters this little known and rarely seen monster of the mid-depths may be the original Kraken, a legendary Scandinavian sea monster.

gibe. Same as jibe.

Gibson Girl. A portable radio for liferafts that broadcasts on a distress frequency. Now replaced by more advanced EPIRB's.

gig. In the U.S. a Naval commanding officer's personal powerboat. Also a multi-pronged fishing spear.

gig stroke. A long, sweeping pull and recovery on the oars of a boat with a 2-second pause after the blade leaves the water before starting recovery.

gigaHertz. A billion cycles per second. *See* Hertz.

gilguy. Any rope temporarily used as a guy or lanyard, such as the light line to hold a halyard away from the mast when the boat is anchored or moored to prevent the halyard from slapping.

gilhickey. Slang for anything whose specific name is not known.

giligan hitch. Any unseamanlike, messy, or inefficient knot, hitch, or bend.

gimbals. An arrangement of metal rings, weights and pivots permitting a chronometer, galley stove, or table to remain level while the boat rolls.

gimlet. To turn something around, as to gimlet or turn the anchor around at the hawse.

ginblock. The iron block with a single sheave used at the end of a cargo boom. Also called a gin or a whip gin.

gin pole. Any improvised hoisting spar, set up as a derrick.

gin tackle. A purchase with a double and a triple block with the standing part of the fall being attached to the double block.

gipsy head. An auxiliary drum on a windlass, winch, or capstan used for handling lines—gypsy for short. Also called a warping head, whipping drum, or winch head and sometimes spelled gypsey. Gypsy is the British word for wildcat.

girding. The accidental, dangerous, broadside pull by a ship on a line made fast to a tug. If the line leads out a beam of the tug she may be capsized and is then said to be girded.

girt. Describes a vessel moored with two anchors whose cables are too taut to permit her to swing. Also to distort the shape of a sail by means of a line stretched across it.

girt band. A strip of canvas sewn across the middle part of a sail to strengthen it.

girth. A ship's or boat's measurement from gunwale (deck edge) to gunwale, around the ship's bottom at any specified frame; used in measuring sailboats for comparative ratings for time allowances in racing. Also the horizontal dimension of a sail from luff to leech.

girting. The procedure of measuring girth.

give way. A command by the coxswain of a pulling boat to his men to begin pulling together. A ship that does not have the right of way under Colregs 72 must give way (change course or speed).

give-way vessel. The vessel that, under Colregs 72 must give way (change course or speed) in deference to the stand-on vessel that has the right of way. Formerly called the burdened vessel. *See* stand-on vessel.

glacon. A fragment of sea ice ranging in size from brash ice to medium floe.

gland. A seal around a propeller shaft, submarine periscope, or any other revolving mechanism to prevent leakage of water, oil, or steam.

glass. Short word for any shipboard instrument made partly of glass such as a barometer, hand-held telescope or long glass, feed water-gauge on a boiler, or magnifying glass used to read a chart. The barometer may be called a storm or weather glass. Night glasses are binoculars with special lenses having good light-gathering properties.

glim. A light or candle once used inside a ship.

glitter. Light reflected from the surface of the sea which, when photographed from a satellite, reveals the seastate.

globe buoy. A buoy mounting a sphere on a staff. Also called a staff and globe buoy.

glue, marine. A special waterproof adhesive used for wooden boat building.

GMT. Greenwich Mean Time.

gnomic projection. A chart that shows all great circles as straight lines.

go-fast. A type of vang used when sailing a boat off the wind.

go about. To tack.

Gold Cup. Popular name for the American Power Boat Association Challenge Cup for the 40-foot class and under.

Golden Gate. A one-design keel sloop. LOA 25′, beam 6′, draft 5′. Designer: George Weyland.

gondola. A long, narrow mostly open boat used for centuries in the canals of Venice.

gongbuoy. Similar to a bellbuoy but has two gongs of distinctive tone that sound as the buoy moves in the seaway.

good ship. As used in the preamble of a charter party means a fully seaworthy vessel.

goose or gooseneck barnacle. *See* barnacle.

gooseneck. A fitting that secures the hinged end of a gaff boom or derrick (the boom plug) to the mast, allowing the spar to move in all directions. Also any pipe or vent making an 180° turn as it emerges from the deck, particularly those used as ventilators. In boats gooseneck ventilators are also called economy vents.

goosewinged. Same as wing and wing. A goosewing jibe is an incomplete one—the boom swings but the head of the sail does not follow.

gore. Any diagonally cut or triangular piece of canvas added to a sail. A sail may be gored or made with a certain goring.

GP 14. A one-design centerboard sloop. LOA 14′, beam 5′ Designer: Jack Holt.

grab, dredge. *See* dredge.

grabrail. Any small section of wood, plastic, or metal railing fitted to the side or top of a deckhouse as a handhold.

grab rope. A safety line or hand rope made fast above a boom or brow. The knotted lifelines hanging from the span wire of boat davits. Any lifeline used in an emergency attached to a lifeboat, liferaft, etc.

graft. To cover a ringbolt, stanchion, block, or other fitting with a weaving of small cord.

grain. A small spear or gig having multiple prongs and barbs.

grampus. Same as killer whale.

granny knot. A false, asymmetrical square knot—one to avoid because it slips and jams. Also called a lubber's knot.

grapnel or grappling iron. A small throwable device with four or five claws used at the end of a line to recover objects in the water or on the bottom. A heavier version is a hawk. British word is creeper.

graticule. The network of longitude and latitude lines on a chart.

grating. Any open framework or latticework, usually of wood, used as a removable piece of decking—something to stand on.

graving dock. A basin or a structure with a gate that can be pumped out. Originally used only for repair and maintenance while a dry-dock was used for building; now the words are used interchangeably.

gravity band. A band with a shackle fitted to the shank of an old-fashioned anchor near its center of gravity.

gravity davit. A mechanical holding and lowering device for ship's boats that depends on the force of gravity to roll the boat to the edge of the boat deck where it can be lowered by boat falls.

gravity waves. Surface waves on water with a wave length over 1.73 cm, whose propogation is mainly due to inertia and gravitational force.

grayback, graybeard. A big curling storm wave, especially when seen from a small boat.

grease ice. A slush of ice crystals, not yet formed into solid ice that reflects little light, thus having a matt or greasy appearance.

great circle. The circle formed at the intersection of the earth's surface with a plane through the earth's center. A great circle course is the shortest distance between places on the earth. A great circle chart showing these courses is used for great circle sailing. *See* rhumb line.

Great Lakes Rules. *See* Inland Rules of the Road.

green flash. A short, one-second glimpse of bright green light on the upper edge of the sun as it drops below the horizon or when it appears at sunrise. It results from the refraction of the different component colors of light in different degrees. Green is seen last, or first at sunrise. Unusually clear weather is required in order to see this phenomenon.

greenheart. A very strong and durable tropical wood resistant to marine borers.

greenhorn. Originally a seaman's term for a landsman, a landlubber.

Greenwich hour angle. *See* hour angle.

Greenwich Mean Time (GMT). Mean or average solar time measured from the meridian (longitude) of Greenwich, near London. *See* time. GMT is used for celestial navigation and, corrected by the zone description, for ship's time. *See* zone time.

gribble. An invertebrate water animal, any of about 4000 species of isopods from one-quarter-inch to a foot in length, that live on wood, including but not limited to wooden boats and docks. Found in fresh water and salt, from the shoreline to the ocean bottom. Also called sea roach.

grid navigation. A system for use in polar regions using grid coordinates instead of latitude and longitude.

grinder. A large pedestal hand- or foot-powered winch on a sailboat. Also the man who turns it.

gripe (s). A device for securing a boat in its davit or cradle. To gripe means to haul in and secure something in its stowage position. A sailboat is said to gripe when she tends to come into the wind, thus carrying excessive weather helm.

grog. The traditional rum and water drink of seamen. Slang for any alcoholic drink, particularly one made of rum.

groin. A jetty or pier of stone projecting out into the water to protect a beach or bank from erosion, or to direct the current in order to maintain a scoured channel. *See* jetty.

grommet. In modern usage, a reinforced hole or eyelet in a sail, awning, canvas bag, etc., to which a line can be rove through or made fast. Also a single strand of rope laid up into a ring. *See* cringle.

gross ton. *See* ton.

ground. The floor of the sea, the bottom. A boat may be said to run aground or ground out. Good holding ground is bottom that will hold an anchor.

groundfish. Fish that live on the bottom such as flounder, cod, halibut, etc. Also called demersal fish.

ground, electronic. A metal plate in contact with the water or a common point where all negative conductors terminate. In a dockside AC system a grounded conductor or wire carries current, does not pass through fuses and switches, and is color-coded white, while a gounding wire is used for safety (shock protection) between the electronic equipment and the ground, carries no current, and is coded green.

grounding. Any contact between a ship's or boat's hull and the bottom on which the vessel comes to rest. *See* stranding.

ground speed. Velocity in knots made good over the ground.

ground swell. Same as swell, not to be confused with ground wave.

ground tackle. The equipment used in anchoring and mooring, including anchors, anchor cables or rodes, connecting shackles and links, etc.

ground wave. Part of a radio wave system that moves along the earth's surface instead of being projected upwards as a sky wave.

grouper. A sedentary and solitary fish of warm water, often very large; edible, curious, and slow that lives near reefs and in underwater caves.

group flashing light. A navigational aid that shows groups of two or more flashes at regular intervals.

group occulting light. A navigational aid showing two or more eclipses or dark periods at regular intervals, the eclipses being shorter than the lighted periods.

grow. An anchor cable was said to grow in the direction in which it was lying. Modern American word is tend or lead.

growler. A piece of floating ice, smaller than a bergy-bit, difficult to detect by radar and thus a hazard to navigation. *See* iceberg.

GRP. *See* fiberglass.

GRT. Gross Registered Tonnage. *See* tonnage.

guard rail. A fence aboard ship, lighter than bulwarks, erected along the deck edge as a safety measure. Also a timber fastened fore-and-aft horizontally above the waterline and serving as a fender. In this sense also called a guard, fender guard, belting, bull rail, or sheer rail.

gudgeon. A steel ring on the sternpost or rudderpost of a ship or boat into which the pins or pintles of the rudder fit and rotate.

guess-warp. A rope or line passed through a thimble on a boat boom, made fast at one end on deck and hanging free when not in use. It is for the convenience of boat crews in hauling out to the boom. Also a rope run along a ship's side as a grabline, guy rope, or to assist in towing astern. May refer to a line run out by boat to a buoy, wharf, dolphin, bollard, etc., to assist in warping (moving) the ship. Also called a guesswarp, guess-rope, or guestwarp.

guest flag. Flag flown from the starboard side of a yacht to indicate that guests are aboard in the owner's absence. It is a rectangular blue flag with a diagonal bar.

Guiana Current. A northward-flowing ocean current off the northeast coast of South America that joins the North Equatorial Current to form the Caribbean Current, the start of the Gulf Stream System.

guillotine. A cable-(chain-) holding device, a hinged bar that can be made fast across the links.

Guinea Current. A branch of the Canary Current that turns southeast and then east at the Cape Verde Islands. *See* Canary Current.

gulf. A very large indentation of the coast line, larger than a bay, an area of water partly enclosed by land.

Gulf Stream System. In general terms it is the ocean current system originating in the Caribbean with the Caribbean Current that flows through the Gulf of Mexico as the Yucatan Current, and then becomes the Florida Current passing close to Florida and north to become known as the Gulf Stream off Cape Hatteras. This stream then flows in a complex pattern generally northeast to become the North Atlantic Current off the Grand Banks. This relatively warm water divides as it approaches Great Britain and Ireland, with some water passing to the north of them and the other going south along the coasts of France and Portugal to form the Canary Current, and join the North Equatorial Current and thus complete the clockwise circulation in the North Atlantic.

gulf weed. Any of the pelagic brown weeds, sargassum, that float in and near the Gulf Stream. Common in large drifts in the Sargasso Sea.

gull. A gregarious, long-winged, web-footed sea bird common to all waters and often found far inland. Also gull is an old word for wear, as a pin wears in a block, causing the sheave to wobble.

Gull. A one-design centerboard sloop. LOA 11′, beam 5¼′. Designer: Ian Proctor.

gulleting. The part of the leading edge of a boat's rudder near the pintles that is cut away to permit them to fit into the gudgeons.

gunkholing. A boatman's word for cruising in sheltered waters, anchoring at night in a quiet cove or other protected anchorage known as a gunkhole.

gunstocking. The broad deck plank of teak or other hard wood inlaid at the curved ends of the deck planking.

gun tackle. One with two single blocks.

gunter. The sliding topmast of the gunter rig, also the triangular sail spread in such a rig. Now rarely seen, the gunter rig is one extended by a gunter yard or gaff secured to a short mast by two iron travelers, gunter irons, which hold the yard upright. A variation of this rig is the gunter lug, similar to a standing lug, very high in the peak with the yard nearly vertical.

guntline. *See* cantline.

gunwale. Upper edge of the side of a boat. Pronounced gunnel.

gurdy. A bearing or roller fitted on the gunwale of a boat to facilitate hauling in lines.

gusset. A reinforcing or connecting steel plate of different shapes used in shipbuilding as a uniting and stiffening member where a gap in the plating exists. In sailboats a gusset may be used in attaching shrouds to the hull. In wooden boat construction a piece used to fasten two timbers together at an angle.

gust. A sudden brief increase in wind velocity. A wind may blow at 20 knots, gusting to 25 knots. Gusts are momentary while squalls may last several minutes or more. *See* flaw.

gut. *See* gat.

gybe. British spelling of jibe.

guy. Any line, rope, or wire used to hold, steady, or support a boom, mast, spar, derrick, etc. Particular name depends on function, such as forward, after, davit, boom, jib-boom, martingale or traveling guy. Sometimes called a vang. *See* vang, lazy guy. The British use guy to describe a breast line which we call a mooring line.

gyrocompass. A ship's compass using a gyroscope.

gyroscope. A rapidly spinning device that maintains itself steady and level and also aligns itself with the axis of the earth, thus pointing to true north.

gyropilot. An automatic steering device using a gyrocompass on which a course can be set and maintained. Also called an iron or a metal mike (slang).

gyro stabilizer. Any mechanism using a gyro to establish a level platform or a level plane of reference, e.g., a stable element.

H

haar. A wet sea fog off the coast of Scotland and England—common in the summer.

hachures. Marks on charts indicating the direction and steepness of the coastal shore line.

hack chronometer or watch. The working timepiece used in taking sights for celestial navigation so as not to disturb and bring topside the major or standard chronometer. Frequent radio time signals now make elaborate combinations of watches and chronometers unnecessary.

hail. A ship is said to hail from a certain port. To hail is to call out as in "boat ahoy." A loud-hailer is a hand-held voice amplifier.

hailing port. The port from which a boat is registered or documented.

half model or half-block model. A solid wooden boat or ship model showing in outboard profile half of the hull form, usually the starboard side.

half-breadth plan. A plan or top view drawing of half a ship divided along the keel line, the other half being symmetrical.

half hitch. One formed by passing the end of a line around the standing part and bringing it up through the bight.

half mast. To fly a flag from the center rather than from the top of a mast is to half mast it. Colors are half masted as a sign of mourning. Also called half staff or at the dip.

half-rater. A class of small, sloop-rigged, open sailboats, once used at the U.S. Naval Academy for sail training.

half seas over. Drunk.

half sheave. A curved metal insert at the top of the mast of a small boat to provide a fairlead. Also called a dead sheave.

Halon. Trade name for a new, very fast-acting and efficient fire extinguisher now widely used in boat engine rooms.

halyard. Any line, rope, tackle, or wire used to raise and lower sails and flags. In many modern sailboats the halyards are run inside the hollow mast and are known as internal halyards.

hambro line. British word for a small three-stranded rope used for lashing and lacing aboard a sailboat.

hammerhead shark. One with a unique laterally expanded head, shaped somewhat like a hammer. Has been known to attack people and is common in the North Atlantic.

hammerlock moor. A procedure to reduce the violent yawing or horsing of a vessel at anchor in a strong wind. A second anchor is dropped when the ship or boat is at one extremity of a yaw, anchor cable is eased and the boat then rides to two anchors.

hamper. *See* top hamper.

Hampton. A one-design centerboard sloop. LOA 18', beam 6'. Designer: V.J. Serio. A Hampton boat is a half-decked, centerboard sailboat, usually 20–25 feet long used for fishing and recreation off New England.

hand. To take in, furl, or stow, as a sail. A hand is a sailor or any member of the crew. To "bear a hand" is to hurry and to "lend a hand" is to assist.

hand lead. A sounding weight, 5–15 pounds in weight, cast and retrieved by hand in shallow water to measure the depth. Spoken: "Led."

hand log. Same as chip log.

handsomely. Carefully, deliberately, as a helmsman may be told to change course handsomely.

handy. Maneuverable, nimble, easy to handle.

hand billy. Traditionally a portable, general-purpose tackle such as a luff tackle once used aboard a sailing ship. Sailboaters refer to any convenient two-block tackle as a handy billy. A portable powered pump used to fight fires or to pump out spaces is also called a handy billy.

hanging keel. Same as bar keel.

hank. A metal or plastic ring, shackle, or hook, often with a spring-loaded closure (piston, plunger, or snap) for securing the luff of a headsail to its stay. Sometimes called a clip, snap hook or piston hank. To hank means to make fast with a hank.

happy hour. A convivial late-afternoon period of relaxation.

harbor. Any area of water, protected naturally or artificially, that provides shelter for a vessel to anchor or moor.

hard. Part of a beach where the sand is firm. Also an adjective meaning full or extreme, as in "hard right rudder" or "hard alee." To harden a sail is to trim it flat for going to windward.

hard alee. A command to put the tiller of a sailboat all the way towards the leeward side in order to bring the boat about, to tack it.

hardtack. An unleavened biscuit or bread made of flour and water; a durable ship's biscuit. Also known as sea biscuit or pilot bread. Normal soft bread is sometimes known as soft tack.

hardwood. In the nautical sense any timber from a tree that has leaves instead of needles.

hare along. To sail fast, usually down wind.

harmattan. A steady dry and dusty wind blowing off the Sahara across the Gulf of Guinea and the Cape Verde Islands.

Harmsworth Trophy. Popular name for the British International Trophy for Motorboats.

harness, safety. Worn by all prudent sailors when topside at night, underway or in heavy weather in a small boat. Straps over the shoulders and around the chest are connected to a line with a snap hook to make fast to a lifeline, shroud, stay, etc.

hatch, hatchway. Any opening in a vessel's deck, usually rectangular, used for the passage of people and/or cargo.

hatch coaming. The steel, wood, or fiberglass rim built around the hatch to keep out water and to provide a support for the hatch cover.

hatch hood. A removable canvas cover for a companion hatchway.

haul. A proper nautical word for pull or drag as in "haul in the anchor." The hauling part of a tackle is the moving or free end in contrast to the standing part. When the wind changes direction clockwise it hauls or veers. *See* back. A ship hauls up, off, or offshore—here haul means go. To haul down a sail means to pull it down.

hauling line. Old word for heaving line.

haul out. To take a boat out of the water for storage, repairs, etc., is to haul it out. The procedure is called a haul out. Also a ship's boat hauls out to a boom when in the water but not in use.

haven. An enclosed and protected harbor.

hawk. A multipronged device, similar to a grapnel, used at the end of a cable to recover a lost anchor or other object on the bottom. Also a wind direction indicator at the top of a mast.

hawksbill turtle. A large sea turtle weighing up to 150 pounds and long hunted for its shell, the source of tortoise shell.

hawse. Part of the bow where the hawse pipes are located through which the anchor chain passes. Also the distance between the ship and the anchor when the anchor is on the bottom.

hawse buckler. The metal cover for the hawsepipe that keeps out water.

hawsepipe. A metal tube leading down from the deck out to the bow plating through which the anchor chain passes. Often called hawse for short. Modern ship anchors are housed and secured at the lower end of the hawsepipe.

hawser. Any large fiber or wire rope over 5 inches in diameter. The British call a mooring line a hawser.

hawser-laid rope. Same as plain-laid or right-handed rope.

hawser rudder. A length of buoyant manila hawser streamed astern; used as a jury rudder by hauling on guys at its end run forward on each quarter.

head. Foremost or projecting part or the highest part, as in ship's head, pier head, rudder head, davit head, head of a sail, etc. The nautical word for toilet. Down by the head describes a vessel having more draft forward than aft. Head on means bow to bow. A precipitous cape or promentory is a headland or head. The expanding, seaward part of a rip current is its head. The wind heads (opposite is frees) when it shifts towards the bow of a boat sailing close-hauled. *See* header.

headboard. The fitting at the head of a triangular sail to which its halyard is made fast.

header. A wind shift in sailing that requires a course change away from the wind; the opposite shift is a lift.

heading. The direction in which a ship is pointed; also known as the ship's head.

headfoil. A grooved tube fitted over the headstay to receive the luff rope of a headsail instead of hanks. If it has a double groove a headsail can be hoisted before the old sail is lowered.

headledge. Either of the transverse coamings of the hatch of a boat. Also either of the upright posts at the ends of a centerboard trunk.

headline. Any mooring line leading forward of a vessel's pivot point.

headreach. The distance made to windward by a sailboat when tacking. Headreaching is sailing to windward.

headroom. The distance in a boat between the sole or deck and the overhead.

headrope. That part of a boltrope sewed to the head of a sail.

headsail. Any sail set forward of the most forward mast. Same as kite. *See* foresail.

headsheets. Sheets attached to the headsails.

headstay. In a small craft, the stay from the top of the forward mast to the top of the stem or to the bowsprit. In large sailing ships it extends to the end of the jibboom. Often same as forestay.

headway. Forward movement of the boat through the water. The opposite is sternway or sternboard.

head wind or sea. Wind or sea more or less opposed to the intended course of the ship.

heart. A circular or heart-shaped, wooden block used as a deadeye. Also a slack twisted strand forming the core of a shroud-laid rope or the fiber rope in the center of wire rope.

heave. To draw, pull, or haul as on a rope. To move into position as "the ship hove in sight." To rise and fall; the vertical bodily movement of a ship in a seaway—distinct from pitch. To heave the lead is to cast it and take a sounding with a hand lead.

heave down. Same as careen.

heaver. A short tool or bar used for tightening line, as when splicing.

heave short. To haul in on the anchor cable until the anchor is at short stay, just short of breaking ground.

heave to. To stop forward progress. In very heavy weather a ship may choose to reduce speed to a minimum by using storm canvas or reduce engine speed. Thus a ship may be hove to or lie to. In light or moderate weather a vessel may heave to to maintain station, haul fishing gear, etc.

heaving line. A light line weighted with a monkey fist at the end that is thrown across from the ship to the pier. A messenger is attached and a mooring line is then pulled across.

heavy. Heavy weather is a storm or a rough sea. In a storm a ship may be said to be making heavy weather of it. A top-heavy ship is one that is unstable because of high weights.

heel. The temporary inclination or leaning of a ship to port or starboard caused by wind and sea or by the inertia of a ship that heels or leans in a high speed turn. It is a dynamic condition and not static as list is and not to be confused with rolling. Also the lower end of a mast rudder or boom is its heel. *See* list.

heel and toe. One after the other, as in a heel and toe watch (watch on and watch off) also referred to as watch and watch.

heel block. One acting as a fair lead to a winch at the lower end of a cargo boom.

heeling error. That part of the deviation or magnetic compass error due to the inclination of the ship. It is corrected by heeling magnets: vertical magnetized iron bars placed in the compass binnacle.

heel tackle. Tackle used for holding in position the heels of sheer legs or similar gear.

height of eye. The distance above the water of the observer's eye, a consideration when measuring the altitude of a celestial body. A table in the Nautical Almanac is used to correct sextant altitude for height of eye.

helm. Normally the tiller or wheel but sometimes the rudder as well. In powered vessels orders to the helm or helmsman are always given as right or left, not starboard or port, and indicate the direction the ship's head will take. In sailboats the tiller may be put up to windward or down to leeward. A sailboat may carry lee or weather helm while a steam vessel carries right or left rudder.

helmsman. One who steers the ship, same as steersman.

Heron. A one-design centerboard sloop. LOA 11′, beam 4½′. Designer: Jack Holt.

Herreshoff anchor. *See* old-fashioned anchor.

Highfield lever. (Now often written hi-field lever). A handle where the running backstay is made fast to the deck by which the backstay can be quickly slacked, or pulled taut when going about.

high frequency (HF). 3 to 30 megahertz (MHz) used for AM, FM, and citizens band (CB). Wavelength is 10 to 100 meters.

Highlander. A one-design centerboard sloop. LOA 20′, beam 6½′. Designer: G.K. Douglass.

high pressure area. An air mass of high atmospheric pressure that helps govern the weather at sea. In and around it the wind blows clockwise in the northern hemisphere, counterclockwise in the southern. Also called an anticyclone.

high seas. All the ocean outside territorial waters. *See* territorial waters. Also wind-driven storm waves. *See* sea.

high water. The maximum height of a rising tide. High water is a more nautical expression than high tide.

high water full and change. *See* lunitidal interval.

hike, hiking. To lean out, on, or over the gunwale of a sailboat to counteract excessive heeling. Hiking boards and straps are often rigged to assist and magnify this effort, and a hiking stick attached to the tiller permits the helmsman to hike out. In maximum hiking a crewman swings out in a strap supported by a wire or trapeze secured at the masthead. The British term is sit out and they use a toe strap, which is called a hiking strap in the U.S.

hiking stick. A swiveled extension of the tiller used by the helmsman when hiking out.

hitch. A knot whose loops normally jam together under strain yet remain separable when strain is removed. *See* knot.

HO. Hydrographic Office of the Navy, now part of the Defense Mapping Agency Hydrographic Center.

hobbyhorsing. Excessive pitching into a head sea, a common probblem for small boats.

Hobie Cat 16. A sloop-rigged catamaran. LOA 16½′, beam 8′. Designer: Hobie Alter. There is a Hobie Cat 18 that has a centerboard.

hockle. Boatman's slang for a kink in a line or wire.

Hoey. *See* protractor.

hog. A ship hogs when the bow and stern drop below the level of the midships section; opposite is sag. A hogging line is one that is passed under a vessel on a collision mat and secured on the opposite side.

hog-piece. A fore-and-aft plank or timber bolted to the inside top of the keel of a small boat.

hoist. 1. To raise or lift. 2. The height of a sail rig. 3. The vertical side of a flag nearest the halyard to which it is bent. 4. A tackle used for lifting something. **5.** To hoist in a boat means to hook on, raise it and stow it. **6.** The length of the luff of a sail.

hoist, flag. A group of signal flags flown together in a single vertical line making up a signal or message.

hoisting pad. A fitting fastened to the bow and the stern of a ship's boat for hoisting purposes.

holding ground. A classification of the bottom as to its anchor holding properties; good, fair, or poor.

holding tank. Any tank designed to hold sewerage, etc., until it can be pumped out.

hold water. A command to oarsmen to immerse their blades and hold steady in order to slow or stop the boat's run.

holiday. Nautical term for any accidentally neglected, unpainted, or unscrubbed area of the deck or bulkhead.

hollow sea. A very steep and dangerous sea, usually caused by the tidal current running against the wind and forming waves with concave fronts.

home. In the direction of the ship, as the anchor comes home when it is hauled in.

home port. For a private yacht it is the port designated by the owner and approved by the appropriate documentation office.

honey barge. Slang for garbage scow.

hook. Any bent piece of steel used for a specific purpose such as a fishhook, chain hook, cargo hook, swivel hook. A snap hook closes with a spring lever; also called a safety hook. Hook or mud hook is slang for anchor. A hook is also a spit of land, a narrow cape whose end curves inland as does Sandy Hook, New Jersey. Also a deformation in a planing boat's hull that forces the bow down at speed, as well as any dent or depression in a wooden boat's hull. *See* rocker.

hooker. A mildly derogative, sometimes, affectionate word for a boat.

hoop. A movable ring of wood or metal to which the luff of a sail is fastened and which slides up and down the mast. Replaced in most modern sailboats by slides that move in a track.

hopper barge. One used to receive mud and sand (spoil) removed from the bottom by a dredge. A dredge that has a compartment to receive spoil is a hopper dredge. Also a double-hulled barge used to carry bulk cargo, either open or decked over, is known as a hopper barge.

horizon. The apparent intersection of the sea and sky, known as the apparent or visible horizon. For celestial navigation the horizon is a plane passing through the center of the earth and perpendicular to a line connecting the observer's position and the earth's center.

horn. 1. One of the side pieces that forms the jaw of a gaff. 2. The outer end of a crosstree or one of the arms of a cleat. 3. A noise-making device, *see* foghorn. 4. A projecting fitting on the stern of some vessels that holds and supports the rudder. 5. In shipbuilding, to align the frames and bulkheads with the keel is to horn them.

horn cleat. One with a single projecting piece or horn about which a line can be made fast. *See* cleat.

horse. In a sailboat, any rope, bar, or track on which something can slide, as the bar or traveler placed athwartships on which the main sheet travels.

horse latitudes. Areas of high atmospheric pressure just north of the Northeast Trade winds in the northern hemisphere and south of the Southest Trades below the Equator, at about latitude 30°. They are marked by calm or light winds, especially in the summer. *See* doldrums.

horseshoe. Boatman's name for a common lifering, shaped somewhat like a horseshoe, and carried topside.

horsing. A corruption of hawsing, the sometimes violent swinging of a vessel at anchor in a strong wind. Same as sluing or slewing.

houndband. The ring around the upper part of the mast, used for attaching the shrouds.

hounding. That part of the mast below the hounds.

hounds. 1. Traditionally, the projections or wooden blocks at the side of a mast supporting the trestletrees. 2. Hounds of the rigging are the eyes of the shrouds as they pass over the trestletrees. 3. In modern boats, the point where the shrouds and the spreaders meet the mast. 4. The point on the mast where the jib halyard block is made fast.

hour angle. That arc in degrees on the equinoctial marked by the observer's meridian and the hour circle of the celestial body. The Greenwich hour angle is the angle or arc measured from Greenwich at longitude $0°$ west to the longitude of the celestial body.

hour circle. The projection of a meridian or line of longitude upon the celestial sphere.

hour glass. A primitive clock, same as sand glass. Also a fouled spinnaker whose middle is twisted so that only the top and bottom of the sail are filled.

house. A structure on deck or a compartment topside, as the cook house in old sailing ships, or the chart house or pilot house on modern ships. To house (here pronounced houz) something is to bring it down from aloft, to store it or to put it away. An anchor is housed when it is secured for sea in the hawsepipe.

houseboat. One designed for comfortable stationary living or suitable for cruising in sheltered waters.

houseline. Traditionally a three-thread tarred cord spun from left to right and laid from right to left; stronger than marlin and smaller than roundline. Now largely replaced by synthetic small stuff.

housing. That part of a sailboat's mast that is below the deck.

housing chain stopper. A length of chain fitted with a turnbuckle, one end secured to the deck and the other fitted with a pelican hook that seizes the chain to the anchor, and holds the anchor up snug into the hawse. Sometimes the turnbuckle is made fast directly to the deck.

hove. Past and past participle of heave, as "the ship hove in sight," or "the line was hove taut."

hub. The central part of a ship's or boat's propeller to which the blades are attached and which keys onto the propeller shaft.

hulk. Usually a bare hull, unfit for sea, used as storage in port. Also a dismasted wreck.

hull. The body of a ship or boat. A boat is said to be hulled when her skin is pierced by something such as a rock. *See* displacement hull, planing hull, vee-bottom hull.

hull balance. That characteristic of good sailboat design that ensures no excessive turning tendency when she is heeled over to the wind.

hull down. Describes a boat over the horizon with just her top hamper showing.

hulling. *See* a-hull.

hull speed. That speed for which a boat's hull is designed as the maximum effective speed.

Humboldt Current. Another and less accurate name for the Peru Current.

hurricane. The Atlantic, Caribbean, and eastern Pacific word for a cyclone or typhoon; a very strong and dangerous tropical storm of devastating power. Any storm at sea with wind velocities over 65 knots.

Hurricane Warning. An official notification from the National Weather Service (NWS) that a hurricane is expected in a specified area within 24 hours. *See* storm warning.

Hurricane Watch. A warning by the National Weather Service that a hurricane is possible in a specified area at an indicated time.

hydraulic current. Current flowing through a narrow passage joining two bodies of water that have different times and ranges of high and low waters.

hydrofoil. A high-speed vessel partly lifted over the water's surface by submerged foils acting in a similar fashion to airplane wings (foils) that provide lift in the air.

hydrography. In a limited sense, the science of determining the condition of navigable waters and charting them as an assistance to navigators. In its broad sense, hydrography is the scientific analysis of the world's seas and oceans. *See* oceanography.

hydroplane. A fast boat in which the hull has steps to lift most of it above water when it reaches the required speed. At this point the boat is planing or is on the step. A boat that does not plane is a displacement boat or hull.

hyfield lever. Another spelling of Highfield lever.

hyperbolic. Describes radionavigation systems (Omega, Decca, Loran C) that use curved lines of position.

I

iceberg. A large floating mass of ice that has broken off a glacier in the Arctic or from the great ice shelf of the Antarctic. An iceberg or berg is over 5 meters high; smaller masses are bergy bits or growlers.

ice blink. The reflection in the sky of the sunlight's glare on the ice.

ice fog. One composed of ice crystals forming at very low temperatures in clear calm weather at high latitudes.

Ice Patrol. The internationally organized and funded watch for ice that might endanger North Atlantic shipping. The U.S. Coast Guard does the patrolling, usually only in early summer.

IHO. The International Hydrographic Organization in Monaco.

IMCO. The International Maritime Consultive Organization, part of the United Nations Organization.

impeller log. One that uses a propeller to generate an electric current with a frequency that is a measure of the boat's speed.

index arm or bar. The movable part of a sextant, carrying the index mirror or glass that indicates degrees of arc or angle. *See* sextant.

index error. A constant error in the angle measured by a sextant due to the horizon glass and the index glass not being parallel when the pointer on the vernier scale indicates zero. *See* sextant.

Indian Ocean. Now considered to be the waters bounded by Antarctica, Asia, Australia, and Africa.

indicator cock. *See* seacock.

inertial navigation. The determination of position by using the inertial or stable properties of a gyroscope and accellerometers measuring and converting minute components of acceleration into course and distance from a known point of departure.

Inglefield anchor. A stockless, double-fluked anchor whose arms can rotate separately up to 45° from the shank.

Inglefield clips. British interlocking C-shaped metal hooks whose tension keeps them closed when used to connect lines or gear such as signal flags to their halyards. Similar in use to snap shackles.

inhaul. Any line or rope used to pull something towards the boat in contrast to an outhaul.

in irons. Said of a sailboat that, when tacking, cannot get through the wind and thus fill its sails on the new tack. She is said to be in stays or to have missed stays. In irons also applies to a tug that cannot move freely because of the way she is made fast to another vessel.

Inland Cat. A one-design centerboard catboat. LOA 14½′, beam 5½′. Designers: Bell and Larimore.

Inland Rules of the Road. The International Rules (Colregs 72) do not now apply to harbors, rivers, lakes, and other inland waters of the U.S. Among the special rules that do apply are the Army Corps of Engineers Rules, Great Lakes Rules, Inland Rules (title 33 of the U.S. Code), the Motor boat Act of 1940, Pilot Rules, and the Western Rivers Rules.

Inland Lake Scow. A fast sloop or catboat (16–38′ overall) with shallow draft, broad beam, nearly flat bottom, square bow, and twin bilge boards and rudders. Also called bilgeboard scows.

Inland Waters. Those areas, shown on most coastal and harbor charts, in which the Inland Rules of the Road apply. If not so indicated on the chart, inland waters are those inside a line drawn roughly parallel to the coast passing through the outermost aids to navigation such as buoys. Not to be confused with territorial waters.

inlet. A relatively short narrow waterway connecting two bodies of water or merely extending inland from the sea or other body.

inshore. Close to the coast, as opposed to offshore.

in stays. While tacking, a sailing vessel is in stays momentarily when sails are flapping prior to the boat falling off on the new tack. *See* in irons.

integrated circuits. A combination of electronic components in a single package.

intercardinal points. Northeast, southeast, southwest, and northwest, the four points on the compass between the cardinal points.

intercept. As used in celestial navigation, the difference between the observed and the calculated altitudes of a celestial body. Its determination leads to plotting a line of position.

Interclub. A one-design, centerboard cat-rigged dinghy. LOA 11½', beam 4½'. Designer: Sparkman & Stephens.

Interlake. A one-design centerboard sloop. LOA 18', beam 6'. Designer: Francis Swiesguth.

interlock. An important safety device that cuts off the electricity when the door or cover of an instrument such as radar is removed.

International Code of Signals. A universal system of communication at sea using flags, light displays, or flashing light transmission in code. A multilingual signal book explains the use of the 40 flags.

International 110. A one-design keel sloop. LOA 24', beam 4', draft 3'. Designer: Ray Hunt.

International 14. An international development class—one of the first planing centerboard sloops. LOA 14', beam 5½'.

International 210. A one-design keel sloop. LOA 30', beam 6', draft 4'. Designer: Ray Hunt.

International Low Water (ILW). A datum or reference plane below mean sea level calculated by multiplying half the range between mean lower low water and mean higher high water by 1.5.

International Offshore Rule (IOR). The regulations issued by the International Yacht Racing Union by which ocean racing sailboats are measured and rated in order to provide equitable handicaps. It is the basic measurement standard for sailboat racing at home and abroad, administered since 1966 by the Offshore Racing Council, representing 13 countries.

International One-Design. A class keel sloop. LOA 33½', beam 7', draft 5½'. Designer: Bjarne Aas.

International 101. *See* Aphrodite 101.

International radio silence. Three-minute periods of silence on the distress frequency starting 15 minutes and 45 minutes after each hour so that ships in distress may be heard.

International Regulations for Preventing Collisions at Sea. Commonly known as the International Rules of the Road. Last revised in 1972 and effective because ratified by the U.S. Congress in 1977. Short title: Colregs 72.

International Rules of the Road. *See* above.

international waters. Those outside territorial limits and thus outside the jurisdiction of any country. Traditionally considered to be 3 miles, although for control of fishing most countries now claim control out to 200 miles.

International Weather Code. A five-figure group of numbers used by ships at sea as well as shore stations in reporting and in receiving weather data.

International Yacht Racing Union (IYRU). The governing body for all international racing.

interrupted quick-flashing light (i. qk. fl.). A navigational light showing a number of quick flashes followed by a period of darkness.

inversion. A weather condition of warm air overlying cooler air common to the west coast of temperate zone land masses; important to seamen because it causes fog. In California, for example, cold air is blown ashore by the prevailing westerly winds displacing and passing under the warm air causing the temperature gradient of the air to be inverted.

inverter. An electrical device often used in boats to change 120 volts to 110 volts so that appliances and power tools may be used.

inwale. A piece of wood fastened inside the frame of an open boat along the top strake of planking. If outside the gunwale it is an outwale.

inward. Towards the land, as inward bound.

I/O. Inboard/Outboard. *See* stern drive.

ionosphere. A layer 50–100 miles above the earth that reflects some radio waves thus producing skywaves. *See* ground wave.

IOR. International Offshore Rule.

Irish pennant. Any loose unsightly rope or line aloft or on deck that should be secured, stowed or made fast. Also called a dead-man.

Irminger Current. One of the terminal branches of the Gulf Stream System flowing west of the south coast of Ireland.

ironbound. Describes a steep coast with no shelters or anchorages.

iron mike. Slang for automatic pilot.

irons. *See* in irons.

Islander 28. A one-design keel sloop. LOA 28′, beam 10′, draft 5′. Designer: Robert Perry.

Islands 17. A one-design centerboard sloop. LOA 16½′, beam 6′. Principal designer: Mike Krug.

isobar. A line on a weather chart showing equal atmospheric pressure.

isobath. A line on a bathymetric chart showing equal depths.

isogen. A line on a chart connecting points or places of the same magnetic variation.

isolator. A device in the shore power line of a boat at dockside to ground stray currents that cause galvanic corrosion.

isophase. Describes a flashing aid to navigation that has equal periods of light and of darkness.

isthmus. A narrow neck of land joining two land masses.

IYRU. International Yacht Racing Union.

J

J24. A one-design keel sloop used for cruising as well as racing. LOA 24′, beam 9′, draft 4′. Designer: Rodney Johnstone.

jack. Short for Union Jack flown at the bow of a warship. Also a mast funnel is called a jack.

jackass. Any device or cover that keeps water out of the hawse-pipes.

jackass rig. Any unseamanlike confused arrangement of gear.

jack-in-a-basket. A cylindrical daymarker made of vertical slats mounted on a pole, used to mark a shoal or the edge of the channel.

jack block. Block kept aloft for hoisting and lowering topgallant yards in a square-rigger.

jackline. One threaded between the mainsail slides on the mast and the cringles on the luff of a sail or between the hanks and the luff of a boomed headsail.

jack pin. A belaying pin.

jackrod. A length of metal rod or small pipe welded to the ship's structure to which awnings, weather cloths, canvas covers, etc., are made fast. Also known as a jackstay.

jackrope. One used to secure the foot of a sail to a boom.

jackstaff. A short flagstaff in the extreme forward part of the bow.

jackstay. Any wire or rope used aboard ship for a wide variety of purposes from supporting a sail or awning to passing to a wreck to take off people.

jackyard. Any extension of a yard, gaff, or spar.

jacob's ladder. A portable rope ladder with wooden rungs slung from a boat boom or over the side to bring aboard a pilot. Also called a pilot ladder or jack ladder and, less accurately, a sea ladder; *see* ladder.

jag. 1. To lay out a rope or wire in loops and to secure them with stops. 2. To caulk a seam in a steel plate or a leaky rivet. 3. A short pull or tug as: "take a jag on that jib sheet."

jam cleat or jamb cleat. One designed to hold a line but able to release it quickly if necessary.

jammer box. A group of adjacent stoppers through which most of the lines from forward in a sailboat are led (sheets, halyards, etc.) aft to a single winch.

jamming fiddle block. One whose slot design permits self-cleating or holding; usually used with vangs.

Japan Current. Same as Kuroshio.

Javelin. A one-design centerboard sloop. LOA 14', beam 5½'. Designer: Uffa Fox.

jaw. 1. Forward end of a gaff or boom which half encircles the mast and whose prongs are called cheeks or horns. Also called a throat. 2. The length of a strand of rope as it makes one full turn. *See* long in the jaw.

jaw rope. Line holding the jaw to the mast; passed through beads to reduce friction as the jaw of the boom is raised and lowered.

jeers. Heavy tackles with multiple blocks used to handle the heaviest yards in a square-rigger.

jellyfish. A marine invertebrate related to coral and the sea anemone; sometimes luminescent, often umbrella shaped, free floating with a transparent body surrounded by passive tentacles studded with tiny stinging barbs. Also known as medusa.

jenny. Same as genoa jib.

jerking line. Same as snatch line.

jerk string. A light line attached to the jib of a sailboat to control the fore-and-aft location of the jib's draft. A jib so rigged is called a vary-luff jib.

jet drive. *See* waterjet.

Jet 14. A one-design centerboard sloop. LOA 14′, beam 4½′. Designer: Howard Siddons.

jetsam. *See* jettison.

jettison. To throw overboard, especially to lighten an endangered ship. The material jettisoned is called flotsam if it floats, jetsam if it sinks, and lagan if it is buoyed for future recovery.

jetty. A waterfront structure such as a wharf or pier built to influence current or protect the entrance to a harbor or river. If its primary use is to protect from erosion it is a groin; if it is used mainly to break the force of the waves it is a breakwater. *See* bulkhead, seawall, training wall.

jewel block. A small single block usually made fast to a yard or masthead and used for reeving flag halyards.

Jersey Sea Skiffs. *See* Seabright skiff.

Jew's harp. A ring or shackle at the shank head of an anchor to which anchor cable is made fast. Also any lyre or harp-shaped shackle.

jib. A triangular sail rigged forward of the most forward mast and of other headsails. Balloon and genoa jibs are large headsails carried by sailboats in moderate or light winds. A deck-sweeper jib is one with a foot so low that it touches the deck.

jibboom. A separate wooden extension of the bowsprit in old wooden ships; part of the bowsprit in modern ships.

jibe. A sudden and often unscheduled change of tack when running free in a sailboat in which the wind swings the boom quickly across the stern and over to the other side as the stern passes through the wind. Accidental jibes can be dangerous but if planned they are routine—the same as wearing. Racing sailboats have special techniques for jibing with a spinnaker set, such as: end-for-end pole jibes (for one-designs), vim jibes, Windigo patented system, etc. Also spelled gybe.

jib head. A piece of wood, plastic, or metal forming the head of a jib in order to facilitate sail handling.

jib-headed. Describes a sailboat with triangular sails instead of the older four-sided gaff rig. Also called a Bermuda or Marconi rig.

jibe-ho. The warning given by the skipper during a planned jibe that the boom is about to swing across.

jib iron. Same as jib traveler.

jib netting. A triangular safety net under the jibboom.

jib-stick. A light pole or spar used to hold the jib outboard (or a staysail) when the sailboat is running before the wind.

jib topsail. A high-clewed headsail used either alone or set above a staysail in a double-headed rig. Also called a jibtop.

jib traveler. An iron ring used to secure the tack of a jib to the bowsprit that was not made fast to a stay; not common today. Also called a jib iron or a tack ring.

jib tricing line. A small line fastened to the center of the jib, used in taking in the jib or spilling its air.

jiffy reefing. *See* slab reefing.

jig. 1. A small general-pupose tackle used aboard a sailboat. Also called a jigger. 2. A fishing lure that spins and flashes, used in jigging.

jigger. A small sail set on a jigger mast: the mizzenmast of a yawl or ketch. The aftermost mast on a four-masted ship, sometimes called a spanker. *See* mast.

jigger bumkin or bumpkin. A spar overhanging the stern of a yawl, fitted with a block for the jigger sheet. Also called a jigger boom.

jog. The thin end or scarf of a timber used in boat building. Also called lip, nib, or scarf.

jogging. In boat building the notching of the boat's frame. Also running at slowest speed (steerage way) in heavy weather.

joggle. In steel shipbuilding means to bend, crimp, or fit a plate or bar around some other material.

johnboat. A square-ended and flat-bottomed boat, also called a jonboat.

joiner. A shipbuilding word used to describe work and fittings that involve sheet metal. Joiner work also describes the fitted wood-work in a boat.

joint. In boatbuilding, when parts come together squarely or end to end they form a butt joint. An expansion joint is one that per-mits expansion or contraction in order to reduce stress. A flange joint involves overlapping flanges or edges while a scarf or lap joint involves scarfing.

jolly boat or jolly. A small rowing or sailing boat carried aboard ship for recreation.

Jollyboat. A one-design centerboard sloop. LOA 18′, beam 5½′. Designer: Uffa Fox.

jonboat. Same as johnboat.

J-stroke. That used by the man in the stern of a canoe to counter the turning effect of the bow man's paddling. Also called a fishhook or steering stroke.

jumbo. On schooners an old name for a large forestaysail or jib.

jumbo boom. An extra heavy cargo boom—a heavy lift boom.

jumper. Any rope, line, or wire that maintains something in posi-tion, such as a jumper stay or jumper guy.

jumper stay. A truss-like stay on the forward upper side of the mast of a sailboat. It supports the top of the mast and is held away from the mast by a jumper strut, also called a forward spreader or jumper-stay spreader.

Junior Clipper. A one-design keel sloop. LOA 26′, beam 7′, draft 5′. Designers: Stephens Brothers.

junk. Old condemned rope and cordage used to make small stuff and caulking. Now rare. Also a traditional Chinese sailboat.

jury. In its nautical sense an adjective meaning temporary or im-provised as a jury rig of any kind, a jury anchor, rudder, mast, etc.

K

kalema. A heavy surf, usually the result of distant storms, that breaks on the coast of Guinea.

Kalia Outrigger. A one-design centerboard sloop. LOA 15½', beam 8'. Designer: Ron Holder.

Kamchatka Current. The branch of the Japan or Kuroshio current that flows northeast towards the Aleutian Islands.

kapok. The silky fibers that surround the seeds of the tropical ceiba tree; used as buoyant stuffing in lifejackets and lifebuoys.

kaus. A moderate to strong southeasterly wind usually marked by rain and squalls that blows in the Arabian Gulf in the winter. Also spelled quas and also called a shaski.

kayak. A small wooden-framed, skin-covered canoe used by Eskimos in the far North, usually paddled by a man.

keckling. The chafing gear made of old rope.

kedge. To move a boat gone aground by laying out an anchor, usually by boat, and then heaving in on that anchor line. The procedure is called kedging. Boatmen often refer to the old-fashioned anchor as a kedge anchor.

keel. A ship's or boat's centerline, fore-and-aft structure running along the bottom, and from which the frames and side plating or planking arise. A boat is on an even keel when it draws the same amount of water fore-and-aft.

keelhaul. Historically, it meant to punish a man by pulling him under the ship from side to side by means of ropes. Now a slang term for a severe reprimand.

keel plate. A boat-stabilizing device, several feet long and several inches high, in the form of a plate fitted along the keel to dampen the roll and sometimes to slightly increase speed.

keelson. Originally a long structure inside the boat over the keel designed to strengthen it. Now any interior strength member, fore-and-aft or athwartships, used to strengthen the hull or support a heavy weight.

keeper. Any locking or securing device.

kellet. Any weight suspended from an anchor rode to reduce the angle that the rode makes with the bottom as it leads to the anchor, thus improving the anchor's holding power. Also called a sentinel.

kelp. Any of the very large seaweeds or algae that grow on the bottom in moderately deep and cold water near the coast.

kentledge. Pig iron or metal scrap used as ballast.

ketch. A small two-masted sailboat with the shorter mizzenmast or jigger abaft the mainmast, and stepped forward of the waterline aft or the rudder post. *See* yawl.

Kestrel. A one-design centerboard sloop. LOA 15½', beam 5½'. Designer: Ian Proctor.

kevel. Old word for cleat. Also spelled cavil or cavel.

Kevlar. A synthetic fiber used in modern rope and sail making and in hull laminates.

key. *See* cay.

kicker. Same as kicking strap. Also slang for outboard motor or a sailboat's inboard motor.

kicking strap. Originally, any line used to restrain something, such as the short line around the spokes of a steering wheel used in heavy weather. Also called a martingale or kicker for short. In modern usage a line from the spinnaker pole to a cleat aft that keeps the spinnaker from lifting. Also a line or tackle on a boom used to restrain it when sailing downwind or to flatten the sail of a racing dinghy. The British call a boom vang a kicking strap. *See* vang.

killer whale. The largest member of the dolphin family; grows to 30 feet. A predatory marine mammal that feeds on fish and sea mammals such as seals, highly intelligent and no threat to man unless it is injured or frightened. Also known as grampus or orc.

killick hitch. One used to make fast the anchor rode.

kill switch. One that automatically cuts off the motor of a fast motorboat, by means of a lanyard attached to the driver, should he/she be thrown out.

Kingfisher. A one-design centerboard sloop. LOA 12′, beam 4½′. Designer: Phil Rhodes.

king plank. A centerline hardwood plank in a planked deck from which the other boards start as they are laid.

king post. *See* sampson post.

king spoke. The radial spoke of a steering wheel that is vertical when the rudder is amidships; usually marked by a turk's head or a brass cap.

Kitchen rudder. A steering and reversing mechanism for small craft consisting of two adjustable blades that form an aperture just abaft the propeller. This permits the boat to go astern without reversing the propeller.

Kite. A one-design centerboard cat-rigged dinghy. LOA 11½′, beam 5′. Designer: Carter Pyle.

kite. Formerly the highest and lightest sails on a square-rigger set only in very light winds above the royals, such as skysails, moonsails, moonrakers, stargazers, skyscrapers, raffees, hopes-in-heaven, puffballs, savealls, trust-in-God, Christ disturbers, cloud ticklers, angels, etc. Now a general term for all light headsails such as spinnakers and genoas. In powerboat racing to kite is to fly through the air out of control; a crash.

kite drag. A sea anchor made of two or more spars and some canvas.

Knarr. A one-design keel sloop. LOA 30′, beam 7′, draft 4½′. Designer: Erling Kristoffersen.

knee. A timber or steel plate used to connect parts of a boat.

Knickerbocker. A one-design keel sloop. LOA 26′, beam 6½′, draft 4½′. Designer: Sparkman & Stephens.

knockabout. Generally a small sloop having no bowsprit and rigged only with a mainsail and a jib. A knockabout yawl, ketch, or schooner is one without a bowsprit.

knockdown. A sailboat is knocked down by wind and sea when she is forced over on her beam ends with sails in the water.

knot. Any combination of loops, mostly interlocking, used to fasten ropes together or to anything else or to enlarge the end of the rope. A bend is a special form of knot that can be cast off easily when necessary. A hitch is a knot whose loops normally jam together under pressure but remain separable when the strain is released. A knot is also a unit of speed—1 nautical mile per hour.

knotmeter. An advanced recording yacht speed indicator using a paddle wheel, a transducer and a digital averaging readout or display dial.

Kona wind (weather). Usually a southerly storm wind in the Hawaiian Islands that at times interrupts the normal northeast trade winds.

Kuroshio or Kuroshiwo System. Similar to the Gulf Stream System, this series of ocean currents in the North Pacific flows northeast along the coasts of Taiwan and Japan where it is known as the Kuroshio or Japan Current. As the main stream curves eastward it divides into the North Pacific Current moving east, a south moving component, and the Tsushima Current that passes into the sea of Japan. The system originates with the North Pacific Equatorial Current.

L

labor. A vessel labors in heavy weather when her motion is so violent that it places unusual stress on hull and rigging.

Labrador Current. An ocean current in the North Atlantic starting south of Davis Strait and flowing down the coasts of Labrador and Newfoundland until it meets the Gulf Stream; then part of it drifts west and south down the U.S. East coast. It is a cold current sometimes bringing down ice that endangers shipping. Also called the Arctic Current.

ladder. Nautical word for stairs. *See* jacob's ladder.

lagan. Under maritime law anything cast overboard that is buoyed for eventual recovery. Also spelled ligan or logan. *See* jettison.

lagoon. A body of shallow water separated from the ocean by a reef or a spit of land. The reflected scattered sunlight from the shallows of a lagoon is often visible upon clouds from a long distance away and is called lagoon blink. *See* blink.

laid. A descriptive word for rope or wire as plain laid, back laid, cable laid, etc. Laid rope is wire rope made of six strands of seven wires each.

laid deck. A wooden deck in which the planks are put down parallel to the gunwale.

laminar flow. Smooth airflow over the surface of a sail or water flow on a hull.

land. The part of a longitudinal plank that overlaps in a clinker-built wooden boat. *See* landing.

land breeze. The offshore breeze at night resulting from the land cooling faster than the sea. Opposite in direction to the sea breeze that blows onshore during the day. These are called solar winds. *See* breeze.

landfall. An approach to land at the end of a sea voyage. Also the act or moment of first sighting land is called a landfall.

landing. The place alongside a dock, pier or wharf where boats may load or unload. To make a landing is to steer or direct a boat alongside a pier, dock, or wharf or another vessel.

landlocked. Surrounded by land as a bay or protected harbor.

landlubber. Person unfamiliar with the sea or life at sea and thus liable to behave in a clumsy or lubberly fashion when at sea.

landmark. On shore any fixed object whose position is marked on a chart.

langouste. Pacific word for spiny lobster.

lanyard. Originally a rope rove through deadeyes or wooden blocks used to set up or tighten the rigging. Now any small line used to hold or fasten something.

lanyard stopper. A rope used as a stopper or holding gear on a heavy line or hawser being hauled in and about to be taken off the winch and made fast to a cleat. Also called a rope stopper.

lapper. A sail very similar to another headsail, a mule. *See* mule. Also any headsail that overlaps a mainsail.

lapstrake. Describes the clinker or lap construction of a wooden boat in which each plank or strake overlaps the other. A lapstrake boat is a clinker-built boat.

Lark. A one-design decked cat-rigged centerboard dinghy. LOA 11', beam 4½'. Designer: S. Paul.

lark's head. A hitch used for fastening a line to a ring, deadeye or spar when the same tension is desired on both standing parts. Same as cow hitch.

Laser. A one-design daggerboard catboat. LOA 14', beam 4½'. Designer: Bruce Kirby.

Laser II. A similar slightly larger and heavier dinghy—is sloop rigged.

lash. To secure fasten or repair with rope or wire by wrapping close-ly. Wind and sea lash the shore and a whale's flukes lash the sea. A sail adrift may lash about.

latchings. A series of loops of small stuff by which the foot of a sail is fastened to a bonnet.

lateen. An ancient sailing rig in which a triangular loose-footed sail on a long yard is slung on a short mast at about an angle of 45; still popular where sailboats are used commercially and is used in some small pleasure boats such as canoes, catamarans.

lateral system of buoyage. An arrangement of buoys of different shapes, colors, numbers and lights used to indicate the side of the buoy on which a ship should pass to avoid danger when proceeding in a given direction. *See* "red, right, returning." This system is used in the USA. *See* cardinal system of buoyage. *See* System B.

latitude. The angular distance of a point north or south of the equator, measured in degrees, minutes and seconds.

Laughlin plow anchor. A patented small boat anchor with a long shank.

lay. To lay is to go as in "lay aloft" or "lay aft." A ship lays or lies alongside a pier or if she stops at sea she lays or lies to. A boat may be laid up for storage or repairs. To lay out an anchor is to carry it out.

lay of wire or rope. The direction of rotation of wires, fibers, yarns or strands making up the rope.

layline. A course that permits a close-hauled sailboat to clear a weather mark in the existing wind. Same as fetch line.

lay on the oars. A command to the crew of a rowing boat or shell to stop rowing and hold the oars straight out horizontally. To lay in the oars is to unship them and place them in the boat. To lay out on the oars is to row harder.

lay up. To apply the various layers of fiberglass cloth, roving and resing that make the hull of a fiberglass boat. Also to lay up a ship or a boat is to prepare her for a period of inactivity.

lazarette. A space or compartment in a boat abaft the cockpit.

lazy. Describes any one of a variety of light lines used where little strain is involved.

lazy guy. A line or light tackle used to steady the boom of a sailboat. Also a wire or vang connecting adjacent cargo booms, also called a schooner guy.

lazy jack. A bridle of light line from the topping lift or mast of a sailboat to each side of the boom between which the sail is contained as it is hoisted and lowered. Also called a boom guy.

lazy sheet. A secondary line secured to the tack and clew of a spinnaker which can be used to free the primary line when jibing. Sometimes called a lazy guy.

lead. The direction in which a rope lies which when free for running has a fair lead. Also a measure of balance in sailing vessels: the distance between the center of effort and the center of lateral resistance expressed as a fraction of waterline length. Spoken: leed.

lead block or leading block. One rigged to provide a fair lead, usually when a line changes direction. Lead blocks are used in sailboats in handling sheets in connection with a slide or traveler.

lead, depth measuring. A sounding or hand lead. The small hand lead is the one used today to measure depths down to 20 fathoms. The lead itself is a sinker with a concave bottom that was traditionally armed with tallow to reveal the nature of the bottom. Pronounced led.

lead line. The rope attached to the sounding lead. Fathoms, referred to as marks and deeps, are marked by bits of cloth and leather.

leads. The parts of a fall or tackle between two blocks. The leading part is the hauling part. Spoken: "leeds."

leadsman. The sailor who stands in the chains to take soundings with a hand lead. He reports the depth in fathoms by marks and deeps as the ship moves forward: for example, "by the deep six," and a half five," "no bottom at 13" etc.

leather. That part of the oar that fits against the oarlock. *See* oar.

ledge. In wooden ships or boats a piece of the deck frame that extends athwartships.

lee. The side away from the wind. If the wind is from port, upon the port side, then that side is the weather side and the starboard side is the lee side. A boat may anchor in the lee of an island or other piece of land. Note that the lee shore is one on which the wind blows. *See* leeward.

leeboard. A flat wooden or steel device lowered over the side of a sailboat to provide lateral resistance when sailing close hauled; serves the same purpose as a centerboard or daggerboard.

lee-bow. A verb meaning to sail a boat across the current so that the current on the lee bow reduces leeway or side-slipping.

leech. The after edge of a fore-and-aft or triangular sail; opposite the luff.

leecloth. A canvas strip made fast to the sides of a bunk in a sailboat to keep the occupant from falling out. Also lee canvas.

lee shore. Any land or coast towards which the wind is blowing; thus a danger in heavy weather to a boat under sail alone or a vessel anchored.

leeward. The direction away from the wind, as a boat approaches a ship at sea to leeward as it comes alongside. Spoken: looard.

leeway. The sideways movement of a boat to leeward of her steered course due to pressure from wind and sea. Also called drift or sag.

leg. 1. A portion of a vessel's tack or plotted course along the same heading; same as board or tack. 2. Part of a rope bridle, boom crutch, or sheerlegs. 3. One of the shores used to hold a boat upright if she is stranded by a receding tide. 4. A segment of a boat race course between 2 turning marks.

legging. The procedure for pushing a canal boat through a very narrow tunnel; men lying on their backs on deck push with their legs.

leg-of-mutton sail. A fore-and-aft triangular sail whose tack extends down below the boom.

Lehman 12. A one-design centerboard cat-rigged dinghy. LOA 12', beam 4½'. A slightly shorter version is the Lehman 10 (interclub).

leste. A hot, dry, easterly wind of the Canary and Madeira Islands originating in the North African desert.

Lido 14. A one-design centerboard sloop. LOA 14', beam 6'. Designer: W.D. Schock.

lie. A boat lies off when it is stopped near a ship or a pier. A ship or a boat may lie to or heave to when stopped and waiting. Sailboats when lying to in heavy weather with some storm canvas set may be said to lie atry. If no sail could be carried they are said to lie ahull. *See* heave to.

lie ahull. *See* lie; also called hulling.

lifebelt. A safety device, a harness attached to a fitting on a boat, worn by boatmen in heavy weather or when cruising at night. Also a buoyant device worn by water skiers, non-swimmers, etc.

lifeboat. In merchant ships a boat carried aboard by international agreement and by law, of specified characteristics, to carry people in the event of a shipwreck or sinking, fire, etc. In the U.S. shore-based lifeboats are manned by the Coast Guard and are designed to withstand very heavy weather; capsizable and nonsinkable. They are being supplemented and replaced at times by helicopters.

lifebuoy or lifering. A buoyant object that can be thrown from a vessel or a pier to someone in the water. May be a simple cork ring with a line attached or a metal or plastic device with a self-starting light.

lifefloat or raft. Any buoyant device, not a boat, designed to support and sometimes shelter a number of people in an emergency. Most modern rafts inflate automatically and provide food, water, and shelter; some are ballasted for stability, others are designed to move away from the scene of the emergency.

lifejacket. Any personal flotation device or life preserver worn to support a person in the water. May be equipped with a whistle, light, shark repellent, etc.

lifeline. Any of several lines rigged on deck, fore and aft, to keep people from falling overboard. Also any protective line rigged on a brow, boom, or dock, or a rope thrown to someone in the water, the grab ropes on a liferaft or lifeboat or those hanging from the span wire of boat davits for the boat crew to grasp as the boat is lowered or hoisted.

lift. 1. A rope or chain used to raise the end of a boom, spar, or spinnaker pole; also called a topping lift. 2. A particular load or piece of cargo that if heavy requires a heavy lift or jumbo boom. 3. Broadside movement of a ship turning due to the effect of the rudder. 4. A shift of wind when sailing that allows a course change into the wind or permits the sail trim (sheet) to be eased without the boat changing course. Also known as a freer. *See* header.

lighter. A broad, usually rectangular, open vessel for transporting cargo as well as for loading and unloading ships. In sheltered waters a lighter is normally towed or pushed but it can be self-propelled. The cargo is usually carried in the open whereas in a barge or scow it is usually at least partly decked over. Lighter, barge, or scow are words often used interchangeably in accordance with local usage. To lighter is to move something by lighter and the fees involved are called lighterage.

lighthouse. A structure on or near the shore showing a strong white or colored light, flashing, or occulting over a specified arc or sector.

Light Lists. Lists published by the U.S. Coast Guard describing all lighted aids to navigation in the waters of the U.S. and its possessions. It includes lighthouses, buoys, daybeacons, ranges, fog signals, and radiobeacons. *See* Lists of Lights, another publication for lights abroad.

Lightning. A one-design centerboard sloop. LOA 19′, beam 6½′. Designer: Sparkman and Stephens.

light, occulting. A navigational light whose periods of darkness or eclipse are less than its periods of light. Its dark periods are all of equal duration and are repeated at regular intervals.

lightship. A permanently anchored vessel showing a lighted aid to navigation at critical junctions of ocean traffic. Most have been replaced by large automatic lighted buoys—there is still a lightship off Nantucket at this writing.

lights, navigational. Lights installed on lighthouses, lightships, buoys, and beacons; may be white or colored and may show all around the horizon or in certain sectors; may be fixed, flashing, or occulting or in any combination, singly or in groups. Their characteristics are found in the Light Lists (U.S.) or in the Lists of Lights (foreign). Also a term for the running lights. *See* lights, ships.

lights, ships. Running lights most commonly shown by ships underway, under both the International (Colregs) and the Inland Rules are: range, masthead, stern, and sidelights. There are many special lights, some not common to both Rules, such as: anchor, flare-up, towing, fishing, not under command, man overboard, pilot, dredge, and submarine construction lights, as well as lights shown by vessels surveying or servicing aids to navigation. There are also special lights shown by warships.

lima coast. One characterized by many lagoons or limans.

liman. A shallow coastal lagoon with a muddy bottom; also an area of mud (topsoil or silt) deposited near the mouth of a stream.

limb. The upper or lower edge of the sun or moon that is aligned with the horizon when measuring the altitude of that body by sextant is known as the upper or lower limb. Also the graduated arc of a sextant from which the reading of the observation is made.

line. 1. The equator. 2. A shipping business; its ships are liners.

line, as cordage. Often synonymous with rope. Any rope used aboard a boat is called a line. *See* rope.

line of position. In celestial navigation, after solving the spherical triangle using the measured altitude at a known time, the result is a line of position that is part of an arc. Somewhere along this line is the ship's position as determined by the intersection of another line of position. Also called a position line. In piloting a single bearing would provide a line of position.

liner. A merchant (cargo or passenger) ship that travels on scheduled routes as a public carrier at regular intervals. *See* tramp.

line squall. A sudden and violent storm marked by a line of black clouds along the horizon.

line-throwing gun. *See* Lyle gun.

lip. *See* jog.

lipper. A slight ruffling or roughness on the surface of calm water. Also a light spray from small waves.

list. The static fixed inclination or leaning of a vessel to port or starboard due to imbalance of weight. *See* heel, roll.

Lists of Lights. Published by the Defense Mapping Agency Hydrographic Center to describe the lighted aids to navigation and fog signals (but not lighted buoys within harbors), of foreign waters and limited sections of the U.S. coast. *See* Light Lists.

Little Bear. A one-design centerboard sloop. LOA 11½′, beam 4½′. Designer: Robert Baker.

littoral. Pertaining to the seashore.

littoral current. Current along the shore such as a rip or longshore current. Also called a longshore current.

Liverpool splice. A wire eye splice made around a thimble with the end tucked with the lay and without locking turns.

Liverpool smoke head. A device at the top of a boat's smokestack permitting the escape of stove gases while keeping out rain.

lizard. A short length of rope having a thimble splice at one end. A traveling lizard moves on a fixed wire or rope span.

Ljungstrom rig. A Swedish sailboat rig having a double triangular mainsail whose vertical axis is wound around a rotating unstayed mast.

Lloyd's Register of Yachts. *See* North American Yacht Register.

LOA or l.o.a. Length overall of a boat expressed in feet or meters.

loading coil. In an antenna one that makes it longer electronically without a change in its physical length.

Local Apparent Noon. Midday as indicated by the actual position of the sun at its maximum altitude, as shown on a sundial, in contrast to midday as measured by the mean or average sun. It is the best time for the navigator to take a sun line to measure his/her latitude.

local attraction. Any magnetic disturbance of a compass due to iron in the vicinity but not in the ship or boat.

local time. That determined by the time zone of the observer.

lock. A structure having movable gates for boats to pass up or down to different water levels in a canal, river, or tidal basin.

Lodestar. The sailor's name for Polaris, the North Star.

log. A device for measuring ship or boat's speed, distance, or both. Modern logs are either pitot-static (which measures differences in pressure generated by ship's movement); impeller type (which uses a turning propeller to generate an electric current); or electromagnetic (which uses an induction coil to develop a signal voltage that varies with speed). Log is also short for logbook.

logbook. A written record of a ship's or boat's activities.

loggerhead turtle. A large edible sea-going turtle of the U.S. Atlantic coast that lays its eggs on southern beaches. An endangered species.

logging race or log race. More accurately a contest in which the powerboats predict their time of passage over the course and the winner is the boat that has predicted most accurately. Also called a predicted log race.

loll. A ship that has a list that makes her unstable is said to loll.

Lonars. An improved Loran C navigational system, being developed by the U.S. Navy.

long blast. One of more than 6 seconds.

long glass. A hand-held telescope, same as spyglass.

longitude. One of the two major navigational coordinates, the other being latitude. It is a measure of angular distance on the earth, east or west of the prime meridian of Greenwich to the point for which the longitude is expressed, measured in degrees, minutes, and seconds.

longshore current. Current produced by waves deflected at an angle by the coast. Also called a littoral current.

long splice. One that provides a minimum increase in the circumference of the lines spliced together.

long ton. A ton weighing 2240 pounds or 1016 kilos.

loof. That part of a ship where the sides begin to converge towards the stem, the rounded part of the bow.

loom. 1. The glow of light from just below (beyond) the horizon. 2. The shaft or central part of an oar between the blade and the handle. 3. Sometimes a loom refers to a small trunk or passage for wires and piping in a boat.

looming. A mirage causing the elevation of distant objects above the horizon. It is due to the refraction of light waves in layers of atmosphere of different characteristics.

loose. To let go, as a sail. A loose-footed sail is one without a boom.

loose boat. *See* fast boat.

LOP. Line of Position.

lop. A state of the sea marked by short steep waves.

LORAN. LOng-RAnge Aid to Navigation; a system of radio position finding using shore stations that emit simultaneously high-frequency radio waves. By measuring the time difference in receiving the signals a ship can locate herself on a LORAN line of position. Loran C is the latest model, and Loran A is being phased out.

lorcha. A sailing junk of the Far East having a European hull and a Chinese lugsail rig.

low. A cyclone or area of low atmospheric pressure that brings rain and storms in contrast to a high or anticyclone that is associated with good weather.

lower the boom. Slang; to administer severe punishment or reprimand.

low frequency (LF). 30–300 kiloHertz (kHz) used in RDF, radio beacons, Loran C and Decca.

lubberly. Unseamanlike or clumsy.

lubber's knot. A granny or false square knot–should not be used.

lubber's line. Reference mark on a compass or radar scope indicating the ship's head.

Luders. A one-design keel sloop. LOA 26', beam 6', draft 4'. Designer: A.E. Luders Jr.

luchet. *See* tabernacle.

luff. The forward edge of a fore-and-aft sail, next to the mast. *vb.* 1. To luff or flag when sailing is to bring the bow up into the wind until forward motion is slowed and the sails shake. 2. To hold your luff is a command to the helmsman to keep the boat pointing up close to the wind. 3. To luff an opponent in a sailing race or to engage in a luffing match is to prevent, if possible, an opponent from passing you to windward by forcing her to luff up.

luffing davit. *See* davit.

luff puller. A cunningham or line attached to the sail to flatten the luff.

luff spar. A hollow spar made fast around the jibstay to provide support for the jib of a sailboat.

luffrope. The rope or line sewn into the luff or leading edge of a sail, traditionally on the port side of the edge. In some small sailboats the luffrope of the mainsail fits into the groove or slide on the mainmast.

luff tackle. A general-purpose tackle consisting of a double and a single block. The standing part is made fast to the single block while the hauling part comes out of the double block.

luff upon luff. A purchase consisting of two luff tackles used together.

lug. 1. A small piece of steel or angle iron used in shipbuilding to make various small fittings or pad eyes. 2. Any fitting on a mast or spar that includes an eye. Also called a lug piece. 3. The yard on which a lugsail is set. Short for lugsail.

lugger. A small coastal two- or three-masted, lug-rigged sailboat, now rare except in the developing countries.

lugsail. A four-sided, fore-and-aft sail with the head shorter than the foot and the luff shorter than the leech. It is bent to a lug or yard that is raised and lowered with the sail and may be loose-footed. Widely used for small craft abroad. Major types are: dipping lug that has no boom (the yard must be dipped around the mast when tacking), the standing lug with a boom whose forward end pivots at the mast, and the balance lug that has boom and lug both projecting forward of the mast.

lunar distance. A special moon sight to determine longitude without having accurate time. Also called a lunar.

lunch hook. A boatman's light anchor used mainly for short stops when cruising such as anchoring for lunch.

lunitidal interval. The time between the moon's upper or lower transit and the time of high or low water at a particular place.

lurching. The abnormal, deep, and sometimes sudden rolling of a boat in a seaway.

lutchet. *See* tabernacle.

luting. A mixture of putty, white lead, and oil used on the contacting surfaces of planks and timbers in wooden boat-building.

LWL. Load Waterline–the waterline at which the boat floats. Also the length of the hull along the waterline.

Lyle gun. A trade name for a line-throwing gun.

M

mackerel. A broad and often confusing name for nearly 60 species of deep sea, wide-ranging popular food and game fish. Included are tuna, albacore, bonito and wahoo. They live in large schools and are being seriously overfished.

mackeral sky. One of the cirro-cumulous clouds whose design resembles the bars or ripples on the back of a Spanish mackerel. Off the British Isles and the U.S. this sky may predict good weather, but in the Mediterranean it may mean bad weather.

McNamara lace. Fancy curtains and trimmings for boats made from unlaid canvas threads.

maelstrom. A powerful and destructive whirlpool. Also a very confused and broken sea as in a severe tide rip.

Mae West. Slang for an inflatable life jacket as well as a parachute spinnaker.

magic box. *See* muscle box.

magnetic compass. A free-floating magnet is attracted to the earth and aligns itself with the earth's magnetic field thus pointing to magnetic north and forming a magnetic compass.

magnetic chart. One showing lines of equal magnetic variation.

mainmast. Traditionally the principal and heaviest mast of a full-rigged ship, the second one from forward. In a yawl or ketch the most forward mast; in a schooner the after mast if there are two, the center mast if there are three masts.

mainsail. Traditionally the principal sail or course on the main-mast. In a square-rigger the lowest sail on the mainmast. In a modern sailboat it is the largest sail set abaft the mainmast.

mainsheet swivel block. Block secured in or near the cockpit that anchors the mainsheet gear. It must swivel 180°.

make. To accomplish, to do. A ship makes leeway, she makes good 10 knots, she makes water when she leaks, the mate makes sail, or makes a line fast to a cleat. Tides make or are making when they rise in maximum height between neap and spring tides. If the tides fall they are said to be taking off.

making iron. A caulking iron, a chisel-like tool with a groove used in finishing a seam after the oakum is driven in. Also called a creasing iron and a common iron.

mako. A shark. *See* shark.

Malibu Outrigger. A one-design centerboard proa LOA 19'. Designer: Warren Seaman.

man. To man a ship is to provide a crew. A boat's crew mans its boat.

Mañana. A one-design keel sloop. LOA 29', beam 6½', draft 4'. Designer: A. Mason.

manhelper. A long pole with a paintbrush attached for painting the side of a ship. Also called a long arm.

manila hemp. A fibrous material from the abaca plant, once widely used for rope and cordage, now largely replaced by synthetic fibers.

manrope. The side or guard rope of a ladder or any rope used as a safety line or lifeline.

manta ray. A huge skate, as much as 20' across, that appears to fly under water as it flaps its winglike fins. Strong but unaggressive it is feared by divers into whose hoses it may blunder. Often seen near the surface in tropical waters, it sometimes leaps clear of the water, presumably to free itself of parasites. Also called devilfish.

Marconi rig. A triangular sail same as Bermudan or jib-headed rig.

mare's nest. Slang for any mess or disorder on board.

mare's tails. A popular name for the tufted cirrus clouds that usually accompany good weather.

marina. A harbor facility providing fuel, food, ice, showers, washing machines, telephones, etc., for the convenience of small-boat owners having permanent or temporary berths. Also includes at times a seaside park.

marine. As an adjective it describes anything to do with the sea.

marine borer. Any of the wood-piercing organisms, especially the teredos, which attack wood underwater.

Marine Check Radar Detector. A trade name for a portable, battery-powered device that detects and gives the bearing of any radar. Useful for small boats who have no radar.

mariner. Person who goes to sea, such as a sailor or seaman, one whose vocation is the sea.

marine railway. A device that moves on partially submerged railroad tracks; used for hauling out boats for repair.

marine salina. A body of salt water separated from the sea by a sand or gravel barrier through which the salt water percolates.

mariner's anchor. An old-fashioned anchor.

marine soap. Same as saltwater soap; usable in saltwater.

Marine Weather Services Charts. Charts covering all U.S. waters, issued by the National Weather Service (NWS) and available from the National Ocean Survey. They show NWS broadcast stations and frequencies, storm warning display locations, and Coast Guard and Marine Police Stations.

maritime. Pertaining to the sea and all associated with it.

mark. 1. A line, notch, piece of cloth or leather, a limit or a danger. A load line mark or Plimsoll mark indicates maximum allowable draft of a ship. 2. A mark on a leadline is a measure of depth. 3. A daymark or dayshape indicates a shoal or obstruction. Also called a landmark or shoalmark.

mark, sail racing. A buoy, other floating object, or a stake that a sailboat must pass on a specified side when racing. Line marks show the starting and finishing lines, rounding marks determine how far the boats must go, and guide marks outline the allowed racing area.

marl. To fasten or secure with a series of marline hitches as a sail to its boltrope.

marlin. One of the large oceanic billfish, a gamefish that weighs over 1000 pounds.

marline. Small stuff or cord used for lashings, mousing, and seizing.

marline spike. A round, tapered steel tool, larger than a fid, used in splicing wire and rope, screwing shackle pins, etc.

marry. To join two lines together, either before splicing or side by side before seizing.

martingale. One of the ropes or chains in a large sailing vessel under the bowsprit and jibboom used to counteract the stress of the headstay upon the end of the jibboom; extended by the dolphin striker. Also a kicking strap or kicker when used to hold a boom down.

mast. The wooden, metal, or composite pole or structure rising vertically from the ship's deck; used to support sails, signal gear, cargo handling gear, etc. In two-masted vessels such as schooners the higher mast is aft, and they are called foremast and mainmast. Three-masted vessels have a mizzenmast aft (also the name for the after mast on a ketch or yawl).

mast carling. *See* sailing thwart.

mast bed. In wooden boats the pieces of wood in the decking around the masthole.

mastboot. *See* mastcoat.

mastcoat. A heavy canvas fitted around the base of the mast where it meets the deck; keeps out water. It is called a petticoat or mastboot in small vessels.

Master. A person in command of a merchant or fishing vessel, qualified by experience and examination, and certified by proper authority. His courtesy title is Captain.

masthead. The part of a mast from the topmost standing rigging to the cap or truck at the top. To masthead something is to hoist it as far as it will go; sometimes called full-mast or two-block.

masthead float. Float at the masthead of a catamaran used to prevent capsizing if the boat is knocked down.

masthead fly. A wind direction indicator.

masthead rig. A jib-headed rig in which the headstay is made fast to the top of the mast. In a 7/8ths rig the headstay is made fast 7/8ths of the way up.

masteye. A metal ring made fast to a mast, usually with a strap.

masthead light. A 20-point (225°) white light at the forward masthead of a ship showing in an arc from dead ahead to two points (22.5°) abaft the beam on both sides; required by the Rules of the Road (Colregs).

mast partner. The timber at the deck line of a boat through which the mast passes.

mast step. The timber at the bottom of a boat upon which the mast rests.

mast trunk. *See* tabernacle.

match hook. *See* sister hook.

match race. A sailing race without time allowances such as that for the America's Cup in which the object is to defeat an opponent boat-for-boat rather than to make a winning time against a handicap. There are usually just 2 boats.

Mathew Walker knot. A good stopper knot, formed by passing each strand around the rope in the direction of the lay, and then tucking it upward through its own bight or loop.

Maya. A one-design keel sloop. LOA 23′, beam 6½′, draft 4′.

Mayday. The internationally known, authorized distress signal by voice radio—SOS is the equivalent in code.

meal flag. Any flag that indicates that the owner, officers, or crew are dining.

mean. A middle or average quantity or position between extremes, such as mean tide, mean draft, etc.

mean time. Time based on the mean sun, an imaginary body whose movement in relation to the earth is regular and uniform. *See* time.

measurement rule. A formula for handicapping sailboats of similar but not identical dimensions so that they may race together equitably.

meathook. Boatman's name for a loose broken strand on a wire rope. Also called a fishhook.

Mediterranean moor. *See* moor.

medium frequency (mf). 300–3000 kiloHertz (kHz), 1000–100 meter wavelength used in commercial and marine broadcast.

medusa. *See* jellyfish.

meet her. A command to the helmsman to shift the rudder or to use more rudder in order to stop the swing of the ship; usually followed by a specific course to steer or object to steer for.

meeting. As defined by Colregs, two ships approaching head to head so that at night both sidelights would be visible.

megaHertz (MHz). *See* Hertz.

mf. *See* medium frequency.

Melody. A one-design centerboard cat-rigged boat. LOA 10′, beam 4½′. Designer: W.C. Ashcroft.

meltemi. The strong northerly wind that blows across the Eastern Mediterranean in the summer. Also called the etesian wind.

mend. In the old days of sail meant to refurl a sail that was badly made up and secured.

menhaden. A small North Atlantic fish of the herring family caught for fish meal and oil.

Meon anchor. Similar to a Danforth with deep flukes that pivot around the stock at the bottom of the shank; designed in the U.K. for big ships.

Mercator charts. Those that result from a Mercator projection—used in latitudes below 75°.

Mercator projection. A method of projecting a sphere, such as the earth, onto a flat surface. The parallels of latitude are shown at proper intervals as straight lines and the meridians of longitude at right angles to them. Visualize a cylinder tangent to the sphere at the equator. Thus we have Mercator sailing in which any rhumb line appears as a straight line.

mercury or mercurial barometer. One that measures atmospheric pressure by the varying height of a column of mercury. *See* barometer.

Mercury. A one-design keel sloop. LOA 18′, beam 5½′, draft 3′. Designer: Ernest Nunes.

meridian. An imaginary great circle passing through the poles and corresponding to a line of longitude.

meridian altitude. The altitude of a celestial body when on the observer's meridian.

meridian distance. The difference of longitude in time or arc between two places.

Mermaid. A one-design keel sloop. LOA 20½′, beam 6¼′, draft 3¼′. Designer: Petersen-McNickles.

Merry-Mac. A one-design centerboard catboat. LOA 13½′, beam 5′. Designer: E.D. McIntosh.

mess. Food or meals served aboard as well as the compartment in which they are served.

message. The proper nautical term for any rapid form of communication (electronic, visual, or messenger) to and from a vessel.

messenger. Any line used to haul in or handle a heavier rope.

messroom. A dining room aboard ship.

metal mike. Slang for automatic pilot.

Metcalf. A one-design centerboard cat-rigged dinghy. LOA 13′. beam 4½′. Designer: C.W. Lapworth.

mic. Short for microseconds, a common word in electronic navigation. A microsecond is a millionth of a second. Pronounced mike.

middle ground. A shoal or shallow area with deep water around it; sometimes found in buoyed channels and marked by a middle-ground buoy.

Midget Ocean Racing Club (MORC). The governing North American organization for small cruising and racing sailboats under 30 feet.

mid latitude sailing. one of the sailings that uses the middle or mean latitude of the area that the ship will traverse.

mile. A nautical mile by international agreement is 6076 feet or 1852 meters or 1 minute of arc at the Equator. A statute or land mile is used when navigating lakes and rivers–5280 feet.

millibar. A thousandth part of a bar used as a measure of atmospheric pressure under the metric system. A bar is 29.92 inches of mercury at sea level and 32°F.

mind your rudder. A caution to the helmsman to steer more precisely or to be careful in applying rudder under special circumstances.

Minifish. A one-design, lateen-rigged daggerboard boat. LOA 12′, beam 4′. Designer: Fred Scott. Minifish II is cat-rigged.

minus tide. A low tide that is below the average of mean low water.

mirage. At sea abnormal atmospheric conditions such as the presence of dry desert air can cause refraction and thus distortion of light, radio, and radar waves.

miss stays. In tacking a sailboat, failure to bring the ship's head through the wind so that she can fall off and fill her sails on the new tack. As a result the boat is in irons.

mistral. A strong dry northerly wind of the Mediterranean, particularly strong in the Gulf of Lyon where the funneling effect of the Rhône Valley increases its velocity. Similar to the bora of the Adriatic and the tramontana of Italy.

mitchboard. Boom crutch or rail used to support the boom when the sail is lowered.

miter. The seam in a sail, usually the headsail, that joins the cloths running in different directions. In a miter cut the cloths are perpendicular to the leech and to the foot of the sail. The miter of a jib or its luff perpendicular is the distance from the luff to the clew along a line perpendicular to the luff.

mitten money. An additional pilotage fee charged in cold weather.

mizzen. Pertaining to the mizzenmast, the aftermost mast on a 3-masted schooner, ketch, or yawl.

Mobjack. A one-design centerboard sloop. LOA 17′, beam 6½′. Designer: Roger Moorman.

moderate breeze. *See* Beaufort Scale.

modern log. A speedometer in a boat.

moderate speed. As defined in the Inland Rules of the Road, the speed not to be exceeded in reduced visibility, at which a ship can stop within half the range of visibility.

modulate. To vary the frequency or amplitude of a radio wave by imposing another signal upon it.

mold. A wooden pattern or frame from which steel beams and plates can be cut and shaped. The design of the ship is laid down full size in a mold loft.

molding. Any decorative or useful strip of metal or wood such as the half round on the outside of a boat at deck and gunwale. Also called a rubbing strip or piece or nosing ribband.

mole. A strong, protective masonry structure forming the wall or breakwater of a harbor and usually fitted on the inside with facilities for loading and unloading ships and boats.

monkey. A vague and usually irrelevant adjective used to describe something unusual or undersize or difficult to label otherwise. A ship is said to be monkey sparred or rigged when her rig is considered too light or unorthodox.

monkey block. A loose term for any small block, usually with an attached swivel.

monkey fist. A heavy-weighted knob at the end of a heaving line.

monkey loop. Slang for the indefinite circle of position resulting from a number of celestial observations that do not produce a fix.

monkey pipe. *See* chain pipe.

monkey rail. A light, decorative wooden fence above the main deck aft on a ship. Also an overhead handhold below decks.

monkey rope. A lifeline made fast to a man going over the side.

monkey tail. A short line attached to the block to assist a man in hooking on when hoisting a boat. It is then used to mouse the hook.

monocoque. Describes a smallboat hull, usually of plastic, that is made as a single skin with few ribs or stringers.

monohull. A sailboat with a single hull, as opposed to multi-hull.

monotype. A racing sailboat built to a one-design class.

monsoon. Specifically a seasonal wind of the Far and Middle East (China Sea, Indian Ocean, Red Sea) that changes direction and intensity in winter and summer as the adjacent land masses lose and gain heat. Monsoon is used in a more general sense for a seasonal wind anywhere in the Orient.

Monsoon Current. An Indian Ocean current flowing in a generally eastward direction off India and Ceylon.

moondog. *See* parhelion.

moor. 1. To secure a ship alongside another or to a pier, dock or to a mooring buoy. 2. To anchor with more than one anchor. A Mediterranean moor involves dropping an anchor or two anchors in succession inside a harbor, then backing down and adjusting scope so that the stern can be made fast just off the pier or seawall and a brow rigged aft.

mooring anchor. Any heavy device, mass, clump of cement, or anchor used to secure a mooring buoy firmly to the bottom.

mooring buoy. A large, floating, well-anchored structure with a heavy ring to which a ship's wire or anchor chain can be made fast. For boats it is a light floating object to which the mooring anchor is attached and which the boat can pick up and make fast to. Known for short as a mooring.

mooring line. Wire or rope used to secure a ship or boat to a pier or to another vessel.

mooring whip. A device to hold a boat away from the pier made of several flexible poles rigged out at an angle over the boat and attached to the boat by short lines. The same device can be used to keep a yacht's dinghy away from the stern.

moray eel. A snakelike, finless, tropical saltwater fish that swims like a snake and hides in the coral or rocks during the day. Its sharp back-slanting teeth can be dangerous to an unwary swimmer groping in a hole for lobster. Grows to 12 feet and is related to the conger eel of cold waters with which it is sometimes confused.

MORC. Midget Ocean Racing Club. Pronounced morsey.

Morse Code. The series of dots and dashes representing letters of the alphabet and used in radio and flashing light communications.

Morse lamp. An electric, directional, hand-held light for sending messages by code; also called a blinker gun or light.

Moth. A popular development class centerboard catboat. LOA 11', beam 3½'. Original designer: Joel Van Sant.

Mother Carey. The traditional and fictitious owner of certain sea birds found in open waters, especially petrels which are known as Mother Carey's chickens. Mother Carey's goose is the giant fulmar.

motorboat. A craft propelled only by a motor; a powerboat.

Motorboat Act, 1960. *See* Inland Rules of the Road.

motor, outboard. A portable internal combustion or electric motor fitted with a steering propeller and attached to the stern of the boat. Slang name, kicker.

motorsailor. A cross between a sailboat and a cabin cruiser. It sails well, has a reasonably powerful motor, and has more comfortable accommodations above the main deck than has a sailboat.

motor well. A cutout section or opening in the bottom of a boat into which an outboard motor can be fitted.

mouse. To mouse a hook is to fasten small stuff or wire across the opening to prevent the escape of the line or wire the hook is holding. Also to seize both shanks of sister hooks or to secure similar pieces of gear. The small stuff is called mousing.

MSD. Marine Sanitation Device.

mug up. A hot drink such as coffee and a snack.

mule. An upper staysail such as the one used in a ketch above the mainsail. Also a small genoa, a dual-purpose sail for cruising and racing, longer in the luff and with less overlap than a #3 genoa.

multihull. A collective term for boats with more than one hull such as catamarans, trimarans or proas.

Murman Current. A warm ocean current running southeast of the coast of the Kola peninsula.

muscle box. A compact enclosed system of blocks for tensioning lines such as halyards in sailboats. Critical amounts of tension, important for optimum sail efficiency, can be duplicated by using a reference scale. Also called a magic box.

mushroom anchor. A special anchor shaped like a mushroom used to anchor mooring buoys. It holds well in a muddy bottom.

mussel. A long, tapering bivalve, usually dark in color, similar to an oyster. A delicacy abroad, mussels are not widely eaten in the U.S.

Mutineer. A one-design centerboard sloop. LOA 15', beam 6'. Designer: J.R. MacAlpine-Downie.

mutton sail. *See* spanker.

muzzler. A strong wind or gale blowing from dead ahead.

Mylar. Trade name for a relatively inelastic synthetic line or rope.

Mylar sailcloth. A non-woven film, shows considerable promise because of its durability.

N

Nacra 5.2. A one-design sloop-rigged catamaran. LOA 17′, beam 8′. Designer: Tom Roland.

nadir. The point on the celestial sphere directly under the observer and opposite to the zenith that is overhead.

nailsick. Describes a wooden hull whose fastenings are too corroded to be reliable.

Napier's diagram. A curve of deviation error on various courses for the magnetic compass; displayed on a board near the binnacle.

Narrasketuk. A one-design centerboard sloop. LOA 20¼′, beam 6½′.

narrows. A navigable, relatively short passage in a river, bay, sound, etc., with a limited width; not as long as a reach.

narwhal. An Arctic sea mammal of the dolphin family, distinguished by a long, round ivory tooth or tusk in the front of its head; believed to have been the inspiration for the mythical unicorn.

National Ocean Survey (NOS). Formerly the Coast and Geodetic Survey, a government office that produces charts of the U.S. as well as tide and current tables, Coast Pilots and Notices to Mariners. It is part of the National Oceanic and Atmospheric Administration (NOAA).

National. One-design A-class centerboard sloop. LOA 17′, beam 5½′. Designer: W.F. Crosby.

nautical. Pertaining to ships, shipping, navigation, and seamen. Not as broad in meaning as maritime since the latter relates to the sea and everything associated with it.

Nautical Almanac. Tables of positions of celestial bodies used in navigation, times of sunrise, moonrise, etc., and other data of interest to navigators. Prepared jointly by the U.S. Naval Observatory and the Royal Greenwich Observatory near London, U.K.

nautiphone. A sound-making device used as a fog signal by shore stations; similar to a diaphone but using an oscillating metal diaphragm instead of compressed air to make the sound.

navaid. Aid to navigation.

naval. A word that according to U.S. usage pertains to the U.S. and foreign navies. Older and British usage has a broader sense in which the word includes most maritime and nautical matters, as in naval architect and naval stores.

navigable semicircle. That area near a hurricane or typhoon away from its direction of advance and thus subject to less violent weather. The opposite, the area towards which the storm is advancing, is called the dangerous semicircle.

navigate. To control or direct the course of a ship or aircraft; to make a passage or voyage.

navigation. The art and science of directing the movement of ships and aircraft. It can be celestial, using heavenly bodies, bathymetric, by depth of water, or electronic. Piloting and dead reckoning are the earliest means of navigation.

navigation calculator or computor. A small, battery-powered, handheld solid-state device for working out sights; that is, solving the astronomical triangle. Data from sight reduction tables and the Almanac are programmed, requiring as input only time and the corrected observed altitude. An accurate digital or quartz watch is often included and many other standard calculations can be made.

navigation lights. *See* lights. The term is also a synonym for running lights.

NAVSAT. Navy NAVigation SATellite system that provides accurate all-weather world-wide position-finding for ships and aircraft. It is highly accurate, passive, and uses Doppler shift to measure the signals emitted by the satellite and calculate the position of the observer. It is also called Transit and is available to all.

Navstar. An advanced global positioning system (GFS) using satellite broadcast signals. Highly accurate and partly coded for security, it follows NAVSAT as a second-generation system.

NAYRU. North American Yacht Racing Union, once important to boatmen because it organized and supervised ocean and coastal racing in the U.S. and Canada. Now replaced by the U.S.Y.R.U., the U.S. Yacht Racing Union.

navy anchor. *See* stockless anchor.

navy top. *See* Bimini top.

neap. The tides which twice in a lunar month rise and fall the least from the mean level; in contrast to spring tides that rise and fall the most. A vessel that has run aground at high water is said to be neaped or is beneaped.

nearshore currents. Those caused by surf. Included is the shoreward mass transport of water by the breaking waves, longshore currents parallel to the beach that include feeder currents, rip currents flowing outward perpendicular to the beach supported by feeder currents, and the expanding heads of the rip currents. Nearshore currents are also called inshore currents. *See* longshore current, rip current.

neck. The stream of a rip current. Also a narrow piece of land between two water masses, an isthmus.

nib. *See* jog.

Nicopress. Trade name for a popular metal collar used to make a loop at the end of a wire.

niggerhead. A gipsy or warping head; the drum end of a winch around which turns of line are made when hauling. Also the heavy bitts for making fast a towrope as well as a bollard on a pier or dock for making fast mooring lines.

night glasses. Binoculars with large fields, and good light-gathering qualities for use at sea at night.

nimbus. *See* cloud.

nip. Sharp turn or bend in a rope or wire. To nip is to stop or seize a taut rope against another as in a tackle, to jam a rope in a block.

NOAA. National Oceanic and Atmospheric Administration.

nock. The upper forward corner of a quadrilateral fore-and-aft sail where the head and luff join. Also called throat.

nodal point. The place where the rise and fall of the tide is at a minimum despite maximum current.

NOMAD. Naval Oceanographic Meteorological Device, an automatic weather-reporting station anchored at sea.

nondisplacement craft. A ground- or surface-effect machine such as a Hovercraft or a planing craft or a hydrofoil.

noon. The time of the sun's passage across the upper branch of the meridian. At local apparent noon (LAN) a latitude is most easily determined by sextant.

norman. Any pin or bolt of wood or metal used to hold or contain rope or cable, such as the horizontal pin through the top of a bitt.

North American Yacht Register. A listing of U.S. and Canadian Yachts, replacing Lloyd's Register of American Yachts.

North Atlantic Current. That most northerly part of the Gulf Stream System originating off the Grand Banks as the end of the Gulf Stream. It flows in a complicated and varying pattern north, northeast, and east towards Europe as well as south. The easterly and southerly drifts eventually join the North Equatorial Current.

Northill folding anchor. Trade name for a popular, collapsible boat anchor.

North Cape Current. *See* Norway Current.

North Equatorial Current. The major east to west flow of water in the north Atlantic in the Trade Wind belt north of the Equator. It is fed by southeasterly currents off the coast of north Africa and, powered by the trade winds, piles up water in the Caribbean Sea where, as the Yucatan Current, it provides the major source of the Gulf Stream System. A similar current with the same name flows westward in the Pacific and is the source of the Japan Current. Another flows westward just north of the Equator in the Indian Ocean from October to July.

Norway Current. A continuation of the North Atlantic Current, by now slowed and widened to a drift that moves north along the coast of Norway. This warm drift becomes the North Cape Current as it moves northeast and then east into the Barents Sea.

North Haven Dinghy. The oldest dinghy racing class in the U.S., in existence since 1887. Gaff-rigged. LOA 14½', beam 5'. Now almost extinct.

NOS. National Ocean Survey.

nose. The stem or most forward part of a boat. Also the metal fitting protecting the stem of a boat.

nose port. A small, usually rectangular glass or plastic window set into a boat's hull above the waterline. It cannot be opened.

nosing ribbon. Same as molding.

notch block. Same as snatch block. *See* block.

Notice to Mariners. Published weekly by the Hydrographic Center of the Defense Mapping Agency and prepared jointly by the National Ocean Survey and the Coast Guard. Contains chart and Light List corrections, warnings of wrecks and other obstructions to safe navigation and other matters of importance to mariners. Local notices are published by each Coast Guard headquarters. *See* Daily Memorandum.

not-under-command. Describes a ship which, through some exceptional circumstance, is unable to maneuver as required by the Rules of the Road. During the day such a ship must show two shapes in a vertical line, at night two red, 32-point (all around) lights in a vertical line. The lights are also called breakdown lights, and in warships are flashed if a man should fall overboard.

nuggar or nugger. The traditional trading sailboat of the lower Nile, two-masted, lateen-rigged.

null. Zero output, as from as RDF when its antenna is lined up with the incoming signal, thus indicating direction.

number tax. A license fee or royalty paid to the class association by the builder of a class boat. After the boat is inspected and accepted by the class association it is given a number to be displayed on the mainsail and under which it may race.

nun buoy. Buoy shaped like a truncated cone, even numbered in U.S. waters. It is anchored to the right of the channel when entering from the sea and painted red; thus the rule: "red, right, returning." *See* can buoy.

nut. The iron ball on the end of the stock of an old-fashioned anchor.

NWS. National Weather Service.

nylon. A very strong, rot resistant and elastic synthetic fiber used widely afloat for ropes, cordage, and sail cloth. Nylon hawsers, under stress have considerable stretch, and if parted can backlash with dangerous force.

O

oakum. Caulking material traditionally made from rope fibers picked from old cordage. It was driven down between the planks of wooden ships with caulking tools and then the seams were payed or sealed with tar.

oar. A bladed wooden pole used to propel a boat by rowing. The parts in order are the handle, loom, or shaft (see loom), neck and blade, or peel. If the blade is rounded that part is called the feather. The part of the shaft or loom that fits into the oarlock is called the leather because traditionally it was covered with leather to resist wear.

oarlock. Any device on the gunwale of a boat for holding an oar while it is being pulled; a grommet or a swiveling crutch, fork, or ring. British word is crutch or rowlock.

OBC. The Outboard Boating Club of America.

occlusion or occluded front. A common weather phenomenon in which the leading edge of a cold air mass overtakes a warm front. The latter is thus occluded, closed out, or dispensed with as the cold air comes in below it and displaces the warm air on the earth's surface.

occulting. *See* light, occulting.

ocean. The intercommunicating body of salt water occupying the depressions on the earth's surface; divided into various parts by the continents and the Equator. The five oceans are the Atlantic, Pacific, Indian, Arctic, and Antarctic, covering 70% of the earth's surface.

ocean current. A large mass of water moved by wind as well as temperature and density differences and subject to Coriolis force. Some are narrow and fast stream currents, others are wide and slow drifts.

ocean engineering. That engineering specialty concerned with the development of new equipment, systems, and techniques, to enable man to exploit the undersea resources.

Oceania. The South Seas, specifically that area bounded by Hawaii, Easter Island, New Zealand, and New Guinea. The eastern part is Polynesia, with Micronesia to the northwest, and Melanesia in the southwest.

oceanography. The study of all aspects of the sea, including its physical boundaries, the chemistry of sea water, marine biology, and submarine geology. In a strict sense oceanography is the description of the marine environment, whereas oceanology is the study of the ocean and its related sciences.

ocean station. *See* weather ship.

ocean sunfish. *See* sunfish.

octant. An instrument similar to a sextant but using an arc of 1/8th of a circle (45°) instead of an arc of 1/6th.

octopus. An invertebrate sea animal with eight arms equipped with suction discs. It has a strong, parrotlike beak, moves by jet propulsion and ejects ink in self-defense. Although it can weigh 150 pounds and stretch 25′ across its tentacles, it is a shy and friendly creature with no record of an unprovoked attack on man.

O'Day 12. A one-design daggerboard catboat. LOA 12½′, beam 5′.

offing. A vessel gains her offing from the shore when she is a safe distance from the coast and no longer needs a pilot.

offset. In shipbuilding and repair, a measurement taken off the plans.

offshore. At sea away from the coast. Ships and boats cruise offshore or cruise along the coast. Also a direction: towards the sea, as an offshore wind that blows away from land. Compare onshore, inshore.

off soundings. Outside the 100-fathom curve. If inside 100 fathoms a boat is said to be on soundings.

off the wind. A sailboat not close hauled or on a reach. Otherwise she would be on the wind. *See* close hauled.

ohm. Measure of resistance to the flow of electricity, a measure of impedance.

oilers or oilies. Slang for oilskins.

oilcock. *See* seacock.

oilskins. Traditionally the heavy, yellow, waterproof jacket and trousers worn at sea in wet weather. Modern raingear is light, is made in many styles, and is produced in various bright colors including an orange that is the most visible in the water if a person goes overboard. Also called slickers, oilers, oilies or foul weather gear.

O.K. Dinghy. A one-design centerboard cat-rigged dinghy. LOA 13′, beam 4½′. Designers: Knud and Alex Olsen.

old-fashioned anchor. The common and traditional anchor of the past with a central shaft or shank, a ring or shackle at one end (often called the Jew's harp) to which the anchor rode is attached, a crosspiece, the stock, and a crown or lower extremity from which two arms branch perpendicular to the stock, each curving up to a broad palm or fluke ending in a bill or pea. It is called a stock anchor in the U.S. Navy and a fisherman's anchor in the U.K.; also often referred to as a kedge, mariner's, yachtsman's, or Herreshoff anchor. *See* anchor.

Omega. A long-range, worldwide, very low frequency (10–14 kHz) hyperbolic radio navigation system developed by the U.S. Navy to provide a global all-weather positioning system for ships, aircraft, and submarines.

omnirange. A radio aid to navigation providing direct indication of magnetic bearing (omnibearing) of a station from any direction. Also called omnidirectional range or beacon. Omni/VOR is a VHF aviation radio navigation system usable by boatmen when within line of sight of the transmitter. Often called omni.

one-design. Describes an organized class of nearly identical boats for cruising and racing.

One-Ten (110). A one-design keel sloop. LOA 24′, beam 8′, draft 4′. Designer: C.R. Hunt.

onshore. The direction towards the coast from the sea. Compare offshore.

on soundings. Within the 100-fathom curve.

on the bow or quarter. Towards the bow or quarter. *See* broad on the bow.

on the wind. Same as close hauled. If not close hauled a boat is sailing off the wind or reaching.

ooching. An illegal procedure on the part of a crew member in a sailing race who lunges forward and then stops suddenly in an effort to move the boat forward.

ooker. Slang for a cunningham.

open. Range lights or marks when not in line are said to be open. A bay or other body may open in a certain direction which indicates accessibility as well as a possible lack of shelter.

open hawse. *See* hawse.

Optimist Pram. A one-design, sprit-rigged centerboard pram. LOA 7½′, beam 3½′. Designer: Clark Mills.

Orion. A one-design sloop with keel and/or centerboard. LOA 19′, beam 6½′, draft (in keel model) 1½′. Designer: Robert Baker.

Orlon. Trade name for a modern synthetic fiber sometimes used for cordage and sails.

oscillator. An electronic device for changing DC to AC current.

Osprey. A one-design centerboard sloop. LOA 15½′, beam 6′. Designer: O'Day Corp.

outboard. Away from the centerline; towards the side of the boat. Opposite direction is inboard.

outboard/inboard. *See* sterndrive.

outboard motor. *See* motor, outboard.

outdrive. Another word for sterndrive.

outfoot. To sail faster close hauled is to outfoot an opponent.

outhaul. A line used to pull something outboard or away from the boat. Compare with inhaul. In a sailboat a line secured to the clew of a sail to pull it out along the boom. Also a metal fitting on the boom of a small racing sailboat to hold the clew cringle.

out oars. A command to the crew of a rowing boat to let the oars fall into the oarlocks with the blades held horizontally.

outpoint. To sail closer to the wind than another sailboat is to outpoint her.

outrigger. A balancing float, attached to a boat or canoe to keep it upright against the pressure of the wind on the sail. Any gear that supports something beyond the vessel's side such as that on a racing shell that supports the oarlocks. Spreaders are sometimes called outriggers.

outward bound. Said of a boat departing on a voyage.

overboard. Over the side; into the water.

overfalls. Short breaking waves marking the meeting of contrary currents, the passing of a strong current over a shallow irregular bottom, or the meeting of a current and an opposing wind. Also called rips or rip tides.

overhang. The projection of a boat's bow or stern beyond the waterline endings.

overhaul. 1. A nautical term for spreading a tackle, thus moving the blocks farther apart. The opposite is round in. 2. To overhaul a rope is to move it back towards the nearest block to ease the strain. 3. A vessel passing another overhauls it. 4. A boat is periodically overhauled when it is hauled out and painted, repaired, etc.

overhead. The proper nautical word for ceiling when the latter is used in its conventional sense. *See* ceiling.

overlap. The extension of the foot of a genoa abaft the luff of the mainsail.

overrake. Said of heavy seas that sweep over a wreck, over the bow of an anchored boat or over a boat in a storm.

over-stood. *See* under-stood.

overtaking vessel. According to the Rules of the Road a vessel that is approaching from astern and passing another ship from a direction more than two points abaft the beam of the overtaken vessel.

oxball. Small ornamental sphere at the top of a flagstaff or mast. On a mast it forms the truck.

Oyashio. A cold ocean current flowing southwest from the Bering Sea along the southeast coast of Siberia and the Kuril Islands, then curving south and east to join the North Pacific Current.

P

Pacific Catamaran. A one-design centerboard sloop-rigged catamaran. LOA 19', beam 8'. Designer: Carter Pyle.

Pacific Ocean. The largest of the world's oceans, named by Magellan who encountered a very rare calm day as he passed around the tip of South America from the Atlantic to the Pacific.

packing gland. *See* stuffing box.

pad. A small piece of plate fastened to the deck or bulkhead to which a removable bolt, hook, or other fitting may be made fast.

paddle. A short oar used to propel a small boat or canoe by being swung freely with both hands; may be single-or double-bladed.

pad eye. A small ring of metal fastened to the deck or a bulkhead.

painter. A small rope or line used on boats usually attached to the bow where it is used for making fast.

palm. 1. The flattened end of the arm of an old-fashioned anchor. Also called a fluke or wrist. 2. A sailmaker's leather semi-glove worn over the palm of the hand and used to force the needle through the canvas.

pampero. A violent storm blowing mostly from July to November offshore of Argentina.

pan. The voice radio prefix for an important message that does not have the priority of an emergency. Spoken: "pawn, pawn, pawn."

pan ice. A piece of ice from several to hundreds of yards in size, formed by the effect of wind and sea on field ice.

pancake ice. The roughly circular pieces up to 6 feet in diameter which appear before the solid floe is formed.

papagayo. A strong, dry northeasterly wind blowing off the west coast of Central America.

parachute flare. A warning or distress signal fired from a hand-held gun. A small parachute delays its descent.

parachute spinnaker. A large, light, triangular racing sail, used in light air, sometimes fitted with holes to achieve balance. Also called a balloon spinnaker or a Mae West.

parallax. In navigation, the error in the sextant altitude of a celestial body caused by the observer being on the surface of and not at the center of the earth. Correction is found in a table and must be applied in order to get true observed altitude.

parallel. The imaginary line around the world corresponding to latitude and longitude lines. Parallel sailing means sailing east or west along a known latitude line, that of the objective.

paraselene. *See* parhelion.

parcel. An old method of protecting rope by winding strips of canvas around it with the lay. This parceling is done after worming and before serving and the whole procedure was to worm, parcel, and serve. *See* serve, worm.

parhelion. An optical illusion, a bright light, or mock sun appearing near the sun; also called a sun dog. A similar phenomenon at night is a paraselene or moon dog.

parrel. Rope, chain, or metal collar by which a yard or gaff is kept close to the mast yet free to move up and down. A parrel moves freely on parrel beads or balls, also known as trucks. Also parral.

part. 1. The different sections of a tackle such as the standing part (fixed) or the moving part known as the hauling part. 2. To part means to break—a sailor always parts a line.

partners. Pieces of timber inserted between beams in wooden boat construction to form a frame for the mast. In modern boats partners around a through-deck mast may be made of fiberglass.

pass. To pass a line or to pass a stopper is to put it in place and make it fast.

passage. A one-way trip or crossing; part of a voyage. Also a narrow navigable channel through reefs or islands or between two bodies of water. In this sense may be called a pass and in New England a hole.

passage sail. Any sail designed for a long steady strong wind, stronger than a normal working sail.

passageway. Nautical word for corridor or hallway aboard ship.

patch. A repair for a hole in the hull or in piping in a boat. For piping a soft patch of gasket material wrapped with wire is sometimes effective.

patent anchor. A general term for a stockless anchor; sometimes sold under trade names such as Danforth.

patent block. A modern block in which the traditional simple pin holding the sheaves has been replaced by a shaft with roller bearings.

patent log. Same as screw log or taffrail log.

patent sheave. *See* roller sheave.

paunch. A thick antichafing mat made by weaving strands of old rope.

pay. 1. In the nautical sense to pay out a line is to let it out under control. 2. A boat under sail is said to pay off when she turns away from the wind to fill her sails after coming about on a new tack.

P.D. On most charts it indicates a reported hazard to navigation as Position Doubtful.

pea. The point or extreme end of a fluke of an anchor. Also called a bill, peak, or pee.

peacoat. A heavy woolen short coat worn by sailors. Called a peajacket in the Merchant Service and a reefer in the Navy.

peak. 1. The upper, after end or corner of a fore-and-aft four-sided sail. 2. The outboard end of the gaff from which the colors are flown underway. 3. The extreme internal ends of a ship are called the forepeak and the afterpeak. 4. The pea or bill of an anchor fluke.

peak cleat. A piece of wood fitted in a pulling boat and used for resting the inboard end of an oar when oars are elevated at the same angle.

peak oars. A command to oarsmen in a pulling boat to raise their oars to the same elevation.

peapod. A colloquial word for a very small light boat towed astern, or secured on deck, of a larger boat.

pedal boat. A small pleasure craft, usually rented at resorts, propelled by pedaling.

pedestal. A vertical free-standing column of wood or metal that supports a boat's steering wheel and houses the associated gear.

peel. Broadest part or blade of an oar or paddle.

pelagic. Pertains to the open sea, such as pelagic fish.

pelican. Any of the large, pouched, coastal birds, who often fly in formation and who dive into the water to capture fish.

Pelican. A one-design cat-rigged centerboard pram. LOA 11', beam 4½'. Designer: H.S. Glander.

pelican hook. A quick-release device consisting of a hook closed by a ring or bail shackle. When this bail is knocked away the hook opens and the anchor chain or whatever is released. Also called a slip hook, cable stopper.

pelorus. In all modern ships is a compass repeater set in gimbals on the wings of the bridge or elsewhere with a wide arc of vision on which a bearing circle, azimuth circle or alidade can be positioned. The whole assembly used for taking true bearings is a pelorus.

penalty pole. Spinnaker pole longer than distance from stemhead to mast.

pendant. Any single rope or chain secured at one end to a mast, spar, sail, etc., and having at its other end a thimble to which a whip or tackle is made fast. There are many special-purpose pendants such as a brace, burton, clearhawse, and fish pendant whose names explain their use. Pendant is the British spelling for pennant, meaning flag.

pendant tackle. A two-fold purchase hooked to a pendant and usually used for moving weights on deck.

Penguin. A one-design centerboard catboat. LOA 11½′, beam 4½′. Designer: Phil Rhodes.

penguin. A flightless, fast-swimming, fish-eating bird of the Antarctic.

peninsula. An elongated portion of land nearly surrounded by water and connected to a larger body of land.

Pennant. A one-design keel sloop. LOA 26′, 31′, or 35′. Designer: J. Schneider.

pennant. A special flag, usually longer than wide (having a greater fly than a hoist) such as a commission pennant. An Irish pennant is a loose untidy object such as a rope's end adrift aboard ship. Also pennant is often spelled pendant by the British but pronounced pennant. A line used to pull up a centerboard or one connecting a boat to its mooring buoy.

perch. An aid to navigation, mounted on a buoy, or ashore, and consisting of a pole or staff on which may be mounted a ball, cage, cross, etc., marking a shoal, rock, reef, or turning point in the channel.

perigee. The orbital position of an earth satellite, such as the moon when it is closest to the earth. Compare apogee.

period. The time that a lighted aid to navigation takes to complete one cycle of its characteristic impulses; one of the principal means of light identification.

period of roll. The time that a ship takes to make one roll from one side to the other and return when rolling freely in calm water. From this time in seconds a ship's stability can be estimated. A short period of roll indicates good stability.

perpendicular. In ship measurements a line drawn at right angles to the keel.

Personal Flotation Device (PFD). A general term for all types of life jackets, belts, vests, and other devices to prevent drowning.

Peru Current. A cold ocean current flowing north along the west coast of South America until near the Equator it turns west to join the South Equatorial Current. Also called the Humboldt Current.

petal. A small clip on a stanchion for securing a wire or lifeline.

petcock. *See* seacock.

petrel. A small, black, white-rumped, tube-nosed bird of the open sea that often follows boats, flying close to the surface. Also called Mother Carey's chickens and stormy petrels.

petticoat. *See* mast coat.

PFD. Personal Flotation Device.

Phantom. A one-design lateen-rigged daggerboard boat. LOA 14', beam 4½'. Designer: Howmar Boats, Inc.

PHRF. Performance Handicap Racing Fleet. An organization that provides ratings based on past racing performance.

pier. A structure built at an angle to the shore and used for mooring boats and ships or used for sightseeing and pleasure. It may be T-shaped. *See* dock, wharf. The British use pier as a synonym for jetty.

pierhead. The seaward end of a pier.

pigtail. The end of a rope or line, the end of a lashing.

pile. A wooden, steel, or concrete pole or stake used in pier, wharf, or cofferdam construction, for ship moorings or to cushion the entrance to ferry slips. Sometimes called a dolphin or a rack.

pillar. Any vertical support member below decks, usually supporting a deck. Also known as a stanchion.

pilot. A qualified, licensed person with local knowledge, who directs a ship in a harbor, channel or narrow passage. A volume of sailing directions is known as a pilot.

pilotage. The act or business of piloting. Also the fee involved.

pilot, automatic. A device that steers a vessel or aircraft on any course selected.

Pilot Chart. One that contains important information on ocean currents, ice at sea, force and direction of seasonal winds, storm tracks, etc., issued monthly by the Defense Mapping Agency Hydrographic Center.

pilotfish. A small, brightly banded fish that accompanies sharks, living off their scraps and giving the appearance of guiding the sharks by often swimming in front of them.

pilothouse. The space in the ship's bridge structure enclosing the steering wheel and engine controls. Also called the wheelhouse.

piloting. That part of navigation that involves contact by sight, sound, or radar with the land.

pilot ladder. A handy, light, flexible, and portable ladder slung over the side of a ship to assist the pilot. *See* ladder.

Pilot Rules. Rules of the Road issued by the U.S. Coast Guard that supplement the Inland Rules for U.S. waters.

pilot's luff. In sailing to windward a luff made to clear an obstruction without tacking.

pin. *See* belaying pin, clevis. Slang for mark among racing sailboatmen.

pin rail. *See* fife rail.

pinch. To sail a boat so close to the wind that her sails shiver and headway is slowed.

pinching string. A knotted line used in sailboats with the mainsheet traveler to bring the boom to weather for higher pointing.

pinky. A New England fishing schooner of the 19th century now being revived by hobbyists. Also called pinkey or pink.

pinrail. *See* fife rail.

pintles. The heavy pins or bolts on the forward edge of the rudder that fit and rotate in the gudgeons secured to the sternpost or rudderpost.

pipe berth. A bed or bunk in a boat or ship made of canvas stretched over a frame of metal tubing and hinged so that it can be folded up.

pipe down. Sailor's term meaning to be quiet, make less noise.

pipe up. Sailor's term meaning to speak louder or start a song. The wind pipes up as it increases in strength.

piping the side. The act of giving honors to an important person arriving or departing aboard a Naval vessel.

Pirateer. A one-design centerboard sloop. LOA 13′, beam 5½′. Designer: J.R. MacAlpine-Downie.

piracy. Robbery and murder on the high seas, still a positive danger to yachtsmen from drug smugglers in local U.S. waters and from others in remote parts of the world.

pirogue. A small, double-ended, flat-bottomed open boat for fishing and hunting along the Gulf coast.

pitch. Traditionally, tar or glue used to seal the caulking between wooden planks. The vertical oscillation of a boat in a seaway on its transverse axis; an up and down movement distinct from heave or surge.

pitchpole. A boat pitchpoles when it is thrown end over end in very large seas, usually as the result of being struck from aft by an enormous storm or rogue wave with a vertical face.

pitch, propeller. The angle a propeller blade makes with a plane perpendicular to the axis of the propeller. This angle varies along the length of the blade. Also expressed as the distance the propeller would move forward in one revolution if it were screwing into a soft solid.

pitch ratio. The pitch divided by the diameter of the propeller.

Pitometer log. *See* pitot-static log.

pitot-static log. A speed-measuring device having a rodmeter assembly that detects both dynamic and static pressure; the former due to boat speed and the latter due to the depth of water. Thus boat speed and distance traveled can be recorded. Examples are the Pitometer log and the Bendix underwater log.

pivot or pivoting point. The point about which a ship pivots when turning.

plain laid rope. A three-strand, right-hand laid fiber rope. If laid left-handed it is backhanded or back-laid rope. Also called right-handed or hawser-laid rope.

plain sail. The sails normally carried in average or moderate weather. In light air more sails and lighter ones are set while in heavy weather the heavy canvas or storm sails are used.

plain sailing. Originally meant to sail in a rhumb line instead of great circle sailing.

plane. A boat planes when its hull rises and friction is reduced.

planets. Heavenly bodies such as Venus, Jupiter, Mars, etc., which, like the earth, revolve around the sun and change position daily. Brighter than stars, they are most useful for celestial navigation.

planing hull. One that rises above the water and planes. *See* displacement hull.

plank. There are many special-purpose planks used in boat building such as carvel, clinker, spline, strip, cross, garboard, and others whose names also identify their use.

plank keel. A flat wooden keel sometimes used in building small boats that have almost vertical garboard strakes.

plank-sheer. In wooden boat building a horizontal fore-and-aft timber that forms the outer edges of the upper deck.

plankton. The minute plant (phytoplankton) and animal (zooplankton) life floating or drifting submerged in the ocean. The basis for all ocean animal life—the start of the ocean food chain.

Planning Guide. *See* Sailing Directions.

Plan Position Indicator (PPI). A radar screen that displays a map-like view of the surrounding land and anything on the water that returns a radar beam.

plate tackle. In a decked sailing canoe the gear used to move the centerboard.

plating. An arrangement of steel or aluminum plates such as deck plating, shell plating, skin plating, tank top plating, etc.

pledget. A roll of oakum used for caulking the seams of planks.

Plimsoll marks or lines. Load waterline or loadline marks painted on the side of a ship indicating the maximum draft to which it may be loaded under different conditions.

plot. A diagram of ship or boat position and movement. To plot a position is to find or locate one and then indicate and label it.

plotter. Basically a combined protractor and straight edge made in various designs under various trade names used in piloting and plotting lines and measuring courses and bearings on a chart.

plotting sheet. Special blank sections of chart, large scale, showing only latitude and longitude lines for plotting the lines of position and the resultant ship's position from celestial navigation.

plow anchor. A stockless anchor whose flukes are plow shaped. It is efficient for small boats but not easy to stow in a hawsepipe. In large sizes it is used to anchor mooring buoys, platforms for the offshore oil business, etc. Called a ploughshare or CQR anchor in the U.K. where it originated. Also called a spade anchor.

plowsteel rope. A particularly strong wire rope made of open-hearth, high-carbon steel.

plug. 1. A boat plug is removed in order to drain the bilges when a boat is lifted clear of the water. **2.** The master pattern for a fiberglass part, around which the mold such as a hull, from which the female mold is taken.

plumb bow. *See* bow shapes.

plumber block. Same as plummer block.

plummer block. One of the pillow blocks supporting the tunnel shafting or propeller shaft bearings.

pneumercator. An instrument for measuring the level of liquid in a tank using air pressure.

pod. A small group of ocean mammals. A large group is a school. Also short for peapod, a small, double-ended boat.

pogy. Another word for menhaden.

point. 1. One of the 32 divisions of the magnetic compass circle, each point equaling 11¼ degrees of arc. Before the introduction of the gyro compass and its 360° scale points were in wide usage but are now mostly used in indicating relative bearing as "ship two points on the port bow." **2.** A projection of land from the coast. **3.** A sailboat points high if she sails close to the wind. **4.** Dewpoint is the temperature at which the moisture in the atmosphere condenses. **5.** Flashpoint is the temperature at which a combustible mixture burns. **6.** To point a line or rope is to taper the end.

pointer. A timber or steel beam fitted diagonally into the fore and after ends of a ship, extending from the deck to the keelson or dead-wood.

pointline. In a square-rigger the light line or cord, often 21-thread manila, used in making reefpoints.

point oars. A command to the crew of a pulling boat when the boat is aground. Oars are lowered into the water, downward, and at the command "shove off," the boat is freed.

pokey pusher. Slang for a trolling motor, a small, quiet and slow outboard motor made from an electric motor run by a storage battery.

polar. Pertaining to the Arctic or the Antarctic, north or south of latitude 66° 33', N or S.

polar chart. A great circle projection whose point of tangency is one of the geographical poles.

Polaris. The north or polar star, an historic guide for navigators, whose direction is always within a degree or two of true north, and whose altitude is nearly exactly equal to the latitude of the observer. Also called Lodestar, Stella Maris, Polestar.

polar whale. The bowhead or Greenland right whale.

pole. That part of a mast above the shrouds, also a flagstaff. Sometimes loosely used as a synonym for mast as in "she ran before the gale under bare poles."

Polestar. Same as Polaris.

pollywog. A person who has not crossed the Line (Equator) and who must be initiated at the Crossing the Line ceremony and thus become a shellback under the kindly tutelage of Father Neptune.

pontoon. A cylindrical float used to support a pontoon boat or houseboat. Any flat, rectangular, bargelike floating structure used in loading and unloading ships and supporting derricks, cranes, portable bridges, etc.

pontoon lifeboat. A wide and shallow boat built of steel or wood and having several watertight compartments.

pooped. For a boat to be pooped means that a large sea or wave has broken over the stern when running before the seas.

porpoise. A relatively small (up to 12′) toothed whale that feeds on fish and squid. Since there is some confusion between the words porpoise and dolphin, even among naturalists, the two words may be used interchangeably unless the specific animal, for example the bottle-nosed dolphin, can be recognized.

port. 1. A harbor or shelter for ships and boats. 2. An opening in the side of a vessel in the form of an airport, cargo port, or side port. A freeing port is one that permits the escape of water.

portfolio. A collection of charts covering a specific area and assigned a number by the issuing office.

porthole. An opening in the side of a vessel fitted with a hinged glass and often a metal cover; same as airport. British word is scuttle or side scuttle.

portlight. The fitting inside a porthole or airport holding the hinged glass cover that can be closed or dogged down. Sometimes used synonymously with airport, but the latter is more accurately the opening, not the fitting. Sometimes an airport with a fixed glass.

port side. The left side of a boat looking forward (note that port and left both have four letters) opposite to starboard, the right side. A sailboat is on the port tack when the wind is coming over the port side before striking the sails.

Portuguese Current. Part of the huge North Atlantic gyral (including the Gulf Stream) that circulates clockwise. It flows south along the coast of Europe to join the Canary Current. A side branch passes into the Mediterranean through the Straits of Gibralter.

Portuguese man-o-war. A jellyfish with long stinging tentacles found floating on the sea worldwide.

position buoy. An anchored marker showing the location of a wreck or other hazard to navigation.

potrero. An accretionary ridge offshore separated from the coast by a lagoon and barrier islands, as along the Texas coast.

pounding. The motion of a boat in a head sea when there is heavy contact with the oncoming waves. If it is so violent that damage may result it is called slamming.

pound net. A fixed fishing enclosure of vertical netting supported by stakes that can menace a small boat close to the beach. Also called a fyke or fike net.

powerboat. One designed to be propelled by power, a motorboat.

power curve. A chart showing the horsepower needed to drive a certain hull at various speeds.

power factor. In a reactive electrical circuit it is the ratio of watts to volt-amperes.

powerhead. The upper unit of an outboard motor from which power is transmitted to the lower unit and propeller.

power skiff. A small, powerful, open boat used to assist the fishing trawler or seine boat in making her set.

PPI. Plan Position Indicator.

pram. A light dinghy or small boat with a square, cut-off bow used by yachts as a tender.

prao. *See* proa.

pratique. Technically a vessel's certificate of health but commonly used to mean permission granted by foreign port authorities for a ship or boat to communicate with the shore after a quarantine inspection or certification (if required). Now often granted by radio after assurances that there are no communicable diseases aboard.

prau. *See* proa.

predicted log race. *See* logging race.

prepreg. An aircraft-quality fiberglass cloth impregnated with epoxy resin used in some modern boat construction.

preventer. Any rope or wire used for additional security to keep something in place, such as a preventer backstay or preventer shroud.

pricker. A small marlinspike.

pride of the morning. A light mist or fog hanging over the sea at sunrise; soon dispelled by the sun of a fair, bright day.

prime meridian. The imaginary great circle passing through the poles and through the original site of the Royal Observatory at Greenwich, England, at zero longitude and zero time zone, from which longitude and time are measured.

primer bulb. A flexible bulb in the gas line to an outboard motor that when squeezed and released forces gas into the motor.

prime vertical. A great circle passing through the zenith as well as through the east and west points of the observer's celestial horizon.

priming. A shortening of the interval between successive high tides. Also called acceleration; the opposite is called lagging.

Prindle. A one-design sloop rigged catamaran. LOA 16', or 18', beam 8'. Designer: Geof Prindle.

prism, tidal. The total amount of water, excluding fresh water, that flows in or out of a harbor with tidal movement.

private flag or signal. One a boatman may fly in any boat he owns or charters.

privileged vessel. *See* stand-on vessel.

proa. A general word for the native craft of Indonesia, Mayalsia, and the Philippines. It is an open boat with a narrow main hull, and a small float or outrigger out on one side. Now adapted for use as a small racing sailboat, the Malibu Outrigger, in the U.S. Spelled prao in Portuguese and prau in Malay.

projection chart. A representation of the spherical earth on a flat sheet of paper.

prolonged blast. A signal of 4–6 seconds on the ship's whistle as specified by the International Rules of the Road.

propeller. A rotating device used to propel a boat. Two, three, or four blades are spaced evenly around a hub or boss into which a power rotated shaft is fitted. A propeller is right-handed when it turns clockwise, is viewed from aft, and the boat is moving ahead.

propeller pitch. *See* pitch.

propeller slip. *See* slip.

protest. In a boat race, a formal charge that a competitor has violated a rule.

protest flag. International alphabet flag B shown by a boat during or just after a race if a protest is made. Flag is noted by the Race Committee who must rule on the matter before declaring a winner.

protractor. A transparent plastic semicircle whose curved edge is marked in degrees. A Hoey or single-arm protractor has a swinging rule attached, used for plotting bearing lines and courses on a chart. A three-arm protractor has three swinging arms that can each be lined up on the bearing of a landmark or aid to navigation. The pivot point or center of the instrument then marks the ship's position obtained without using a compass if relative bearings are used.

prow. The extreme forward part of a vessel, the bow; a poetic word rarely used by sailors.

psc. Per standard compass.

pudding. Chafing gear usually made of yarn or matting, used to protect a boat, spar, towline, etc., from rubbing. British spelling is puddening.

pudding fender. A small fender or bumper made of old rope and covered with matting or canvas; now usually replaced by a hollow and strong plastic cylinder or ball. Sometimes called a dolphin.

Puffer. A one-design daggerboard sloop. LOA 18½′, beam 5′. Designer: Fred Scott.

pull. To pull a boat is better nautical usage than to row a boat. A rowboat is used on a lake; a pulling boat is used at sea by a sailor who pulls an oar. However he does not pull on a rope, he hauls on it.

pulpit. Traditionally a platform on a bow extension or bowsprit for a harpooner, particularly one who spears swordfish. In modern boats the rail around the most forward part of the deck as well as that space itself is often called the pulpit.

pumping. Frequent rapid trimming and releasing of sails regardless of wind direction. Also known as fanning and is of questionable legality in sailboat racing.

punt. Any small, flat-bottom, usually square-ended boat used for odd jobs such as painting the side of a ship.

purchase. A general word for any arrangement of blocks and ropes (tackle) that produces a machanical advantage. The latter is also called purchase and, disregarding friction, is the number of moving parts (ropes or lines) at the moving block.

purchase block. One having two or more sheaves and used in a multiple tackle for moving heavy weights.

purse seine. A fishing net built like a long shallow curtain; the top is buoyed with floats and the lower end is weighted. A purse rope pulls the bottom together when the net has been pulled around a school of fish.

pusher mast. The seventh mast on some seven-masted schooners. On other schooners it was the fifth or sixth mast from forward.

pushing lights. Two amber 12 point (135°) lights displayed in a vertical line at the stern of a vessel pushing a tow. This is in accordance with the Rules of the Road.

put. To move, bring about or take action. A sailboat puts about when tacking. A ship puts out to sea and may put into port.

pyrometer. An instrument that measures heat. In boat engines it measures the temperature at the exhaust manifold to detect overheating before damage can occur.

Q

quadrant. A portable device used to measure angles that has an arc length of 90°; similar to a sextant but smaller.

quadrantal deviation. A deflection of the magnetic compass caused by the induced magnetism of the ship's horizontal iron. It is corrected by the quadrantal spheres.

quadrantal spheres. Round iron balls mounted on each side of the compass on the binnacle. Sometimes called the navigator's balls.

quadrant or quadrental davit. One in which the lower end of the arm is a quadrant of steel fitted with gear teeth that enable the arm to be cranked out away from the ship's side in order to lower the boat.

quadrant, rudder. A fitting shaped like a quadrant of a circle that is used to attach the rudder chains and cables to the rudder stock.

quadrature. The relationship between two celestial bodies, the moon and the sun when they are 90° apart in reference to the earth. When the moon is in quadrature or 90° from the sun their effect on the tides is less (neap tides) than when the moon and sun lie in a line to produce their maximum or spring tides.

Quad Trainer. A one-design centerboard dinghy rigged as a catboat or a sloop. LOA 11', beam 4½'. Designer: Conference for National Cooperation in Aquatics.

quarantine. The detention period for a ship or boat entering port, unless she has been granted pratique. *See* pratique.

quarter. 1. The part of the stern 45° or four points on each side of the centerline. 2. A direction; an object may be described as being sighted broad on the port quarter (225° relative). 3. To quarter the wind and sea is to bring them astern on the quarter.

quarter bitts. Bitts located topside on each quarter of a ship used for securing mooring lines.

quarter boat. Any boat hung on davits near the ship's quarter.

quarterdeck. Traditionally, that part of a ship aft and topside from which the master or captain conned the ship. It was the domain of officers and the scene of ceremony and punishment.

quas. *See* kaus.

quay. Usually a solid masonry structure, a landing place along the shore for ships and boats. Often called a wharf if made of wood and sometimes loosely called a pier, dock, or mole.

queen staysail. A triangular sail set on the main topmast stay of a two-masted schooner.

quick-flashing light. A navigational light that flashes continuously and quickly, not more than 60 flashes per minute. *See* flashing light.

R

rabbet. A shoulder or recess; a channel made to receive the edge of a board.

rabbet plank. *See* hog-piece.

race. 1. Any fast, visibly turbulent water such as a tide race or a propeller or screw race. 2. A propeller is said to race when it is lifted partly out of the water in a heavily pitching ship or boat and it speeds up.

racing-jib traveler. *See* traveler.

rack. 1. Any device designed to keep things from going adrift in a seaway such as a pot rack on the galley range or a table rack or fiddle. Ships are made fast to a piling called a mooring rack, and the piles that shoulder a ferry into her slip are a ferry rack. 2. To seize two ropes together side by side to prevent their relative movement is to rack them.

racking. Spun yarn or small stuff (seizing) used to rack two lines together. Also the lateral stress and deformation of a ship's hull due to violent rolling.

racking stopper. *See* stopper.

racon. A RAdar beaCON, a transponder, that returns a coded signal giving identification of the beacon as well as range and bearing when triggered by a ship's radar. *See* ramark.

radar. RAdio Detection And Ranging, an electronic device used to obtain ranges and bearings as well as a visual presentation of ships, aircraft, landmarks, etc., by means of the reflection of pulses of radio energy. Of great value to seamen in low visibility.

radar alarm. A device for boats not fitted with radar to detect and to track by direction radar signals from ships that could endanger them in low visibility.

radar reflector. Any device used to ensure a strong reflected radar signal from boats, buoys, etc. Also called a corner reflector, it is usually a folding, geometric shape of metal hoisted in the rigging.

raddle. To interlace lengths of rope as in making boat gripes.

radio. Used as an aid to navigation in the form of radio direction finders (RDF), radio beacons, radio fog signals, and particularly voice radio now common on all ships and most boats.

radio beacon. An aid to navigation that broadcasts an identifiable signal whose direction from the ship can be determined.

radio direction finder (RDF). A radio receiver using a directional or loop antenna that determines the bearing of a radio signal such as a radio beacon or a commercial radio broadcasting station.

radio navigation. A system of navigation by which radio waves are received and evaluated to determine the ship's position, for example, Loran. It includes radar and satellite navigation. Electronic navigation, a broader term, includes depth finders, inertial systems, Doppler equipment, etc.

radiosonde. A device carried by balloon that is used to record weather information at various altitudes and transmit this information by radio to ships and shore stations.

radiotelephone. Basic voice radio communications for boats—medium, high, and very high frequency, including single sideband (SSB) and citizens band (CB).

radio time signal. A broadcast at frequent intervals on a variety of frequencies of Greenwich Mean Time; useful to navigators who can thus get a time tick accurate to 1/10 second. All information is in a U.S. government publication, H.O. 205, Radio Aids to Navigation.

raffe or raffee. A triangular sail once set above the upper skysails of a schooner carrying a square topsail.

raffle. In the nautical sense, a tangle of cordage, blocks, spars, and other debris associated with a wreck or a lesser accident involving some of the topside rigging carrying away.

raft. Any floating device used for transport on water made of floats and having no hull or interior space. Boats that moor together side by side are said to be rafted or nested, or may be said to raft up.

rail. The nautical word for fence. Also a plank, timber, or piece of metal forming the top of a bulwark. A hand rail, ladder rail, or safety rail is often present to assist those using a ladder. *See* fender rail, guard rail, sheer rail, toe rail.

railway. A track or metal strip on a mast on which the clips of a sail are fastened and on which they travel as the sail is hoisted and lowered. *See* marine railway.

Rainbow. A one-design keel sloop for class racing and family sailing LOA 24′, beam 8′, draft 3′. Designer: Sparkman and Stephens.

raise. In a nautical sense means to bring into view, as "We shall soon raise Fire Island." 2. The wind raises a choppy sea. 3. One attempts to raise another boat or station by radio.

rake. The inclination forward or abaft (backwards) of a mast, funnel or other piece of tophamper or hull above the waterline. To rake is to remove old caulking from a seam in a wooden boat using a raking tool.

rake of a propeller. The difference between the angle of slope of its blades and the perpendicular.

rakish. Having a smart appearance suggestive of speed.

ram bow. The bow of a boat that slopes aft above the waterline.

ramark. RAdar MARKer beacon that transmits a signal indicating the direction of the beacon.

RAMOS. Remote Automatic Meteorological Observing System.

ramp. To sail a boat rather full when on the wind is to ramp her.

range. The effective range of visibility of a navigational light. The direction indicated by two marks or lights when in line to show something in line such as a channel. The boat following the range is either on, opening, or closing the range. The markers that show the channel are also called a range. To range an anchor rode is to lay it out on deck or on the pier. A ship coming alongside a pier or another ship is said to range alongside.

range light. In accordance with the Rules of the Road, a white light abaft and above the masthead light. The two form a range that reveals a direction, in this case the course of a ship at night. For seagoing steam vessels it is a 20-point light, showing ahead and on each side.

range of tide. The difference in feet between high and low water.

Ranger 22. A one-design keel sloop. LOA 22½′, beam 8′, draft 4′. Designer: Gary Mull.

ranging. Said of a ship or boat at anchor that is moving or horsing around its anchor in a blow as the vessel changes her heading.

RAOB. A weather RAdio OBservation system of land stations and ships that receive data sent by radiosonde.

rap full. With all sails filled and the sailboat not quite close-hauled; same as clean full.

Rascal. A one-design centerboard sloop. LOA 14′, beam 6½′. Designer: Ray Greene.

RATAN. RAdio and Television Aid to Navigation, a system in which a central station transmits a radar picture by television of a harbor or congested waterway to ships which can thus ensure that they are on a safe course.

ratchet block. One whose sheave is controlled by a ratchet, often used in a mainsheet system since the sheave can only move in the trim direction.

rate. The daily change in a chronometer's error.

rat guard. A conical metal shield fixed around a mooring line to keep rats out of the boat.

rathole. A sailor's private storage or hiding place for personal gear.

rating. A number assigned to a racing sailboat by a handicapping organization or rule such as the IOR that depends on her measurements and determines her racing handicap.

ratline. A short length of rope crossing the shrouds at regular intervals and useful for men going aloft. Pronounced ratlin.

rattail. The tapered end of a rope.

rattle down. To fasten the ratlines to the shrouds by means of eye splices and clove hitches.

Raven. A centerboard sloop. LOA 24', beam 7'. Designer: Roger McAleer.

rave hook. A caulking tool used to remove old oakum from a seam.

rawin. The radar observation of a balloon released from the ground or deck and then tracked to reveal the direction and force of winds up to 100,000'. When combined with radiosonde it is a rawinsonde.

Rawson 30. A one-design keel sloop. LOA 30½', beam 9', draft 5'. Designer: William Garden.

Raydist. A small portable electronic navigation system used in survey work with a range to 350 miles.

Raymond releasing hook. A type of hook used on boat falls that trips itself free when the boat is waterborne.

razing iron. A caulking tool; same as a ripping iron.

RDF. Radio Direction Finder.

reach. 1. The straight portion of a river or canal between bends, rapids or locks. 2. An arm of the sea extending into the land. 3. Sailing with the wind on the beam or nearly so, between close hauled and free, is sailing on a reach or reaching. 4. To close reach is to sail nearly close hauled; to be on a beam reach is to have the wind abeam; to be on a broad reach is to have the wind just abaft the beam; to head reach is to forge ahead while lying to in heavy weather under canvas; to forereach is to forge to windward while tacking. 5. A leg or a distance sailed on a certain course is known as a reach.

reaching foresail. *See* foresail.

reacher. A lightweight, high-clewed jib or spinnaker used when reaching; normally smaller than a spinnaker. Also called a jibtop.

reacher block. One used for changing the lead or direction of headsail sheets. Similar to a turning block but with a swivel.

reaching canvas. Sails designed for most efficiency when reaching —full-cut and relatively light.

reaching jib. Same as balloon jib.

reaching strut. A short spur used on a sailboat to hold a headsail guy away from the shrouds. British word is jockey pole.

ready about. The command given to the crew of a sailboat by the person at the tiller before tacking or coming about. Also a warning to all hands to beware of a swinging boom.

ream. To enlarge a hole, particularly a grommet or cringle in a sail by means of a fid. Sailmakers use a reaming stool with holes of various sizes bored in the top. May be spelled rime.

Rebel. A one-design centerboard sloop. LOA 16′, beam 6½′. Designer: Ray Greene.

recall flag. A signal to racing sailboats that they have crossed the starting line too soon.

rectifier. A device that converts alternating current to direct current.

red lead. An anticorrosive primer paint for metal, traditionally red in color. Sailor's slang for catsup.

red tide. A bloom, or very rapid growth, of a red and toxic animal plankton, a dinoflagellate. The surface water of the sea turns red and is luminescent at night, fish die from a lack of oxygen and shellfish in the area become poisonous. A local and temporary phenomenon.

red, right, returning. An expression remembered by navigators, pilots, and ship and boat handlers, meaning that the red channel buoys are to be kept to the right or starboard hand in U.S. waters when entering a channel from seaward.

reduction to the meridian. The correction of the observed altitude of a heavenly body near the meridian to obtain its meridian altitude and thus the latitude of the observer.

reef. A reduction in the area of a sail. To reef is to reduce sail area, usually because of an increase in wind that the sailboat cannot handle safely or comfortably.

reef band. A strip of canvas sewed horizontally across a sail as strengthening for the line of reef points.

reef cringle. A rope grommet worked around a thimble in the leech of a sail at the end of the reef band through which the reef earing passes.

reef earing. A short rope used to secure the corner of the reefed sail to yard or boom by passing through the reef cringle.

reefer. A short blue or black woolen coat worn by seamen, same as peacoat or peajacket.

reef, geographic. Any long rock or coral formation near enough to the surface of the sea to be a danger to navigation. Coral reefs are made of dead and living coral, either fringing the shore and separated by a narrow stretch of water (a friendly reef), or a barrier reef off shore separated from the land by deep water, or random reefs known as platform, patch, or table reefs. *See* atoll, coral, shoal.

reefing cleats. Cleats fitted on the boom of a sailboat near the clew used to take the hauling out turns of the reef earing.

reefing hook. A steel hook used on the mast at the gooseneck to hold a reefing cringle.

reefing iron. A caulking tool; same as a ripping iron or reeming iron.

reef knot. A square knot, a simple over and under twice with the ends emerging on the same side of the loop. In reefing one end is often tucked back and under as a bow that could release the knot quickly and thus expedite shaking out a reef.

reef points. The short lengths of line, also called point lines, made fast to a sail at the reef band which, tied with a reef knot, results in a reef being taken in that sail. *See* slab reefing.

reef, sail. To reef a sail is to reduce its area, usually by tying part of it off by reef points or by rolling part of the sail around a wire or rod (roller reefing gear). A sailor puts in or tucks in a reef, and then may shake out a reef.

reeming iron. A wedge used for opening the seams of a wooden boat to permit caulking. Also reefing iron.

reeve. To pass through or lead a line, rope, or wire through an opening such as a block, grommet, etc. Past tense is rove.

reeving line. Any small line fastened to a larger one to assist in putting the heavier line through a block.

reeving line bend. A way of fastening two lines together to facilitate their passing through an opening. It consists of two half hitches with the ends seized to the standing parts.

refraction. In one sense the change of direction of light waves when passing through the atmosphere or when passing through air masses of different characteristics. The first elevates a celestial body above its true altitude, the second produces mirages and the distortion of electronic emissions, commonly observed when passing along a coast where dry and warm desert air meets colder and moist ocean air.

refraction of water waves. The change in direction of waves as they pass over shallow areas or close to land; the part of the wave in shallow water is slowed by the reduced depth. This phenomenon was known to the Polynesians and assisted them in detecting land far away by a slight change in the direction of the swell.

regatta. A boat race or series of races for sailing, power, or pulling boats.

registry. *See* certificate of registry.

relative. In the maritime sense it describes a direction relative to the vessel's fore-and-aft axis rather than to a compass. The latter would be a true direction.

relative wind. Same as apparent wind.

relieving tackle. Any purchase rigged to take the strain off a piece of gear as, for example, the steering gear in heavy weather.

remora. A small fish equipped with a suction disc on the top of its head by which it can attach itself to sharks, debris, vessels, etc.

Remote Automatic Meteorological Observing System (RAMOS). Installed by the National Weather Service, its solar powered instruments report temperature, dewpoint, wind speed and direction, pressure, and rainfall each hour.

render. An old word for easing a line through a block. The line renders as it runs free.

Rennell's Current. A seasonal ocean current, usual in the winter, that sets northward across the western approaches to the English Channel.

resin. Any of a variety of synthetic plastic materials used as adhesives and in laminating. Also rosin.

restricted visibility. According to the Rules of the Road means any "condition in which visibility is restricted by fog, mist, falling snow, heavy rainstorms, sandstorms or any other similar causes."

retained magnetism. Transient or temporary magnetism induced in a ship's iron when the ship remains on the same heading for a length of time.

return block. *See* snatch block.

revenue cutter. Old name for a Coast Guard cutter; from the days when the Revenue Service was independent.

Rhodes Bantam. One-design centerboard or keel sloops. LOA 14', 18', 19', beams 5–7'. Designer: P.L. Rhodes.

rhumb line. A curve on the earth's surface that intersects all the meridians at the same angle and appears on a Mercator chart as a straight line.

ribbon staysail. *See* tallboy.

ride. To lie at anchor, riding easy or hard depending on wind and tide. A boat may be said to ride out the storm.

rider. A wood or steel piece that adds strength and stiffness, as a rider plate or keelson.

ridge rope. The backbone wire or rope that supports an awning.

riding bitts. The heavy bitts forward on a large sailboat to which an anchor rode is made fast.

riding boom. Same as boat boom or guesswarp boom; a hinged spar rigged out from a ship's side in port to which the ship's boats are made fast.

riding lights. Lights displayed by a ship or boat at anchor as required by the Rules of the Road. Same as anchor lights.

riding sail. Any small sail used to steady a powerboat underway as when fishing or to steady any boat while at anchor.

riding turn. A turn of the part of a rope under strain around a cleat, bitts, etc. This turn lies over the others and jams them. Also riding turns are a second layer put over the first in a seizing or whipping.

Ridley turtle. A small sea turtle, rarely over 2 feet in length, found in both the Atlantic and Pacific; an endangered species and protected by law.

rig. 1. A distinctive arrangement of sails and masts, as a schooner, bark, fore-and-aft or square rig. 2. Any arrangement of gear or machinery aboard ship. 3. To rig something is to set it up and arrange it, as the anchor of a boat is rigged for letting go. Booms are rigged in or may be rigged out.

rigger. A shipyard or boatyard workman who raises and lowers gear and equipment.

rigger's screw. A portable vise used in splicing rope and wire. Also called a rigger's vise or a splicing vise and sometimes a rigging screw. The latter is also a word for turnbuckle or bottlescrew.

rigging. Everything nonstructural above decks such as shrouds, sails, spars, and cordage. Standing rigging is fixed in place, while running rigging is free to move.

rigging screw. *See* turnbuckle, rigger's screw.

right whale. Any of several baleen or whalebone whales having a large head and no dorsal fin. Now nearly extinct.

rigol. Same as eyebrow, now often spelled wriggle.

rip. Disturbed water caused by a meeting of currents or by a current flowing over a shoal or an irregular bottom. If tidal current is involved it is a rip tide or tide rip but should not be confused with a rip current.

rip current. A strong, relatively narrow stream setting directly away from the shore upon which heavy surf is breaking. It results from the water piled up inshore by the surf and requires an escape. Sometimes improperly called a rip tide or tide rip—it has nothing to do with the tide—and should not be confused with undertow. A rip current consists of a feeder current running along the beach (itself a warning to swimmers), a neck which is the narrow current setting away from the shore, and the head where the current broadens and dissipates. To escape a rip current one should swim parallel to the beach.

ripping iron. A caulker's tool used to clear wooden seams of pitch and old oakum before recaulking. Also called a razing iron, reefing iron, or clearing iron.

riprap. Rocks, concrete blocks, or stones dumped together to form a breakwater or groin. Also the resultant structure.

riser. A fore-and-aft plank in a wooden boat that supports the thwarts.

roach. As used by boatmen today, the outward (convex) curve, aft, of the leech of a fore-and-aft mainsail or, more loosely, any curved part of a sail. Also used as a verb meaning to induce more curve in a sail.

roadstead or roads. An offshore anchorage with good holding ground and usually some protection from wind and sea.

Roaring Forties. That part of the ocean between 40 and 50 south latitude famous for almost continuous strong winds, gales, and very high seas resulting from the very long fetch the wind has. *See* brave west winds.

Robin. A one-design centerboard sloop or catboat. LOA 11', beam 4½'. Designer: R.L. Rhodes.

rocker. Describes a boat having a rockered keel; one with a slight convex curve looking at the keel from the outside, bow to stern.

rocking. Persistently rolling a sailboat from side. Not permitted when racing.

roddle. That part of a wire rope clip against which the U-bolt is made fast.

rode. The line or rope on which a boat rides when anchored. Also called an anchor cable or line. An anchored boat is said to be tide-rode when she lies to the tidal current, and wind-rode when her position is determined by the wind.

rodmeter. A retractable device that is lowered through the hull as part of a log, containing either a pitot tube, a propeller, or an induction coil, depending on the type of log.

rogue's yarn. An identification thread of a different color run through the center of one strand of a rope.

rogue wave. Unusually high wave, often with an apparently vertical face, occurring in the open sea, rare, but statistically predictable. It can and does poop and pitchpole boats, sweep people off rocks, jetties, and the decks of ships, smash into the pilot house windows of ocean liners, and in general intimidates all prudent mariners. Also called the ultimate wave.

roll. The rhythmic motion of a boat from side to side around its fore-and-aft or longitudinal axis. Period of roll is the time in seconds from one side to the other and return and is a measure of the stability of the vessel. Sway is a sideways, bodily movement of a ship, while lurching is a deep, abnormal, and sometimes sudden roll. Rolling should not be confused with heeling, listing, or lolling. *See* ship motion.

roller. A long, sometimes nonbreaking swell, usually generated by storms at a distance.

roller chock. One with one or more fixed rollers designed to reduce friction on a line moving in the chock.

roller furler. A mechanical device for rolling a jib around its own luff wire. The procedure is called roller furling. *See* Stoway mast.

roller reef. A reef taken in a sailboat's fore-and-aft sail by rotating the boom, thus winding the foot of the sail around the boom.

roller sheave. One fitted with roller bearings to facilitate turning. Also called a patent sheave.

rolling hitch. A knot used where strain is roughly parallel to the spar or rope to be made fast to. It consists of two round turns and a half hitch.

roll tack, jibe. A procedure for quickly tacking or jibing a sailing dinghy that involves a deliberate deep roll of the boat.

rombowline. Used canvas and cordage that can only be used as chafing gear.

Rooster. A one-design cat-rigged boat with a daggerboard. LOA 9½', beam 4'. Designer: M.P. Smith.

rooster tail. The arching plume of water raised aft by a planing boat moving at speed.

rooting. A sailboat running before big seas may bury her bow from time to time and is then said to be rooting.

rope. In general a word for cordage over 1½ inches in circumference and 21 threads; either fiber or wire. Line is smaller (small stuff, marline, etc.) although in the U.S. Navy all cordage is called line except for specific ropes such as wheel rope, bell rope, etc. Boatmen tend to use the term line only when it is being used afloat for standing and running rigging, and use the term rope when it is coiled in the storeroom or when it is used to secure something. Rope may be braided or prestretched. *See* braid, fiber rope, wire rope.

roping. Same as boltrope; also a collective term for rope.

roping needle. A large sail needle used in sewing boltropes.

rorqual. A large baleen or whalebone whale as different from the toothed whales; like its giant cousin the blue whale, close to extinction.

rose. A circular diagram on a chart. *See* compass rose, wind rose.

rose box. A perforated plate or box used as a strainer over a water inlet, as in a bilge pump, to keep foreign matter out. Also called a strum or strum box.

rose lashing. A special lashing used to make a rope fast to the side of a spar, rail or harpoon. Also called a rose seizing.

rosin. Same as resin.

Ross 13. A one-design centerboard sloop. LOA 13', beam 4½'. Designer: Dean Ross.

Rossel Current. A seasonal ocean current flowing westward and north westward along the coast of New Guinea from May to September.

rotary current. The circular movement of the tidal flow offshore or in a bay caused principally by the rotation of the earth, and is thus clockwise in the northern hemisphere.

rotten stops. Light pieces of basting thread or weak string made fast around a sail to hold it together in bundles or stops when it is sent aloft in stops. A sharp pull on the sheet breaks the stops and thus unfurls the sail, usually a headsail.

rough seas. A turbulent sea state in which waves with combing crests 5–8 feet high are produced by winds of force 5–7 on the Beaufort Scale. Rough seas are lower than high seas.

round. In a nautical sense, with down, in, or up, means to haul on a certain slack rope or tackle. To round to, or up, means to turn a ship or boat into the wind or to heave to. Round in is the opposite of round down or overhaul since it means to bring the blocks of a tackle closer together rather than to separate them. The round of a sail is its convex curvature, as well as the extra cloth added to a sail along its borders.

rounding. Old rope or strands fastened around a rope to prevent chafing.

roundline. Traditionally, small stuff of tarred hemp used for heavy service afloat. It was laid righthanded of three strands, each made up of two yarns.

round turn. A complete turn of a line around a bitt, spar, or cleat, rather than a partial turn, thus there is enough friction to permit the line to be held or checked.

rouse. To haul heavily and with great force on a rope or wire. To rouse out is to wake up and alert, as in: "rouse out the anchor watch."

rouse-about block. A large, all-purpose heavy duty snatch block.

rove. Past tense of reeve.

roving. A bundle of parallel fibers of fiberglass usually woven into a coarse cloth and used in making plastic boats and in waterproofing the decks of wooden boats.

row. To propel a boat with oars. The usual nautical word is pull. A sailor pulls on an oar but hauls on a line or rope. A rowboat is properly called a pulling boat by mariners.

rowlock. Strictly speaking a piece cut out of a boat's gunwale to take an oar but now used by the British as a synonym for crutch, the word the British use when we use oarlock. *See* oarlock.

royal. A squaresail traditionally set next above the topgallant sail and used only in light winds on a square-rigger.

rubber banding. Securing or stopping up a genoa or spinnaker with rubber bands instead of light twine.

rubber snubber. An elastic device to keep boat mooring lines taut. Also used to absorb sudden strain on an anchor rode.

rubbing strip. Any external, longitudinal timber or metal strip extending along most of the side of a ship or boat above the waterline as a protection against abrasion on the sides of piers, docks, or other vessels. Often called a molding and also a rubrail or a rubbing fender, piece or strake.

rudder. The flat, vertical wood or metal slab that pivots at the stern of a vessel and by which it is steered. A drop rudder is a portable rudder for sailboats that extends down far enough to be somewhat effective as a keel or centerboard. A jury rudder is a temporary, improvised one.

rudder braces. A collective term for rudder pintles and gudgeons; also called rudder hangings and rudder irons.

rudder carrier. a fitting placed inboard under the tiller to take the weight and thrust of the rudderstock and tiller. It rests on a rudder bearing.

rudderhead. The upper part or continuation of the rudderstock above the blade on which the quadrant or tiller is fitted.

rudder quadrant. A casting or forging that is part of the rudder structure and with which the turning force is exerted by chains or wire ropes that fit into the grooves of the quadrant. Rigged on opposite sides; as the port wire is pulled the one on the starboard side yields.

rudderstock. The part of a rudder that acts as a vertical shaft through which the turning force of the steering engine or the tiller is exerted.

Rule of Special Circumstance. *See* Special Circumstance.

Rules of the Road. Short term for the International Regulations for Preventing Collision at Sea, also known as Colregs. There are Inland Rules as well Pilot Rules, etc.

rumbowline. *See* rombowline.

rummage. A thorough search for contraband aboard ship.

run. 1. The aftermost, narrowing part of a boat's hull. 2. A day's run is the distance sailed in 24 hours. 3. To go, to move, as to run before a gale. 4. To pass through, as in running a line through a chock. 5. To hoist as in running up the colors. 6. A boat may run aground, run down another boat, or run her easting down, which means to sail east on the latitude of her destination.

runabout. A fast open motorboat used for day cruising, water skiing, etc.

runner. 1. A line fastened at one end to a fixed object, such as an eyebolt, and rove through a single block. 2. Any whip or fall used as a working hoist. 3. A ship or boat used for smuggling. 4. Someone who solicits business for a hotel, bar, etc., from sailors ashore. 5. The running or shifting backstays in a sailboat. 6. A light (one-half-oz.) spinnaker, also called a floater.

running. Usually describes something that moves such as a running bowline that forms a free-sliding bight or running rigging. A heavy sea or surf may be said to be running and the movable part of a rope in a tackle is the running part in contrast to the standing part. A boat is running free when sailing before the wind.

running block. One that moves as opposed to a standing block in a tackle.

running lights. Those required to be shown at night in accordance with the Rules of the Road.

running fix. A fix advanced by dead reckoning to a new position.

running rigging. Ropes, lines, and tackle that move or can move in contrast to fixed or standing rigging.;

S

Sabot. A one-design cat-rigged pram with daggerboard or leeboards. LOA 88', beam 4'. Designers: McCollough, Violette & Campbell.

saddle. A piece of timber having a rounded notch on which a boom or other spar is stowed. *See* boom crutch.

saddle plate. A plate on a mast that may support the jaws of a gaff.

safety factor. A multiple unit of measure that represents the relationship between the breaking strength of a rope, wire, chain, tackle or any structure and its maximum designed working load.

safety message. A voice radio transmission, less urgent than pan but asking priority to pass a message concerning the general safety of navigation. *See* security, security, security.

sag, sagging. The droop or bending in the center of a spar or boat that is supported at both ends. The opposite is hog. A sailboat is said to sag to leeward when she is moved sideways because of wind, sea, or current.

sail. Any piece of fabric made of natural or synthetic fiber that is used to propel something by means of the wind. Fore-and-aft sails may be three- or four-sided and have at least one side made fast to a mast or boom. The bottom of a sail is the foot, the top is the head, the luff is the forward edge, and the leech is the trailing edge. The top corner is the head and the lower forward corner is the tack, the clew is at the bottom aft. Sailboats use working sails for normal sailing, light sails for racing in light air, and storm sails in heavy weather.

sail, to. To go on the water even under power is to sail. "The ship sails at dawn." To travel in a ship or to direct a sailboat is to sail. For recreation people often go for a sail.

Sailaway. A one-design centerboard sloop. LOA 11', beam 5'. Designer: Pearson Brothers.

sailboard. *See* boardboat.

sailcloth. Once 100% cotton or linen, now synthetic fibers such as Dacron, nylon, Kevlar are used as well.

saildrive. An auxiliary propulsion system for sailboats in which a unit similar to the lower part of an outboard motor projects below the hull.

sailfish. A warmwater gamefish with a beak similar to that of a swordfish; distinguished by a prominent dorsal fin called its sail.

Sailfish. A one-design lateen-rigged boardboat with centerboard. LOA 12', beam 3'. Designer: Alcort Inc.

sail ho. The traditional cry of the lookout at sea on sighting another ship.

sailhook. A sailmaker's tool for holding the canvas taut while it is being worked on. Also called a bench hook.

Sailing Directions. Publications of the Defense Mapping Agency Hydrographic Center providing detailed information about the coasts of the world and adjacent waters. They now include Planning Guides and Enroute Directions.

sailing master. Anyone in charge of the shiphandling and navigation of a sailboat who is not in command. Boatowners who are not yet experienced often have sailing masters aboard.

sailing on her own bottom. Said of a boat that is fully paid for.

sailing thwart. In a sailboat it is the fore-and-aft plank on top of the thwarts through which the mast is stepped. it is also called a gangplank, a gangboard, and a mast carling.

sail loft. An area or building where sails are made.

sailmaker. Traditionally a man who makes and repairs sails, cutting and sewing by hand with palm and needle.

sail needle. A heavy needle, triangular in cross-section pushed through canvas by means of a leather palm worn by the sailmaker.

sailor. In general terms anyone who goes to sea as a profession or as a hobby. Specifically it is a person who works afloat under officers, mates, or petty officers.

sailor's knot. A square or reef knot.

sailover. A boat race in which only one boat starts and finishes.

sail plan. A side view, drawn to scale, of a sailboat with sails set.

sails, cut of. The cloths or panels sewn together to make a sail run up and down in a vertical cut, at right angles to the leech in a crosscut sail and in both directions in a miter cut. *See* miter.

salina. A salt marsh separated from the sea but flooded at high water.

Saint Elmo's Fire. Same as corposant.

sally. To sally a boat is to cause it to roll by having the crew move from side to side in unison. Useful for helping to free a boat aground.

salmon. A valuable food and game fish of the family that includes trout and char. Salmon maintain a pelagic life but return to their natal river to spawn. The Pacific salmon does not return to the sea after spawning but the Atlantic salmon does.

salt, salty. A sailor is a salt, especially at a certain age, an old salt. Salty means sea-going, nautical, raffish, cocky, and sometimes earthy.

salting. The old custom of filling open spaces in a wooden vessel with salt to inhibit rot, particularly between frame timbers.

salvage. Normally a service rendered voluntarily to save lives and vessels at sea or performed under contract on a no-cure no-pay basis by professionals using special ships and equipment. The property saved is called salvage. Anyone putting a line aboard a stranded vessel may claim salvage unless an agreement is reached beforehand.

sampan. A general word in the Far East for a small boat used to carry people and cargo.

sampson post. Traditionally a short vertical timber or metal bar forward of the mast on a sailboat to which the anchor cable or rode is made fast. Also called a kingpost or deck cleat.

samson line. A three-strand, nine-thread rope for heavy duty, somewhat larger than a round line.

sandspit. A long narrow projecting piece of sandy shoreline.

San Juan 24. A one-design keel sloop. LOA 24', beam 8', draft 4'.

sand strake. *See* garboard strake.

Santana 20. A one-design keel sloop. LOA 22', beam 8', draft 4'. Designer: Shad Turner.

santa ana. A strong easterly desert wind that is sandy, dry, and warm. It periodically blows off the coast of Southern California mostly in the winter and is responsible for remarkable mirages offshore.

Santa Cruz 27. A one-design keel sloop. LOA 27', beam 8', draft 4½'. Designer: Bill Lee.

SAR. Search And Rescue.

sardine. A small fish related to the herring. Also the young of the European pilchard when large enough for canning.

Sargasso Sea. A relatively calm area of the North Atlantic, south of Bermuda to latitude 25° N, between longitudes 40° and 65° W, the vortex of the general clockwise circulation of water part of which is the Gulf Stream System.

sargassum. The yellow floating seaweed of the Sargasso Sea and the Gulf Stream System.

SARSAT. Search And Rescue Satellite-Aided Tracking.

save-all. A rope net or canvas spread under a brow or under a cargo net and used to catch material that might fall overboard.

scale. A large-scaled chart shows a small part of the coast in large dimensions thereby making piloting easier. A small-scaled chart is normally used for passages at sea and shows a large area on a relatively small piece of chart.

scallop. A bivalve mollusk that is highly esteemed for food.

scandalize. To spill wind or reduce sail area by any unusual method such as dropping the peak of a fore-and-aft sail.

scantling (s). The dimensions of all structural parts of a ship such as frames, girders, platings. These are published for various types of ships by the classification authorities. Full scantling means ship construction of maximum strength.

scarf. The joining or scarfing of two pieces of wood or metal end-to-end or side-by-side produces a scarf or jog.

scend. The amplitude of the upward vertical motion of a ship when heaving or pitching. Sometimes spelled send. As a verb—to rise or heave upward.

Schock 22. A one-design keel and centerboard sloop. LOA 22', beam 7½'. Designer: W.D. Schock.

Schock 25. A one-design keel sloop. LOA 25', beam 7', draft 4'. Designer: Seymour Paul.

schooner. A fore-and-aft rigged sailboat, normally with two masts, the foremast shorter than the mainmast.

schooner guy. *See* lazy guy.

S Class. A one-design racing and family keel sloop. LOA 27½', beam 7'. Designer: Nathaniel Herreshoff.

Scooter. A small, simple, low-speed pleasure boat for use in sheltered waters.

scope. The length of the anchor rode from the boat out to the anchor or to a mooring. Greater riding scope is used at anchor in strong winds to reduce the angle between the rode and the horizontal plane at the anchor and thus increase holding power. Also short for oscilloscope, the display instrument of a radar.

score. A groove made in the cheeks of a wooden block to hold the strap. Any groove, notch, or cut-away section in a spar, rudder, or deadeye.

Scotch cut. A miter-cut sail in which the cloths or pieces lie parallel to leech and foot, meeting at a center seam bisecting the clew.

Scotchman. A batten or board made fast in the rigging to prevent chafing.

scouring basin. In a tidal lock system, it is a bay or lock in which water is retained until needed at low water to scour or flush out the dock or channel.

scow. A flat-bottom vessel with square sloping ends and no power. As a general service boat it is stable, easy to build, and to beach. Variations are known as John boat, bateau, flatboat, pram, punt, and square-ender. In U.S. inland waters sailing scows are fast, shallow-draft sailboats with twin rudders and twin bilgeboards. *See* inland lake scow. Large scows are used as barges, lighters, houseboats, and often carry pile-driving and dredging machinery. Scow, lighter, and barge are often used interchangeably in accordance with local usage.

scowing. *See* becue.

screw. Another word for propeller.

screw anchor. An anchor set down into soft mud to hold a mooring.

screw current. The moving water generated by a turning propeller.

screw log. A device streamed astern that is used to measure speed and thus distance. A rotor or screw turns the tow line that registers on a counter. Also called a taffrail log, a patent log, a towing log, or a mechanical log.

scrimshaw. Pictures and designs carved on whalebone or on the teeth of whales or sharks or other animal ivory: the figures or objects thus carved.

SCUBA. Self-Contained Underwater Breathing Apparatus.

scud. Loose, vapory fragments of low clouds moving rapidly, often beneath rain clouds. To scud before a storm is to head down wind with enough sail to maintain steering control.

scull. A light, spoon-bladed oar used to propel a very light racing shell, also (sometimes) called a scull. To scull with an oar is to use it over the stern of a boat.

scupper. A deck drain used to carry off rain and sea water either directly as on the weather deck or through scupper pipes or hoses that discharge through the hull. Also known as a freeing port.

scuttle. 1. A small opening in a bulkhead or in the deck, usually fitted with a cover. 2. The cover that fits over the opening. 3. A ventilating air scoop rigged in a deck opening. 4. The British word for airport. To scuttle a vessel is to sink it deliberately.

sea anchor. 1. Any designed or improvised floating or partly submerged device that is used to hold a boat's bow up to the wind and sea in heavy weather. 2. A drag sail or drift sail. 3. When referred to as a drogue it performs a different function. *See* drogue.

sea bag. The traditional cylindrical canvas bag in which sailors carry their clothes and personal gear.

seaboard. Along the coast; near the sea.

sea breeze. *See* breeze.

Seabright skiff. A small open sailing and rowing boat developed in New Jersey waters. Boats now being evolved from this old design are called Jersey sea skiffs.

sea buoy. The buoy that is the furthest out at sea to indicate a channel or an entrance. Also called the farewell, departure, or landfall buoy.

sea chest. Traditionally a box in which a sailor stows his gear aboard ship.

seacock. Any opening through the hull of a boat that can be opened and closed. Also a valve fitted to the saltwater intake line; a sea valve.

sea cow. A manatee or dugong, an aquatic, weed-eating mammal.

sea dog. An older, experienced sailor.

sea eagle. A fish-eating bird of prey such as an osprey.

sea elephant. The largest of the seals, up to 20 feet in length with a long snout. Also called an elephant seal.

seafarer. A person who goes to sea as his profession or hobby.

sea fire. A brilliant display of bioluminescence near the surface of the sea that is usually seen on a dark night.

Sea Fury. A one-design sloop with twin keels. LOA 21', beam 7', draft 2'. Designer: D.H. Meeusen.

seagoing. Describes a person, boat, or any other object that goes to sea or that is fit and able to do so. Also nautical, salty.

sea horse. A small fish that has a head and upper body suggestive of a horse, a prehensile tail, and that swims upright in warm waters.

sea kindly. Describes a boat that endures heavy weather without excessive discomfort for her crew.

seal. A sea-going, fast-swimming, intelligent mammal that lives on fish.

sea ladder. *See* ladder.

sea legs. The ability to accommodate to a boat's motion at sea. Usually a person acquires his sea legs after a few days and may lose them again when ashore.

sea lion. A seal having small external ears, and up to 12 feet in length (the Stella sea lion).

seaman. In a broad sense, any person who works aboard ship. Under U.S. law a seaman is any person, other than an apprentice, who is employed or engaged in any capacity aboard a vessel owned by a U.S. citizen.

seaman's eye. A mariner's ability to judge speed, distance, wind, and sea in all aspects of boat handling.

seamanship. The art and science of managing, operating, and maintaining ships and boats and their gear.

seamark. In the broadest sense, any object ashore—a landmark as seen from the sea, or a floating object such as a buoy used to assist in navigation and piloting.

sea mosquitoes. Tiny, ferocious, tropical isopods, sort of planktonic crabs, whose claws tear off minute bits of flesh when they attack a diver underwater in large numbers.

sea otter. A saltwater marine mammal that lives in the giant kelp forests of the Pacific Northwest. About the size of a dog, it must eat 20% of its weight daily in mollusks, particularly sea urchins, in order to maintain body warmth since it does not have a layer of blubber.

sea painter. A long line leading from the bow of a lifeboat well forward; used in lowering and hoisting to control the boat alongside.

sea puss. A dangerous longshore current, or a strong rip current, or the channel scoured through a bar by such a current.

Search and Rescue (SAR). The carefully organized and courageously implemented operations of the U.S. Coast Guard in assisting those in danger and distress at sea.

Search and Rescue Satellite-Aided Tracking (SARSAT). An international project using weather satellites as listening and relay stations for EPIRB and ELT signals.

sea return. Interference on a radar screen caused by radar reflections from waves. Also called clutter.

sea roach. *See* gribble.

sea room. Space afloat to maneuver a ship or boat or to ride out a storm.

Seasat. A U.S. ocean-watching satellite that scans 90% of the world's sea surface and broadcasts data on sea state, wind, current, schools of fish, etc.

Sea Shell. A one-design cat-rigged plywood pram with the daggerboard. LOA 8', beam 4'.

seasickness. Nausea, often violent, caused by the disturbance of boat motion of the body's balancing mechanism found in the ear's semicircular canals. There is no real cure for those strongly afflicted except long periods at sea or going ashore. *See* Stugeron.

sea slick. An area of the surface of the sea that has an oily appearance or a different color. If not man-made pollution it is usually caused by blooming plankton.

sea snake. A sea-going reptile, related to the cobra and venomous. Most live in tropical waters or the Indian Ocean and the Western Pacific, some range the ocean, and some live near shore where, as in Malaysia, they are a danger to people bathing and surfing.

Sea Spray. A one-design sloop rigged catamaran. LOA 15', beam 6½'. Designer: Alan Arnold.

sea state. The wave conditions of the surface of the sea. The World Meteorological Organization has a widely accepted table which states: "Read code number for sea state, description and mean maximum wave height. 0 glassy calm 0; 1 calm (ripples) 0–1; 2 smooth (wavelets) 1–2; 3 slight 2–4; 4 moderate 4–8; 5 rough 8–13; 6 very rough 13–20; 7 high 20–30; 8 very high 30–45; 9 phenomenal over 45. Figures for wave height are in feet." *See* wave, wave height.

sea stores. Tax-free goods such as tobacco and spirits for use only when the boat is at sea.

seat. The fore-and-aft bench in the cockpit of a boat.

Seattle head. The galley smoke pipe, Charlie Noble, that is seen on boats. It is a metal pipe in the shape of a T with the two ends of the cross-piece slanted down to keep out spray and rain.

sea turtles. Any of the large marine reptiles whose feet have evolved into flippers for swimming. There are loggerhead, leatherback, hawksbill, green, and Ridley turtles, all endangered species nearing extinction.

sea urchin. An echinoderm, an animal with a hard shell and many spines that lives on the ocean floor and is fond of the holdfasts of kelp. Europeans and Orientals consider their eggs a delicacy and so do sea otter and lobsters.

sea valve. Any valve or cock close to a boat's skin that controls the passage of a liquid. Also called an outboard valve or a skin valve.

seawall. A stone structure, usually solid, built along the waterfront to prevent encroachment by the sea. It often acts as a road and as a pier for boats. *See* jetty.

seaward. Towards the sea.

seaway. At sea; afloat in the ocean. A sea kindly boat is dry and comfortable in a seaway.

seaweed. A general word for marine algae and grass growing in the sea either attached to the bottom as kelp is, or free floating like sargassum.

Sea Witch. One-design centerboard sloop. LOA 12', beam 4½'. Designers: Lockley & Evans.

seaworthy. Capable of safe operation or usage at sea.

sea wrack. Any material cast up on a beach or shore, such as seaweed.

secret block. One which is closed at the top or swallow; the rope or wire enters through holes in the shell of the block. This arrangement prevents fouling adjacent gear.

secure. *vb.* To make fast, lash tight, lock up, stop, or cease. *Adj.* safe, as in, secure berth.

security, security, security. Preface to a voice radio safety message requesting priority to broadcast a message concerning the safety of navigation. Less urgent than pan. Spoken: securi-tay."

seiche. A standing wave oscillation in an enclosed body of water such as a harbor, that often moves boats and ships about so violently that mooring lines are parted as the water level rises and falls rapidly. It is a harmonic vibration in response to waves, storms. or underwater seismic disturbances outside the harbor.

seine. a portable net used to encircle and haul in fish. It is supported by a floatline or corkline and held vertical by a weighted footrope or leadline.

seiner. A boat used for seining.

seismic sea wave. A wave of large amplitude and long period, often very destructive, caused by seaquakes, volcanic explosions, or large earth movements underwater. They are popularly called tsunami or tidal waves although there is nothing tidal involved.

seize. To bind, lash, or make fast a rope to another or to a spar by using small stuff or seizing.

selatan. A strong south wind of the northern Celebes during the monsoon season.

self-bailing cockpit. One designed to drain itself if flooded. Also called a self-draining or self-emptying cockpit.

self-righting boat. A specially designed rescue boat with buoyancy tanks and a heavy keel that is used by the Coast Guard. It rights itself if capsized by a breaking wave.

self-tacking jib. One with a clew that moves on a traveler when tacking, thus eliminating jib sheets. *See* club-footed jib.

selvage. The edges of a net or piece of canvas, particularly the latter when woven so as to prevent unravelling. Also selvedge.

semicircular deviation. *See* deviation.

semidiameter (correction). A correction of sextant altitude needed to determine the altitude of the moon or the sun since they both have a sensible diameter; the upper or lower limb is seen on the horizon through a sextant and not the center.

semidiurnal. Having a period or cycle of half a lunar day. Tides and tidal currents are normally semidiurnal, having two floods and two ebbs each day.

Senhouse slip. *See* pelican hook.

sentinel. A weight used to increase the holding power of the anchor of a boat. *See* kellet.

serve, serving. To wrap around with tight turns as in serving a hawser with marlin. *See* worm, parcel, and serve.

service. The small stuff used in serving.

serving mallet. A wooden hammerlike instrument used to pass a serving around a rope on top of the parceling.

SES. Surface Effect Ship.

set. 1. The direction towards which a current is flowing. 2. A boat deflected from its steered course by wind, sea, or current is said to be set and the amount of the deflection may be called set or drift. 3. A sail is hoisted and set. 4. A ship sets sail after setting the first watch. 5. A draft, hoist, or sling of cargo is a set or sett.

set flying. *See* flying.

sett. *See* set.

set taut, set up. To take in the slack; to tighten as in "set up the jib halyard."

setting pole. One used to push a boat along in shallow water.

settee rig. A four-sided lateen sail with a very short luff.

seventh-eighths rig. *See* masthead rig.

Seven Eleven. A one-design centerboard catboat. LOA 8', beam 4'. Designer: Robert Baker.

Seven Seas. The North and South Atlantic, North and South Pacific, Indian Ocean, the Arctic and Antarctic Oceans.

sextant. A portable, reflecting, hand-held instrument used to measure angles, particularly in celestial navigation, in observing the altitudes of heavenly bodies. By measuring the horizontal angle between seamarks the ship's position can be fixed. A sextant has a length of arc of 60° or one-sixth of a circle although with its reflecting mirror it can measure angles up to 120°. The sextant is the successor to the octant and the quadrant.

shackle. Any metal fitting or link, roughly U- or D-shaped, used to connect or attach wire, rope, chain, sails, etc.; has a removable pin or a spring-loaded pin across its mouth. Sometimes called a clevis. Modern shackles used in sailboats have a great variety of shapes, sizes, closing mechanisms, and trade names. *See* anchor, bending, connecting, kenter, mooring, snap hook, swivel, and upset shackle.

shad. An important food fish found in North American rivers, a member of the herring family but larger and noted for its roe.

shake. 1. Cracks and flaws in timber caused by growth defects or too rapid drying. 2. To shake a sailboat is to bring her up so far into the wind that the sails shiver. 3. To shake out a reef is to release the reef points and set taut the halyard.

shaksl. *See* kaus.

shallow water effect. The difficulty in steering and the increased resistance to forward movement of a ship or boat in shoal water.

shamal. The dry northwesterly wind of the Arabian Gulf that blows for long periods year around.

shank. The main or center shaft of an old-fashioned anchor.

shape. A ball, cone, drum, basket, or similar object made of light metal or canvas as required by the Rules of the Road to be hoisted in the rigging of ships at anchor, fishing, dredging, etc.

shark. A variety of fish with multiple gill slits and cartilage instead of bone as a skeleton. There are some 250 species worldwide of which only a dozen are known to attack people. Of these the great white shark is the worst, followed by the hammerhead. The largest, the basking shark, is a placid giant who feeds on plankton, small fish, squid, etc. Most sharks are scavengers but a few will take bait. Among the gamefish are the blue, mako, white, porbeagle, thresher and tiger sharks.

Shark. A one-design catboat with a centerboard. LOA 14', beam 3'. Designer: W.A. DeLong.

shark billy. A short stick fitted with nails at one end used by divers to fend off small aggressive sharks.

sharpie. A distinctive, long (about 30') flat-bottom, centerboard, often schooner-rigged sailboat found along the east coast of the U.S. It originated in Connecticut about 1850.

Shearwater. A one-design sloop-rigged centerboard catamaran. LOA 16½', beam 7½'. Designer: Prout Bros.

sheathing. 1. A covering of thin copper, zinc or galvanized iron once widely used over wooden hulls to protect them from marine worms. Now replaced by poisonous paints. 2. Extra planking around the waterline as ice protection. **3.** A thin layer of reinforced plastic over a hull or deck.

sheave. A grooved wheel in a block over which a rope or wire passes. Some are a solid disc, others have spokes and are called spoke sheaves. Modern blocks have ball bearings to assist the rotation of the sheave. Pronounced shiv.

sheepshank. A hitch made in a line to shorten it, formed by making a long bight or loop and passing a half hitch over both ends.

sheer. **1.** The upward curvature of a boat's deck from amidships to each end. **2.** A sudden shift or change of heading of a vessel due to natural causes such as shallow water. To sheer off is to steer away from.

sheer batten. *See* sheer pole.

sheer cleat. *See* whaleboat chock.

sheer molding. Molding on the outside of the hull that follows the upper deck line. Also called a sheer rail.

sheer pole. An iron bar or wooden batten seized across the shrouds of a large sailing ship above the upper deadeyes or turnbuckles. It served as the first ratline, was often fitted to hold belaying pins, and was also called a sheer batten.

sheer rail. Same as sheer molding. *Also see* guard rail.

sheer ratline. Every fifth ratline that extended to the after shroud of a large sailboat.

sheers, sheer legs. A tripod arrangement, usually temporary, of spars rigged to lift a weight.

sheet. A rope, tackle, or chain with which a sail is held, hauled flat, eased, sheeted home, or otherwise trimmed. Headsheets are those used with headsails. A sailor never belays a sheet.

sheet anchor. A spare anchor, the largest one aboard, once carried in the waist of a ship for emergencies.

shelf. Timbers that follow the sheer of a wooden ship or boat and are fastened to the underside of the deck beams to strengthen and support the deck.

shell. 1. The wooden, plastic, or metal casing of a block in which the sheaves revolve. 2. The outer hull of a ship, short for shell plating. 3. A light, narrow-pulling boat fitted with oarlocks on outriggers and sliding seats, used for racing.

shellback. Anyone who has crossed the Equator in a boat or ship; an old salt.

shelter cabin. A partial cabin over the tiller or wheel of a small pleasure boat.

SHF. *See* super high frequency.

Shields. A one-design keel sloop. LOA 30′, beam 6½′, draft 5′. Designer: Sparkman & Stephens.

shift. To change or to move, as the wind shifts or the ship shifts berths in the harbor. The cost of such a move assisted by a tug is a shift.

shift the rudder. An order to the helmsman to apply the same amount of rudder to the opposite side.

shifting backstay. *See* backstay.

shifting chock. *See* chock.

shingle. A wedge-shaped piece of wood or plastic fastened to the bottom of a powerboat to improve her trim and thus help her to plane.

ship. Any decked vessel used in the open sea. Traditionally a ship was square-rigged and had three or more masts, while other rigs with various numbers of masts and combinations of sails were called barks, brigantines, schooners, brigs, etc. Modern ships are, for the most part, either Naval or merchant. To ship water is to take it aboard accidentally, to ship a rudder or an oar is to put it into place.

shiphandling. The art and skill of directing the movements of a ship especially under difficult circumstances in congested waters, in poor visibility, strong winds, etc.

shipmate. A fellow sailor in the same boat or ship.

ship motion. Heave (up and down), sway (sideways), and surge (fore-and-aft) are translational movements in which the whole ship moves bodily. *See* scend. Roll, pitch, and yaw are rotational movements about different axes in which the ship's center of gravity is not displaced. Lurching, listing, heeling, and lolling are associated with rolling and are also rotational.

shipping board clamps. Threaded U–shaped fittings with an end-piece that is fastened with two bolts; used to join wire rope or to make an eye. Also called clips.

ship-rigged. Having all masts fitted with yards and squaresails.

ship's company. All hands; everyone on board except passengers.

shipshape. Neat, orderly, well-stowed, free of Irish pennants and stray gear. Sometimes expressed as "shipshape and Bristol fashion."

Ship's Inertial Navigation System (SINS). Developed by the U.S. Navy as a very accurate, all-weather, dead reckoning system of navigation. It uses gyroscopes, accelerometers, and associated electronics to sense and record every change of course and speed of a ship and then computes continuously the ship's position.

ship's name. Every vessel, including registered yachts, must have an assigned name and number. The name and home port should be shown on the stern.

ship's papers. Those required by law that include the ship's certificate of registry, clearance certificate, manifest, bills of lading, charter party, and official logbook.

ship's time. At sea a ship or a boat making a crossing keeps time according to its longitude which determines the zone time. *See* zone time. Traditionally the ship's bell is struck every half hour in groups of two strokes, followed, if appropriate, by one stroke. One bell is 12:30, 4:30 (16:30) and 8:30 (20:30), both A.M. and P.M.; 2 bells for 1:00 (13:00) 5:00 (17:00) and 9:00 (21:00); 3 bells for 1:30 (13:30) etc., until 8 bells are struck indicating noon, midnight, 4:00 (16:00), and 8:00 (20:00). Thus a complete cycle is struck every 4 hours.

ship's stores. *See* sea stores.

shipworm. A marine mollusk that, when young and small, bores a tiny hole into a wooden boat below the waterline and then eats its way, with the grain of the wood, into an adult of 8 inches or so. Metal sheathing was once used as protection, but poisonous paints now protect the hull.

shoal. 1. A submerged ridge, bank, or bar of mud, sand, or gravel near enough to the surface (less than 10 fathoms) to be a hazard to navigation. If composed of rock or coral it is a reef. As water becomes shallower it is said to shoal or become shoal water. 2. A school or concentration of fish. Shoal draft describes a vessel with minimum draft, well suited to shallow waters.

shock cord. An elastic line that stretches easily and is sometimes fitted with a hook at one end. It has various uses on deck for securing lines and halyards from slatting about. Also called a snubber.

shoe. 1. The horizontal connection between the heel of the rudderpost and that of the sternpost in a single screw ship; called a skeg in a boat. It is usually for protection under the keel. To shoe an anchor was an old practice of bolting timbers to the flukes of an anchor in order to improve holding power in a muddy bottom.

shole. A flat piece of wood or steel placed under the keel or the bottom of a shore. Also called a sole block.

shoot. To shoot the sun or other celestial body is slang for measuring its altitude. In sailing to turn into the wind and maintain headway by momentum.

shooter. *See* blooper.

SHORAN. SHOrt RAnge Navigation; a precise short-range electronic system that uses the time divergence of pulse type transmissions from two or more fixed stations. Used in surveying and oceanographic research.

shore. 1. The land along the edge of a body of water. 2. A prop or timber fixed under a boat's bottom or along her side that keeps her upright while in drydock or on a marine railway.

short blast. One on a ship's whistle, siren, or on a boat's horn that, according to the International Rules of the Road, has a duration of about 1 second. *See* blast.

short sheet. A length of line, normally with an open hook at one end, that can be used to hold a sheet or other line temporarily to free a winch for another task, or can do any other odd job about a sailboat.

short stay. Said of an anchor when it has been hauled in to the point of just starting to break ground.

short splice. A method of joining two ends of rope resulting in a strong but thick splice that may not pass through a block.

shoulder. The rounded protruding sections just abaft the stem of a boat.

shoulder block. One with a projection near its upper end so that it can rest against something such as a spar without jamming the rope.

shove off. Nautical expression for depart or go.

shroud. Rope, wire or metal rods providing lateral support for the mast of a sailboat. Often fitted with ratlines so that men can climb aloft.

shroud rollers. Split tubes of wood or plastic fastened to the shrouds to reduce chafing of sails and rigging.

shutter. The detachable portion of the gunwale of a wooden pulling boat in the way of the oarlocks. Also the last plank to be fitted in carvel-planked construction.

side coaming. One of the fore-and-aft coamings or protective low metal edges around a hatch.

sidelights. The red (port) and green (starboard) 112.5° lights required by the Rules of the Road to be visible from ahead on all ships underway at night. Part of the running lights.

sideport. *See* port.

sidereal. Of or pertaining to the stars.

sidereal time. Used by navigators to locate and identify stars; a measurement in relation to a fixed star instead of the sun.

sidescuttle. Same as scuttle, the British word for airport.

sidewall craft. An air-cushion vehicle for over water use only. The skirts on the side are rigid and project just below the surface.

sight. An accurately timed sextant altitude of a heavenly body that is used to determine the observer's position. To sight the anchor is to heave it short and close enough to see whether it is foul or clear. If clear it may be dropped again.

sight reduction table. A compilation of the data needed by a navigator to solve the astronomical triangle after he takes a sight. Published by the Defense Mapping Agency Hydrographic Office, these tables have such numbers as 249 without the old prefix H.O.

Signal of Doubt. *See* danger signal.

simoom. A short and very violent sandy wind storm off the coast of the Arabian peninsula and off the Syrian and Sahara deserts. Also simoon.

single banked. A pulling boat in which one oarsman sits on each thwart; with two men on a thwart the boat is double banked.

single-hander. A sailboat operated by one person. Also the person sailing that boat.

Single Sideband (SSB). A modern and efficient system of voice radio communication using one of the bands of frequencies on either side of the carrier of a modulated wave.

SINS. Ships Inertial Navigation System.

sirocco. The ancient but still used name for the warm, dry, southerly wind that blows off the North African desert to the Mediterranean. The word is also used more generally to mean any hot dry wind.

sisal. A variety of natural fiber derived from the henequen plant found in Mexico and once used for cordage. Next in strength to manila among the natural fibers it is little used today by boatmen.

sister block. One having two sheaves both in the same plane; either side by side as in a sheet block, or one above the other as in a long-tailed block or tandem block. *See* block, fiddle block.

sister hooks. Two partial circles of metal suspended from the same link or eye. When in use the parts close and hold as long as there is tension; used about the deck for securing various lines and small tackles. Also called clasp hook, clip hook, clove hook, match hook, sister clip.

Six meter. A racing sloop designed to rate 6 meters (actual LOA 37′). Now regaining some of its former popularity in international competition. Beam 6′, draft 5½′. A development class. Original designers: Burgess & Gardner.

skeet. A long-handled dipper used to wet down the sides and deck of a boat in hot weather or to wet the sails in very light airs.

skeg. Aftermost and deepest part of the deadwood or after structure of a boat's hull; the projection of the keel on which the rudder may at times be stepped and which protects a propeller. Also a knee timber that connects and braces the stern post and keel of a wooden boat. In modern sailboats often a hull appendage just forward of the rudder helping to support, protect or streamline it.

skew. Propeller blades that are tilted aft are skewed.

skids. Boat skids are a framework on deck that hold the cradle or saddle in which a boat is stowed and held down by gripes.

skiff. Any small open boat of simple construction, usually lapstrake with a sharp bow and a square stern.

skin. The plating or hull covering of a boat; sometimes the inner skin is called ceiling. The last bit of sail left exposed when furling a sail. To skin or skin up a sail is to furl it neatly.

skin boat. A boat made with a wooden frame covered with skins. Still used in the Arctic; and was once common in Ireland and Scotland.

skin drag. The resistance or water drag of something such as a boat moving in water due to the boundary layer of water dragged along by skin friction. Also called skin resistance.

Skipjack. A one-design centerboard sloop. LOA 15′, beam 5¼′. Designer: Carter Pyle.

skipjack. The traditional broad beamed V-bottomed, clipper-bowed, center-board sailboat used on the Atlantic coast, particularly Chesapeake Bay where it originated. It has a raked mast and was once widely used for fishing and oystering; smaller than a buckeye, it is now often used as a yacht.

skipper. Generally and colloquially used to refer to and address any master, captain, owner, or commanding officer. If a yacht has a paid captain he is known as the captain, while the owner or the amateur in charge is known as the skipper.

skysail. A triangular racing sail used between the masts of a schooner.

skyscraper. In a square-rigger a small triangular sail set above the skysail in very light winds. *See* kites.

skywave. A radio wave that has been reflected from the ionosphere in contrast to a ground wave.

slab reefing. Now popular in racing and cruising sailboats, this fast system uses reef holes in the sail instead of reef points. Lines are run from the tack and clew cringles through cheek blocks to a winch and to cam cleats on the boom, and then the lines are passed through the reef holes and around the boom. Also called jiffy reefing.

slack. *n.* To take in the slack is to haul on a line until it is taut. *adj.* Loose as in a slack rope, opposite of taut. *vb.* To slack a line is to let it out, ease the strain but not let it run or cast it off. A sailboat is said to be slack when she tends to fall away from the wind; the opposite of ardent.

slack water. The interval during which the tidal current is zero or very weak, usually during the reversal of the tide, but it can occur at any time. Sometimes called slack tide.

slamming. The pounding of a boat's hull against the seas when she is pitching so heavily that structural damage is possible. More violent than pounding.

slant. A course taken by a sailboat under a favorable wind.

slant of wind. A duration of fair wind.

slat. To flap, as a loose sail or awning shakes and slaps, particularly when a boat is becalmed.

slave jib. One set more or less permanently.

slave station. One of the subordinate transmitting stations in Loran.

sleeper. 1. One of the heavy timbers forming the foundation of a building way or slipway. 2. One of the curved or angled timbers or knees used to strengthen the stern framing of a wooden boat. 3. A deadhead or nearly submerged log.

sleeper seats. Seats in pleasure boats that can be used as beds.

slice. A long hardwood wedge used as a launching tool to raise a boat off the ways before launching.

slide. A small metal fitting that attaches the luff of a sail to a boom or mast track on which it moves as the sail is set or lowered. Also called a clip or car.

sliding keel. *See* centerboard.

sliding way. *See* launching cradle.

sling. Any arrangement of rope, chain, or canvas used at the end of a boom or crane to lift cargo. The load or draft is sometimes also called a sling as well as a hoist or set.

slip. *n.* 1. The open water between two piers or between two structures as in a ferry slip. 2. Short for slipway. *vb.* To release, to let run. To slip an anchor cable was to release it aboard ship, buoying the anchor for recovery later, all in the interest of a quick departure.

slip, propeller. The difference between the distance actually made good by a boat and that theoretically possible due to the pitch of the propeller.

slip hook. Same as cable stopper, pelican hook and senhouse slip. *See* pelican hook.

slip knot. A simple knot that can be released easily, such as a reef knot with a bow. Also a knot in which a loop slides along the standing part as a running bowline.

slip or slippery hitch. A hitch around a cleat in which the end of the line forms a loop under the last turn. A pull on the end will release the hitch.

slip rope. Rope that can be released quickly, such as the one that is passed from deck through the ring on the mooring buoy and back on deck before releasing the cable or wire attached to the buoy. When ready to go the end of the slip rope on deck is let go.

slip stopper. *See* chain stopper.

slipway. The inclined surface of a shipyard that holds the cradle in which the ship is built and on which it is launched by sliding down into the water. The fixed structure is the groundway and the moving part is the sliding or launching way.

slob ice. An accumulation of sludge ice so dense that it prevents the passage of small boats.

sloop. In modern U.S. usage a single-masted sailboat, similar to a cutter but with fewer headsails because a sloop's mast is set farther forward than that of a cutter. The British define sloop as a single-masted sailboat with one headsail. *See* cutter.

slop. Excessive clearance or play, as in a winch bearing.

slot. The area on a sailboat between the after part of the headsail and the leeward side of the mainsail.

slot effect. The guidance of the wind abaft the headsails and around to the lee side of the mainsail thereby increasing the efficiency and pulling power of the sails.

slough. *See* bayou or marsh.

sludge ice. A mixture of small spongy ice lumps, snow and sea water having a greasy appearance; the initial stage in the freezing of sea water. Also called slush ice.

slue, slew. 1. To twist or turn something especially a boom or mast. 2. To sheer or yaw from side to side as a ship at anchor does in strong wind. 3. A towed barge may slew as it takes a sheer in a channel. 4. A backwater or side channel (slough).

sluice. An opening in the lower part of a bulkhead to permit the passage of a liquid.

slush ice. *See* sludge ice.

Small Craft Advisory. A warning of winds 18 knots or higher issued by the NWS.

small. To steer small is to use minimum rudder to keep the course.

small stores. Items of personal convenience such as tobacco and toiletries, sold aboard ship.

small stuff. The general term for line and cordage up to 15-thread ratline stuff, including marline, spunyarn, etc., used for light lashings and seizings.

snap block. *See* snatch block.

snaphook. A metal hank or hook closed by a spring snap generally used for bending on headsails such as jibs to their stays. Also called a springhook, a piston hank or snapshackle.

snapshackle. *See* snaphook.

snatch block. A block whose shell opens to take the loop or bight of a line making it unnecessary to find the end of the line and feed it through. Used on cunninghams, foreguys, preventers, sheets, vangs, etc. Also called a notch block, return block, or snap block.

snatch cleat. One with a single horn instead of two, often used as a fairlead. Same as a thumb cleat.

snatch line. A short line made fast to a spinnaker sheet to assist in trimming.

sneak boat. A very shallow draft scow-like sailboat of the coast of New Jersey and adjacent states. Used also without sails to hunt wildfowl. Also called sneakbox or box. *See* Barnegat Bay sneakbox.

Snipe. A one-design centerboard sloop. LOA 15½′, beam 5′. Designer: W.F. Crosby. The largest class in the world with over 24,000 boats.

snorter. A strong gale at sea, particularly in the winter in the North Atlantic. A variant of snotter.

snotter. A spinnaker pole bell, the fitting that holds a spinnaker pole on deck. Also the fitting that secures the stick-boom of a leg-of-mutton sail or spritsail to the mast is a snotter.

Snowbird. A one-design cat-rigged centerboard dinghy. LOA 12', beam 5'.

Snowflake. A one-design cat-rigged centerboard dinghy. LOA 9½', beam 4'. Designer: C.W. Forsman.

snub. The act of stopping a line from running. *See* check. To snub a boat is to let go the anchor and then hold or check the anchor rode.

snubber. *See* shock cord.

snug. Safe, secure, as in a snug harbor. To snug down means to prepare the boat for heavy weather.

sny. The upward curve of a boat's planking or plating at bow and stern. Also called spile.

SOFAR. SOund Fixing And Ranging.

soft eye. A spliced eye at the end of a shroud or stay that is fitted over the masthead.

softwood. In the maritime sense any timber from trees having needles instead of leaves.

solano. A warm and sometimes dusty southeasterly wind blowing in the summer from Africa towards the coast of Spain.

solar time. Time as determined from the rotation of the earth in relation to the sun. Also called mean solar time in contrast to sidereal time.

solar wind. *See* land breeze.

SOLAS. Safety of Life at Sea conference.

sole. 1. The deck or floor (using the word floor as we do ashore) of the cabin and the cockpit in a boat. Removable sections of the sole are known as floorboards.

sole block. A heavy flat piece of wood placed under the lower end of a spar such as a sheer leg. Also called a shole or shoe.

sole piece. A skeg or heel piece that projects from the after end of the keel for supporting the rudder.

sole plate. The bed plate in a boat on which a piece of machinery is made fast.

Soling. An Olympic one-design keel sloop. LOA 27′, beam 6¼′, draft 4¼′. Designer: Jan Linge.

SONAR. SOund Navigation And Ranging.

SORC. Southern Ocean Racing Conference. An annual series of ocean races between Florida and the Bahamas.

SOS. An international radio signal using Morse Code (... --- ...) indicating distress and asking for help. Mayday is the voice radio equivalent.

soul and body lashing. Lashing that holds something against the boat's motion. A piece of line around the outside of a person's rain clothing with an end that can be made fast to a lifeline.

sound. *n.* 1. A long and wide body of water, larger than a strait or channel, that connects larger bodies of water or a long wide ocean inlet. 2. The air bladder of a fish with which it can control its buoyancy. *vb.* A fish or whale sounds when it dives quickly and heads downward. Also, as a verb, to measure the depth of water or other fluid.

sounding. To take a sounding is to measure the depth of liquid.

sounding lead. A leadline or any heavy weight used with a leadline.

soundings. Depth of water on a chart given in fathoms (traditional), feet (for harbors and restricted waters), or meters (becoming universal with shift to metric system). To be on or off soundings is to be, respectively, inside or outside the 100-fathom line.

SOund Navigation And Ranging (SONAR). A system for measuring distance underwater by means of sound impulses whose reflection from a target provides bearing and, when timed, distance. Also called echo ranging, the basis for echo sounding and fishfinding.

southerly buster. A sudden strong wind of the southern coast of Australia. Also called a brickfielder.

Southern Cross. The five bright stars of the constellation Crux that form a cross visible south of the Tropic of Cancer.

Southeaster. A one-design centerboard sloop. LOA 16', beam 5½'. Designer: R.D. Halsey.

South Equatorial Current. A strong westerly flow in the Atlantic, Indian and Pacific Oceans just south of the Equator. Its counterpart is the North Equatorial Current.

South Freeport 33. A one-design keel and centerboard yawl. LOA 33½', beam 10', fixed draft 3½'. Designer: H.S. Parker Jr.

South Pacific Current. An eastward-flowing ocean current in the South Pacific that passes along the northern edge of the west-flowing Antarctic Circumpolar Current.

South Seas. Another term for the South Pacific.

southwester. Traditional fisherman's yellow or black waterproof hat with a long brim in back. Also called a slicker hat or squam.

spade anchor. *See* plow anchor.

spaghetti factory. Slang for a modern racing sailboat that seems festooned with an inordinate number of sheets, halyards, cunninghams, etc.

spall, spale. In wooden boat construction one of the cross members on which planks rest. Also called a stage bearer or thwart.

span. Any rope or wire running between two points such as on masts or davits that is used to suspend lines or tackle; blocks, fairleads, etc.

Spanish burton. A tackle of two single blocks with both standing parts fastened to the load to be moved. The strap of one block is tailed and rove through the sheave of the other.

Spanish bowline. One having two loops, neither of which will slip.

Spanish windlass. A simple improvised device for shortening a rope by twisting it.

spanker. One of the masts of a square-rigger or schooner. *See* mast. The aftermost fore-and-aft sail on any large sailing ship. If jib-headed the sail was called a storm sail or trysail. Now a symmetrical jiblike reaching spinnaker with narrow shoulders.

spar. General word for a long round piece of wood or steel used as a boom, mast, gaff, buoy, etc.

spar buoy. An anchored spar floating upright marking an obstruction, shoal, or channel.

spar varnish. A special durable clear paint designed for marine use.

SPCC. Strength Power Communication Cable.

speak. To encounter and communicate with a ship at sea.

Special Circumstance, Rule of. An important provision of the Rules of the Road that every mariner should know by heart: "In construing and complying with these rules due regard shall be had to all dangers of navigation and collision and to any special circumstance, including the limitations of the vessels involved, which may make a departure from these rules necessary in order to avoid immediate danger." Also known as the General Prudential Rule.

speed. At sea speed is measured in knots or nautical miles per hour.

speedboat. Any powerboat designed primarily for speed rather than comfort.

speed made good. Speed measured in reference to distance traveled over the ground in contrast to speed through the water.

speed, moderate. *See* moderate speed.

speed of advance. The anticipated speed made good or needed to reach a destination at a desired time.

spencer. A trapezoidal gaff sail, generally loose-footed, once set on the fore and main lower yards of square-riggers.

sperm whale. A large toothed whale, up to 60 feet long whose major food is the giant squid. Like most whales it faces extinction because of killing by man. Also called cachalot. A smaller cousin, the pigmy whale, grows to 13 feet.

spider. A triangular metal outrigger used to keep a block clear of a mast or of a ship's side. Also the portable magnifying glass on the face of the magnetic compass.

spider band. An iron band around a lower mast near the deck of a large sailboat that has sockets for belaying pins. Also called a spider iron or spider hoop.

spile. A small wooden peg used to fill the hole left by a withdrawn spike. Also the same as sny.

spiling. A method of boat construction in which the desired shape of a part is drawn on a template or spiling batten and transferred to the material to be cut out.

spilling line. Any line attached to a sail that is used to spill the wind and gather in the sail prior to reefing or furling.

spindle. The center of a composite or built up mast; the main piece. Also called the heart.

spindrift. Foam and spray blown by the wind off the tops of waves as well as the resultant streaks on the water. *See* Beaufort Scale.

spinnaker. A large, light sail boomed out with a pole and used when sailing before the wind or when reaching.

spinnaker bag. The container in which the sail is stowed and from which it can be hoisted quickly. When used this way or when a special bag is used the container is a turtle, or in the U.K., a spinnaker chute.

spinnaker, double or parachute. A larger spinnaker that is boomed out on both sides; also called a Mae West.

spinnaker pole. A light spar used to hold the spinnaker in place when set. It is governed by an after guy, a pole downhaul and by a topping lift.

spinnaker staysail. A sail sometimes set below a lifted and filled spinnaker. Also called a cheater.

spinner dolphin, shark. A dolphin or shark identified by its habit of often jumping clear of the water while revolving its body before reentry.

spiny lobster. The accepted approved name for a saltwater crustacean valued for food that is not a true lobster since it has no large claws. Locally but inaccurately called a crayfish, crawfish, rock lobster or langusta.

spit. A small, narrow, projecting piece of coast line; often called a sandspit.

spitfire. A small, heavy storm jib usually set in a sailboat at the same time as the storm trysail.

spitkid or spitkit. A spittoon or ashtray aboard ship.

splashboard. A board that fits vertically into grooves on each side of a companionway in a sailboat to keep water from spilling below.

splice. The joining of two pieces of rope or wire by interweaving the strands. There are long splices, short splices, cut splices and back splices as well as many more. This has resulted in the expression: "Different ships—different long splices." To be spliced is the sailors' expression for marriage.

splice the main brace. To have a drink or to serve alcohol.

spline. A long-flexible strip used for fairing curves in boatbuilding drawings. Also a thin strip of wood fitted into a planking seam and smoothed to make a well-finished deck. The result is known as spline planking.

spoil. Mud, sand, and other materials removed by a dredge.

sponge. A simple and passive invertebrate found on the ocean floor nearly everywhere. There are over 500 species, from an inch to 6 feet in length. One that has a tough and flexible skeleton is used as a bath sponge.

sponson. A small structure or platform projecting from a ship's side to provide protection or to increase stability.

spoon bow. An overhanging bow with full round sections shaped like the bowl of a spoon.

spoondrift. *See* spindrift.

sport fisherman. A sturdy, well-powered boat, usually 25–60 feet long, designed and equipped to catch gamefish.

spray hood. A collapsible fabric and frame device in a small boat for rain and spray protection.

sprayrail. An indentation or shelf in the hull of a powerboat near the bow that helps keep spray off the deck.

spreacher block. A two-way lead block that combines the spinnaker and reacher blocks to allow two lines through. It resembles a big fiddle block with a swivel.

spreader. Any wooden or steel fitting used to push out or extend stays or shrouds; commonly used on both sides of the mast of a sailboat to spread the shrouds or mast supports. Also called a crosstree, although technically a crosstree is continuous while a spreader can be rigged on one side only. *See* jumper stay.

spreader boot. A rubber or plastic protective device over the end of a spreader to protect sails from chafing.

spring. 1. A mooring line rigged at an angle with the ship, either a forward or after spring. 2. A line used to change the heading of an anchored boat, being led to an anchor, a buoy, or ashore. A boat may spring a leak if she takes in water or she may spring a plank in a collision.

springhook. *See* snaphook.

spring lay rope. A six-strand flexible composite rope made with alternate fiber and wire strands around a fiber core.

spring stay. The stay between the tops of a two-masted boat.

spring tide. The tide with the maximum range resulting from the combined attraction of the moon and the sun. A spring tide occurs twice in a lunar month, at the new and the full moon. Spring tidal currents are stronger than normal. *See* neap tide.

sprit. A small spar or pole used to extend something. Short for bowsprit. The spar that extends and holds the peak of a spritsail.

Sprite. A one-design centerboard sloop. LOA 10′, beam 5′. Designers: Baker and O'Day.

spritsail. A quadrilateral fore-and-aft sail having a sprit from its lower forward corner to its peak or after top corner. The foot of the sail is loose and the lower end of the heel of the sprit is secured to the mast with a sort of becket called a snotter. Also a triangular sail set between the gaff and the mast of a gaff-rigged sailboat.

spume. Froth or very light spray or foam, often caused by breaking seas.

spun yarn. Small light line made of two to four yarns. Spoken "spunyon."

spur. 1. Any shore or timber used in a drydock to support a vessel. 2. A half-beam in a wooden boat. 3. One of the projections of the arms or crown of a stockless anchor for engaging the bottom.

spyglass. *See* long glass.

squall. A sudden strong wind, usually with rain or snow, not of long duration. Often accompanied by a single black cloud, a black squall, or a long line of black clouds just above the horizon (a line squall) or no clouds (a white squall). A squall is longer than a gust.

squall line. The air ahead of a cold front, marked by heavy showers, strong, shifting winds, and sometimes thunder and lightning. Very dangerous to small boats; also called the instability line.

squam. A rain hat.

square-ender. *See* scow.

square-rigger. Same as a full-rigged ship or a square-rigged ship that has nearly all sails rectangular in shape and set on yards perpendicular to the mast.

squaresail. A quadrilateral, usually rectangular, sail having a foot, a head and two vertical edges called leeches. The lower corners are clews and the upper corners are earings.

squeegee or squilgee. A sort of rubber-shod wooden hoe used to remove water from a wooden deck. Now used mainly in the form of hand-held gadgets to clean windows.

squid. A fast-moving, jet-propelled pelagic cephalopod with a long body, 10 arms, an internal skeleton of sorts, and a pair of fins. They are found worldwide in various sizes and are becoming increasingly important as food since fish are declining in numbers.

SSB. Single Sideband Radio.

stabber. A small sailmaker's pricker or marline spike, often with three sharp edges.

stability. That vital characteristic that enables a boat or a ship to right herself when heeled over; a function of design and loading. A rough indication of a vessel's stability is its period of roll in a seaway. A rapid, jerky roll indicates high stability while a long slow roll, particularly one with some hesitation at the end, indicates marginal stability.

stair. Not a nautical word, although sometimes used by naval architects. Ladder is the proper term.

stall zone. A sailor's term for the area of haphazard wind eddies that develop near the luff of a sail when it is pointed too close to the wind.

stanchion. Any wood or metal vertical support member but usually refers to the posts that support the lifelines.

stand. A vessel stands off a harbor when waiting to enter, and stands out as she departs. To continue on the same course is to stand on. A man stands clear of a tackle under dangerous strain and may stand easy or stand down when he stops work. A sailor stands his watch or may stand by to drop the anchor.

standing. Fixed, not movable. There are standing blocks and running blocks; the standing part of a tackle and the hauling part.

standing lights. Lights kept lit below decks during the night.

standing lug. *See* lugsail.

stand, of the tide. The interval at high and low water when there is no rise and fall. It may last for several hours and may be called a platform tide.

standing wave. *See* wave, standing.

Stand-On Vessel. That vessel which is required by the Rules of the Road to maintain course and speed when it has the right of way. Formerly called the Privileged Vessel. *See* Give-way Vessel.

star. Term for the celestial bodies, including the planets but not the sun and moon, that are used for navigation.

Star. A popular Olympic, one-design keel sloop. LOA 23', beam 5½', draft 3½'. Designer: Francis Sweisguth.

starboard. The right side of a ship or a boat when looking forward. By remembering that port and left both have four letters it is easy to distinguish between port and starboard.

star chart. One that shows the location of stars and planets.

star cut. A way of assembling the panels when making a sail. Also a synonym for the super flanker, a sail.

start. To loosen or ease a line as one starts a sheet. To open and begin using the contents of a cask. A plank or seam is said to be started when it springs a leak.

starting signal. At the start of a boat race a gun is fired and at the same time a flag is hoisted. There is usually a 5-minute warning signal before the start.

starts, of races. In sailing races a boat may make a timed, sitting-on-the-line, running-the-line, dip, or barging start.

station pointer. Another name for a three-arm protractor, especially in the U.K.

stave. To stave in a boat's planking means to crush and damage it. Also stove. To stave off means to fend off.

stay. *n.* 1. Any wire or rope supporting a mast fore and aft. 2. A boat is anchored at short stay when the anchor is out just far enough to hold temporarily—usually just before departure. *vb.* 1. To stay a topmast is to support and steady it. 2. To stay was an old word for tack, and a sailboat when tacking slowly with headsails shaking was said to be in stays or slack in stays.

stay hole. A hole in the luff of a staysail or jib used for the lacing or hanks that attach it to its stay. *See* triatic stay.

staysail. Traditionally any fore-and-aft sail, except a jib, that is set on a stay, but now, in relation to sailboats, it is any additional sail set between masts. Modern sailboats use a number of special staysails as headsails as well, including the genoa, the super, the banana, the windward staysail as well as the tallboy. A topless or baldheaded staysail has its top cut off to avoid blocking the spinnaker's wind.

staysail ketch. A ketch whose mainsail is replaced by a staysail used together with an abbreviated mainsail.

staysail schooner. A schooner in which the usual foresail is replaced by several staysails. *See* fisherman's staysail.

stay tackle. Tackle used for setting up a stay or rigged on a stay for handling weights.

steady. A command to a helmsman of "steady" or "steady as you go" means for him to maintain that course he was on as the words were spoken.

steamcock. *See* seacock.

steam fog. Fog formed when very cold air drifts over relatively warm water. Also known as sea smoke, sea mist, and Arctic frost smoke, it should not be confused with advection fog that results from warm air over cold water.

steamship. Same as steam vessel.

steam vessel. Under the International Rules of the Road any vessel propelled by machinery.

steerageway. The minimum speed of a boat through the water at which she will respond to the rudder.

steering stroke. *See* J-stroke.

steersman. The person who steers the boat; also called a helmsman.

steeve. The angle the bowsprit makes with the horizontal. Also stive.

St. Elmo's fire. *See* corposant.

stem. *n.* The upright post or bar at the bow of a ship where the side planking or plating ends, extending down to the keel. The upper part of the stem is the stemhead; the lower part is the stemfoot where the stem knee is fitted in a wooden boat. *See* cutwater. *vb.* To stem is to make headway against wind or current as in: "The boat stemmed the tide."

stem band. An iron band that protects the stem of a wooden boat.

stemhead. The upper part of the stem.

step. The socket, block, or framing into which the mast of a boat fits when erect or when it has been stepped.

stern. 1. The extreme afterpart of a boat. 2. A boat drawing more water aft than forward is down by the stern. 3. "Stern all" is a command to oarsmen in a pulling boat to backwater on both sides and thus make the boat go astern.

sternboard. *See* sternway.

sterndrive. A modern propulsion system for boats in which the engine is inside the hull, close to the stern, while the rudder and the propeller are just outside or abaft the transom. Also called: inboard/outboard, I/O, outdrive, outboard/inboard, or transom drive.

stern fast. An after mooring line for a boat.

stern frame. A heavy-strength member combining the rudder post on which the rudder is hung and the propeller post through which the propeller shaft passes; also connects the ends of the shell plating. Sometimes called the sternpost.

sternlight. A 12 point, 135° white light showing 67.5° on each side directly aft. Required to be shown by ships by the Rules of the Road in international waters, but in inland waters only required if no other light shows astern.

stern pointer. In a wooden ship or large boat one of the timbers fastened diagonally upon the ceiling of the stern.

sternpost. Same as stern frame.

stern pulpit. Similar to the pulpit forward, located over the transom to assist in tending an after sail, such as the mizzen sail of a yawl. British word is pushpit.

stern shapes. A cruiser stern has no overhang and often has tumble home. An elliptical stern has a projecting counter that terminates at the deck in a rounded shape. A transom stern has a square or flat counter, usually sloping aft. If it has an open-work extension aft it is a lute stern. A canoe stern is one in which the planking comes together, producing a boat known as a double-ender. A tunnel stern has a tunnel in which the propeller turns, designed for shallow water. A counter stern is one with a flat overhang; a ducktail stern slants forward.

sternsheets. The space in an open boat just forward of the stern thwart and abaft the first regular thwart.

sternson. The curved timber uniting the upper deadwood to the sternpost in wooden boats.

sternway. Same as sternboard.

stick. A pole, spar, or mast. The boom of a small leg-of-mutton sail is sometimes called a stick-boom.

stiff. A boat not easily inclined that has a short quick, snappy uncomfortable roll, or has a good ability to carry sail is said to be stiff. It is the opposite of crank or tender. Also a strong breeze or current may be described as stiff. *See* crank.

stingray. One of the flat fish or rays that can inflict a very painful wound with the poisoned barb of its whiplike tail when stepped upon in shallow water. Thus on California beaches it is well to shuffle out to swim rather than step high.

stock. The movable crosspiece with a ball at each end of a stock, or old-fashioned anchor, that lies perpendicular to the shank when the anchor is in use. The stock lies parallel to the shank when the anchor is stowed. Stocks are the shore blocks and timbers on which a ship or boat rests in a building way.

stockless anchor. The modern, patent anchor made with a number of patented variations, housed and secured in the hawsepipe of ships since it has no stock or crosspiece. Examples are the Baldt, Dunn, Norfolk, and British A.C. 14. Called by small boatmen Navy anchor.

stool. Any chock or support for a shaft or for piping. *See* backstay stool.

stop. Any projection on a mast or spar used to support something, or as a preventer for a fitting or piece of gear. Small stuff used to fasten something such as clothes' stops. Stops are used to secure a furled sail to a boom and may stop up a furled headsail to a forestay. In this case they are rotten stops since a sharp pull on the sheet will part the weak strands and the sail will be set flying.

stopper. A short length of rope or chain or any contrivance used temporarily to check the running of a rope, wire, or cable or for holding it while it is belayed. *See* chain stopper. There are bitt stoppers, block stoppers, and cathead stoppers. To stopper is to check or hold a line. A stopper knot is one in the end of a rope to keep it from passing through a fairlead. *See* ball stopper.

stopwater. Any device for stopping a leak, as for example a dowel driven along a seam in wooden boat construction.

storm. Winds of force 10 (a storm) or force 11 (a violent storm) on the Beaufort Scale, 43–65 knots, often accompanied by rain, hail or snow. Higher winds mark a cyclone, hurricane or typhoon; slightly lesser winds are gales. Note that a storm is worse than a gale.

storm glass. The barometer.

storm, magnetic. A disturbance of the earth's magnetic field that affects radio communications.

storm oil. Preferably an animal or vegetable oil that was traditionally disbursed in small quantities to calm breaking seas.

storm sails. Heavy small sails such as trysails that are set in rough weather when the usual sails would blow out.

storm signals. Flags, shapes, and lights displayed ashore at Coast Guard stations and other locations that forecast various degrees of bad weather.

storm surge. A sudden increase in the level of the sea along a coast due to strong onshore winds, often reinforced by very low atmospheric pressure and a high tide.

storm trysail. *See* trysail.

storm valve. A flapper or check valve in the overboard discharge lines that prevents the entrance of water in bad weather.

storm warning. A NWS advisory of winds over 48 knots. If associated with a hurricane it is a hurricane warning. *See* gale warning, Small Craft Advisory.

stove. *See* stave.

stow. To put away, lash in place, roll up or furl.

stowage. The act or procedure of packing away or stowing something. The place where it is stowed, the goods themselves or the cost may also be called stowage. Not the same as storage.

Stoway mast. A patented hollow mast with a long slot facing aft in which the sail is stowed wound on a rotating rod. Sail can be set, reefed, or stowed away with great ease.

strain. To pull or haul on a line is to take a strain. When a sailor rests in his bunk he is said to be taking an equal strain on all parts.

straits. A relatively narrow waterway between large bodies of water as, for example, the Straits of Gibralter.

strake. A range or line of planks or plating adjacent to each other and extending fore and aft the length of the ship or boat. Bilge strakes are those along the turn of the bilge. The garboard or sand strake is next to the keel; next are the broad strakes. The sheer strake follows the sheer line of the boat and is just the topside strake. The wash strake in an open boat is the thin plank fitted above the gunwale to increase freeboard.

strand. A poetic word for shore or beach. To run aground or to be driven ashore is to be stranded. In cordage a strand is one of several twisted yarns or threads that are laid up or twisted together to form rope. A rope is said to be stranded when one of its strands has parted. Stranded wire is wire rope.

strap. A narrow band of flexible material used to secure, suspend, or fasten something. Strop is British spelling.

stratus. Usually a bank of shapeless low clouds; may produce fog or a light drizzle. *See* cloud.

stray line. An additional, sometimes smaller line attached to a rope to assist in handling. Same as messenger.

streaker. *See* blooper.

stream. Any flow of water such as a river or an ocean current. A ship or boat is said to be in the stream when she is not moored alongside a pier but is anchored. To stream something is to let it out to be towed.

stream anchor. A lighter anchor sometimes carried for use as a stern or warping anchor. Also called a stern anchor.

streamers. Short and narrow pieces of cloth that are attached to the sail of a racing sailboat to reveal the direction of airflow near the sail. *See* telltale.

Strength Power Communication Cable (SPCC). Cable used from the surface to a deep diving capsule. Also called the umbilical cord.

stretch. A reach or straight portion of a river, canal or bay.

stretcher. An athwartship strip of wood in a boat against which an oarsman braces his feet.

stretchy luff. A construction for the luff of the genoa of a sailboat that allows the location of the sail's draft to be controlled.

strike. In its nautical sense means to haul down or pass below, as sails or colors are struck or stores arriving aboard are struck below.

string. The highest strake of ceiling planking in the hold of a wooden ship. Also same as telltale.

stringer. Any longitudinal beam or girder inside the structure of a vessel that strengthens the beams, frames or skin.

skin-planking. A method of planking a wooden boat in which planks are edge-nailed to the frames and glued together.

strobe. A highly visible, quick flashing white light that is commonly used by fishermen and yachtsmen as a fog light, anchor warning light, and as a distress signal on personal flotation devices and life rings. Strobes are sometimes used incorrectly as flare-up or flashing lights under the Rules of the Road which does not authorize them.

stroke. The complete movement of an oarsman in a pulling boat.

strongback. 1. A spar against which a boat is secured in the davits. 2. The wooden beam in a stowed boat over which the boat cover is stretched. 3. A wooden beam supporting an awning. 4. A heavy timber foundation temporarily supporting a boat during construction.

strop. *See* strap.

strum or strum box. *See* rose box.

strut. Any bracket or supporting member, specifically the one holding the outboard end of a propeller shaft.

studsail. An additional strip of canvas made fast to the bottom of a fore-and-aft sail, also called a bonnet.

stuff. A word for light cordage.

stuffing box. A device used to prevent leakage around a moving or fixed part projecting through a watertight bulkhead. A propeller shaft passes through a stuffing box while a cable would pass through a stuffing tube. Also called a packing gland.

Stugeron. A British nonprescription drug found effective against seasickness.

sturgeon. A large, river-spawning food fish whose roe is caviar.

S-Twelve (S-12). A one-design cat-rigged boardboat with a daggerboard. LOA 12′, beam 3½′.

suction, bank. In shiphandling in narrow channels or canals or when going alongside a pier or another vessel, bank suction is a force attracting the stern of a ship or boat towards the bank or other vessel when the propeller is turning over.

Sudbury vent. Trade name of an opaque, plastic combination ventilator and skylight (including a water trap) used in small boats.

suit. A sailboat has at least one set of sails, one each of those required. This is a suit of sails and more than one suit makes up her wardrobe or inventory.

sumatra. A squall with violent thunder, lightning, and rain that blows at night in the Malacca Straits, especially during the southwest monsoon.

Sunbird. A one-design centerboard sloop. LOA 12', beam 5½'. Designer: J.V. Puccia.

sun dog. *See* parhelion.

sunfish. A large round ocean fish that appears to be all head and is often seen on the surface. Also called a headfish.

Sunfish. A one-design, lateen-rigged daggerboard boat. LOA 14', beam 4'. Designer: Alcort, Inc. A Super Sunfish is cat-rigged.

sun over the yardarm. The traditional sailor's criterion for opening the bar or having the first drink of the day, usually about 11 A.M.

sun's backstays. A sailor's term for the apparent rays of sun reaching down to the water when the sun is behind a cloud.

super flanker. Smaller than the all-purpose spinnaker, a super flanker or starcut is designed for very close reaching or for heavy air running.

super high frequency (SHF). 3000–30,000 megaHertz, wavelength 1–10 centimeters, used by radars.

surf. The waves breaking on the shore as breakers produce surf. Depending on the slope of the beach underwater, the waves either break heavily and suddenly as on a steep slope (plunging breakers) or rise slowly to a curl and break at the top before gradually tumbling over as on a gradually shelving beach (spilling breakers).

surface effect ship (ses). Any of the new craft, such as Hovercraft, that move over land and sea supported by a downward thrust of compressed air. Old term was ground effect machine.

surfboard. A buoyant smooth plank used by surfers to catch and slide across a breaking wave front. The sport is surfing.

surf boats. Those designed to be launched from shore through surf.

surf currents. *See* nearshore current system.

surfsailing. *See* windsurfing.

surge. 1. To slack or ease a line slowly as in lowering a weight. 2. The fore-and-aft translational movement of a boat in a seiche or seaway. 3. The horizontal oscillation of water that accompanies a seiche. *See* ship motion, storm surge.

surge brakes. Brakes on a boat trailer that operate automatically when the trailer's momentum exerts pressure against the towing hitch.

survival suit. Plastic, waterproof, buoyant, heat-containing clothing designed to permit survival in cold water. Also called an exposure suit.

swab. Nautical word for mop. Swabbing is cleaning a deck with a wet mop.

swage. A hollow tube of metal cold-rolled around the end of a wire as a terminal. Also the tool used to form the terminal. Also used as a verb. Spoken: swedge.

swallow. The opening in a block through which the rope passes.

swallow tail. A flag or pennant with a forked fly.

swallow the anchor. To leave the sea as a profession or major hobby; to go ashore permanently.

swamp. 1. To fill with water as a boat may do in breaking seas. 2. To remove a mooring buoy, sink the attached gear and mark the spot is to swamp the buoy. Done where the mooring area is too exposed to be used in prolonged bad weather.

swash. The rush of water as the movement up onto the beach from a breaking wave. Also called wash.

swash channel. A narrow passage between shoals and breakers.

sway. *n.* The athwartship motion of a ship in a seiche or seaway; a sideways, bodily, translational movement. *See* ship motion. *vb.* To hoist or raise as in swaying up a topmast. To throw one's weight on a line as one sways up the mainsail to get it all the way up.

sweat up. To hoist something such as a sail to the very top.

Swedish mainsail. A tall, narrow, relatively small sail used for going to windward in heavy weather and big waves.

sweep. *n.* 1. A long oar used for steering and sculling. 2. The track on which a tiller quadrant travels. 3. Any long arc of curvature of a ship's structure as well as the curved piece of wood or plastic used to draw the lines before construction. *vb.* To sweep an area or channel is to drag a wire over it at a certain depth; the area is then said to be swept or wire dragged to that depth.

Sweet 16. A one-design centerboard sloop. LOA 16′, beam 6′. Designer: Advance Sail Corp.

swell. The undulation of the sea caused by wind blowing from some distance away or a wind that has stopped blowing. Also called a free wave. Swell is sometimes called ground swell or ground sea especially when it breaks over a bar.

swifter. 1. A piece of line used to bouse or pull together a shroud or lashing. 2. A single shroud. 3. A rope fender encircling a boat below the gunwale to protect its sides.

swig. *n.* 1. To tighten a line by pulling at right angles to it. 2. A sailor might be asked to take a swig on the main halyard. 3. A thirsty sailor might be invited to take a swig of water. *vb.* To swig in or swig up a jib sheet or halyard is to haul on it.

swing. 1. A ship or boat swings at anchor because of wind or current. 2. To swing ship is to steer on various headings while underway in order to correct or compensate the magnetic compass.

swivel block. Block suspended by a swivel and free to turn.

sword arm. A device projected from a ship's or boat's bottom that contains a sensing instrument such as a pitot tube.

swordfish. A large worldwide pelagic food and game billfish having a swordlike beak. Sometimes harpooned while basking on the surface, they are fished commercially by longline.

synoptic chart. A weather map showing isobars or lines of equal pressure, thus revealing the high and low pressure systems from which forecasts can be made.

System A. The proposed uniform international buoyage system for Europe, Africa, Australia, India and certain other Asian waters known as: "System A—The Combined Cardinal and Lateral System (red to port)."

System B. The proposed uniform buoyage system for North and South America and parts of Asia, known as: "System B—The Lateral System (red to starboard)."

T

tabernacle. A vertical trunk built to take the heel of a mast that does not pass through the deck; used as a pivoted mast step for fold-down masts on boats that travel on canals and must pass under bridges. Also called a mast trunk and sometimes a lutchet.

table. The outer part of a keel, stem, or sternpost projecting beyond the planking.

tabling. The hem around a sail.

tack. *n.* **1.** The lower forward corner of a fore-and-aft sail. **2.** The weather clew of a course, or the rope or tackle holding such a clew. **3.** In sailing, the direction or heading of a boat in relation to the wind, i.e., a boat on the port tack is one with the wind coming over the port side. **4.** The distance, duration, leg, or board of a sailboat on a tack. **5.** The main tack is the weather clew of a square mainsail and there are tack blocks, bumkins, earings, lashings and cringles, all associated with the tack. **6.** Short for tackline. *vb.* To tack is to direct the boat's head through the wind so that the wind strikes the sails on the opposite side. This is called tacking or coming about or going about. Also to sail a series of alternate tacks. *See* wear.

tackle. An arrangement of rope, wire, or chain and blocks rigged to increase the holding power and to gain a mechanical advantage, such as a relieving tackle or a mainsheet tackle. In general it means the same as purchase although this is associated with the mechanical advantage of a particular tackle. Spoken: "taykle."

tackle block. One used to make up a tackle.

tackline. A 6-foot length of halyard used as a spacer between signal flags in a flag hoist.

tack ring. *See* jib traveler.

tack shackle. A full swiveling snap shackle fitted at the stemhead to permit instant attachment or release of the tack of a jib.

taffrail. The railing around the fantail of a vessel's stern.

taffrail log. A towed, spinning ship's speed-measuring device with the recording dial attached to the taffrail. Same as screw log.

tail. *n.* A short piece of line attached to a block, a rope, or a chain. *vb.* 1. A ship at anchor may tail into the shore. 2. Men needed to haul on a line may be asked to tail on. A man who puts turns around a winch is a tailer who tails a sheet or other line while the cranker cranks the winch unless it is a self-tailing winch.

tail block. One with a short rope tail.

tailgate. The downstream gate of a lock.

take. To measure, such as to take soundings or to lay hold of, such as to take a turn with a rope or take in the slack. A boat may take her departure when leaving port, and then takes water aboard if she meets heavy weather.

take charge. Go out of control, such as a heavy piece of gear may come adrift in a seaway and take charge, or a line may take charge when it parts.

tallboy. An extremely tall, narrow, flat staysail that may be used when sailing downwind. Also called a ribbon staysail.

take off. Tides on successive days take off when their heights decrease between spring and neap tides. When the heights increase the tide is said to make.

Tallstar. A one-design centerboard sloop. LOA 14', beam 6'. Designer: Robert Baker.

talurit splice. A modern, quick and easy eye splice in a wire rope using a thimble and a collar or ferrule compressed about both parts after the thimble is inserted.

tang. A fitting, such as a metal strap, made fast to a spar or mast to which a stay or a halyard block may be secured.

Tanzer 14, 16, 22. One-design centerboard sloops. LOA 14′, 16′, 22′, beam 5½′, 6′, 7′. Designer: Johann Tanzer.

tar. The sailor's traditional waterproofing and preservative agent made from pine; replaced now by modern chemicals. A sailor was known as a tar.

tarpaulin. Any piece of canvas used to protect or cover something aboard a boat. Tarp for short.

Tartan 27. A one-design keel and centerboard sloop or yawl. LOA 27′, beam 8½′, fixed draft 3′. Designer: Olin Stephens. There is also a bigger Tartan 30 as well as a Tartan 10.

Tasar. A one-design daggerboard sloop. LOA 15′, beam 6′. Designer: Bethwaite & Bruce.

taut. Nautical word for tight as in "a line is hauled taut." In a general sense taut means well-disciplined, orderly, efficient, as a taut ship.

Teal. A one-design centerboard sloop. LOA 15½′, beam 5′. Designer: Hindriks Bulthuis.

tease. To open out and separate yarns and strands of rope.

Tech Dinghy. A one-design centerboard sloop or cat-rigged dinghy. LOA 13′, beam 5′. Designer: Halsey Herreshoff.

tehuantepecer. A violent north wind that blows in the winter across the isthmus and into the Gulf of Tehuantepec in Mexico.

telegraph block. A block through which several signal halyards are rove with a long narrow shell having the sheaves one above the other in the same plane similar to a fiddle block.

telescope. A long glass.

telltale. 1. An inverted compass or compass repeater placed over the master's, owner's, or captain's bunk indicating the boat's course. 2. Any indicator or pointer that shows the rudder angle to the helmsman. 3. A bit of yarn or cloth made fast in the rigging of a sailboat to indicate airflow direction is a telltale, streamer, string, tickler, windtuft, wooly or yarn.

tempest. A literary word for storm or gale, not usually heard at sea.

Tempest. A one-design keel sloop. LOA 22′, beam 6½′. Designer: Ian Proctor.

tender. A small boat carried or towed by a larger boat or yacht. A boat is said to be tender if she has poor stability, same as crank.

tenon. The heel of a mast shaped to fit into the step.

teredos. *See* marine borer.

tern. A seabird similar to a gull but smaller and thinner. It has a forked tail from which it gets its other name, sea swallow.

territorial waters. Those adjacent to the coast of a country and over which it claims jurisdiction. Traditionally this has been 3 miles, the range of a smoothbore ship's gun, but now 12 miles is claimed by some countries, as well as 200 miles in which control of fishing is asserted.

Texas tower. A fixed structure erected offshore for oil or gas drilling or to provide sea and weather data and to act as an aid to navigation.

thick and thin block. One having several sheaves of different sizes to hold different sizes of rope and wire.

thimble. An oval metal fitting secured in the eye of a rope or wire for protection against wear as well as a convenience in forming the eye.

Thistle. A one-design centerboard sloop. LOA 17′, beam 6′. Designer: G.K. Douglass.

thole pin. A primitive oarlock for a pulling boat consisting of a wooden or metal pin set upright in a hole in the gunwale. The oar may be held to the pin by a loop of rope.

thoroughfoot. To coil down a twisted rope against the lay, counter-clockwise for right-hand laid cordage, bringing the lower end up through the coil and then coiling the line with the lay. This will take out the twist, particularly with new rope.

thrash. A beat to windward. Can also be used as a verb.

three-arm protractor. *See* protractor.

threefold or treble block. One having three adjacent sheaves.

throat. 1. The forward end of the gaff of a gaff sail where it embraces the mast (with a saddle, saddle plate, and parrel). Also called jaws. 2. The upper forward corner of a four-sided fore-and-aft sail where head and luff join. Also called nock. 3. On an old-fashioned anchor, the curved part of either arm where it joins the shank. 4. The part of the shell of a block nearest the hook. 5. The midship part of the floor timber over the keel where its depth is greatest. 6. The center part of a knee or breasthook.

thrum. Short bits of yarn sewn to canvas to make mats.

thumb cleat. A piece of wood or plastic, usually triangular, secured to a spar or spreader to keep part of the rigging in place. Also called a snatch cleat.

Thunderbird. A one-design keel sloop. LOA 26', beam 7½', draft 5'. Designer: Ben Seaborn.

thunderboat. A popular name for noisy, large, racing motorboats or hydroplanes.

thwart. A plank or bench at right angles to the keel of a boat on which rowers and passengers sit; it naturally runs athwartships.

tickle. Any narrow passage connecting two bodies of water; a small strait.

tickler. *See* telltale.

tidal basin. The part of a port or harbor where the tidal range is extreme; enclosed and protected by floodgates to keep the water level constant.

tidal bore. *See* bore.

tidal constant. The minutes and feet that are added or subtracted from the data at the reference stations found in the Tide Tables in order to obtain the time and height of tide at another location.

tidal current. Current resulting from the rise and fall of the tide and which reverses direction in confined waters. It can be evaluated from current tables, diagrams, and charts. In the open sea tidal currents assume a circular movement due to Coriolis force. The British term is tidal stream.

tidal wave. A slow-moving bulge of water on the ocean's surface caused by the gravitational attraction of the moon and the sun. Also called tide wave. As this bulge or wave advances on and then retracts from the shore high and low tides result. Tidal wave is an inaccurate term for seismic sea wave.

tide. The rise and fall of the level of the ocean caused by the gravitational attraction of the moon and the sun. A rising tide is a flood tide; a falling tide is an ebb. The time between successive high tides is normally 24 hours and 51 minutes but is about 13 minutes less when the earth, moon, and sun are in a straight line (first and third quarters of the moon). This is called acceleration or priming of the tide. The opposite phenomenon called lag, lagging, or retardation of the tide occurs when the moon and the sun are in quadrature (second and fourth quarters).

tide-rode. Said of a boat at anchor when she lies bow to the tidal current instead of bow to the wind or wind-rode.

Tide Tables. The list of predicted times of high and low water and their heights for some 200 reference posts and 6000 secondary stations. Published by the National Ocean Survey.

tie. A small band of canvas that is used to secure a sail. A boat may be tied up but it is more seamanlike to say made fast or secured.

tier. A row or layer, such as a series of fakes in a hawser or chain ranged on deck clear for running.

tie-tie. A pair of cloth bands used to fasten a kapok life jacket.

Tiger Cat. A one-design sloop-rigged centerboard catamaran. LOA 17', beam 8'. Designer: R.B. Harris.

Tiki 11. A one-design sloop-rigged centerboard catamaran. LOA 14', beam 7'. Designer: MacLear & Harris.

tiller. An arm or lever fitted to the top of the rudder and used to turn it when steering a boat.

tiltbed. A type of boat trailer which, upon the removal of a tilt pin, lowers the stern of the boat so that it can easily be waterborne.

time. Since the earth revolves at a slightly irregular rate it is convenient to assume an average or mean rate, thus mean time. Greenwich Mean Time (GMT) is the time measured at Greenwich near London and used as the point of reference in nautical almanacs and by navigators. When corrected by the zone description it becomes local ship's time.

timenoguy. A rope stretched from one part of a sailboat to another in order to prevent running gear from fouling the rigging.

time signal. A signal sent by radio worldwide to ships at sea on various frequencies at various hours of the day to provide the exact universal time to navigators. Also called a time tick.

tingle. A copper patch used to repair a hole in the hull of a wooden boat.

tobin bolt. A composition bronze bolt used in wooden boat construction.

toe. The point of the palm or fluke of an anchor.

toe cleat. A piece of wood that holds the lower end of an oarlock in place in a wooden pulling boat.

toe rail. A low rail or strip on the deck of a sailboat forward to keep the crew from sliding off when the boat heels.

toggle. 1. A piece of wood or metal fitted crosswise in a loop or in the eye of a line. 2. A movable barb in a harpoon. 3. A metal fitting at the end of a turnbuckle used to prevent bending pressure on the turnbuckle threads.

ton. A unit of weight, both ashore and afloat, or of capacity at sea. A short ton is 2000 pounds, a long ton is 2240, and a metric ton is 2205 pounds or 1000 kilos. For units of capacity, used with cargo vessels, a ton is 100 cubic feet which is a gross registered ton, or 40 cubic feet which is the net registered tonnage, shipping measurement ton, or freight ton.

tongue. 1. A hinged piece of wood placed vertically in the throat of a gaff to bear the thrust of the latter against a mast. 2. The upper part of a built-up wooden mast.

tonnage. 1. A collective word for all the commercial shipping of a country, port, waterway, etc. 2. The charge per ton on cargo in the form of a tax at a port or a canal.

tonnage, displacement. The actual weight of a ship or boat measured by the volume of water displaced, expressed in long tons.

top. A platform aloft on a mast. The top of a mast is the cap except for the highest mast where it is the truck. To top up a yard or spar is to raise one end. To top up or top off a tank is to fill it.

topgallant. The masts, sails, rigging, and yards above the topmast in a square-rigger.

top hamper. Collective term for all gear, spars, masts, and other items above the maindeck.

topmark. The distinctive shape carried by some foreign buoys as an aid in identifying the function of the buoy.

topmast. The mast rigged above the main or principal mast. A topsail is set on a topmast.

topping lift. A wire, rope, or chain used to take the weight off a yard, boom, or sail. Also called a lift or topping line.

topside. Describes anything on the maindeck or above including the surface of the hull above the waterline. Not to be confused with overhead.

Tornado. A one-design Olympic sloop-rigged centerboard catamaran. LOA 20', beam 10'. Designer: Rodney March.

tortoise. *See* hawksbill turtle.

toss. To toss oars is to lift them together vertically at the end of a stroke as a salute or before shipping the oars.

Totem 21. A one-design keel and centerboard sloop. LOA 21', beam 7½', fixed draft 2'. Designer: Bill Nightingale.

touch. To touch the wind is to steer a sailboat very close to the wind causing the luff to shiver.

towing lights. Under the International Rules of the Road a tug when towing or pushing displays various combinations of masthead, range, sidelight, and stern lights as well as a towing light defined as a yellow light showing astern, 67.5° on each side. Under Inland Rules similar but different combinations of lights are displayed by the tug, but not the yellow towing light described above. Under Inland Rules a tug when pushing shows two amber 12-point lights arranged vertically on her stern and showing 67.5° on each side aft.

towing machine. A large powerdriven drum upon which the towline of a tug is wound and held at the pivot point of the tug. Also called a towing winch.

Town. A one-design centerboard sloop. LOA 16½', beam 6'. Designer: P.M. Lowell.

track. The path or course of a ship or of a storm marked on a chart with the intended or assumed direction of movement, resulting in a track chart. Also a metal strip on a mast in which the luff attachment of a sail slides.

trade winds or trades. Constant and steady winds that naturally flow towards the Equator as the sun-heated air there rises and is displaced by cold air from the poles. Their easterly component is due to Coriolis force and thus there are northeast trades in the northern hemisphere and southeast trades in the southern.

trailboard. A carved plank on each side of the stem near the deck edge in a sailboat where the bowsprit starts.

training wall. A jetty or similar structure, often submerged, built to confine the flow of a river or tidal current.

tramontana. The cold north wind off the west coast of Italy similar to the mistral off the south coast of France.

tramp. A cargo ship that does not have a fixed schedule but carries freight where she can find the business.

trampoline. The net of webbing or fabric between the hulls of a small catamaran.

transducer. The device in a depth finder or other electronic measuring instrument that converts electrical energy to sound and vice versa.

transformer. A device that changes alternating current into higher or lower voltage.

transit. 1. The passage of a celestial body over a specified meridian. 2. Two objects, such as range lights or beacons, seen in line with each other are said to be in transit or in range.

Transit. Same as NAVSAT.

transom. 1. The framework of the stern of a ship at the sternpost; it includes the transom floor, frames and beams. 2. A built-in sofa in the cabin of a ship or boat. 3. The outer planking or surface of a square-sterned boat.

transom board. In a small boat the aftermost athwartships piece in the stern.

transom drive. *See* stern drive.

transom flap. An opening in the stern of a boat that permits the escape of water.

transom step. A shelf, usually of wood, across the transom of a boat.

transom stern. One with a square or flat counter, usually sloping outward from the sternpost, as different from a sharp or rounded stern. *See* stern shapes.

trapeze. The wire from aloft that supports a crew member who is hiked out in a small sailboat.

traveler. 1. Any ring, thimble, or strap that moves on a spar, bar, rod or rope, such as a sheet traveler block that moves athwartships on a traveling iron or horse. 2. In modern sailboats the track or bar on which a traveler or block moves. A racing-jib traveler is one on a jib with control lines rigged down through the deck and aft.

traverse table. A table that gives the distance gained both in latitude and longitude for any course steered at a certain speed. Used in traverse sailing. *See* sailing.

trawler. Any vessel that sets or shoots, tows or hauls a trawl fishing net either as a side or stern trawler. Modern power pleasure boats that follow trawler design in search of seaworthiness and economy are also called trawlers.

Treasure Island. A one-design keel sloop. LOA 21½', beam 6', draft 3½'. Designer: W.B. Nichols.

treenail. A hardwood peg used at one time to fasten planks and timbers in wooden boat construction. Now largely replaced by nails, bolts, or screws. Also spelled trenail; pronounced trunnel.

trebling. Extra planking on the bow of a wooden vessel to resist ice.

trestletrees. A fore-and-aft framing that rests on the cheeks of a lower mast or topmast of a sailing ship and supports the weight of the crosstrees and the top. Also called trestles.

triatic stay. A fore-and-aft wire between masts or from a mast to the top of a mast. If used to support signal halyards it is a signal or cap stay.

trice. To lift a sail, awning, or spar by means of a tricing stay, line, or pendant, or to temporarily hold or support something.

trick. A spell or a turn of duty, as a helmsman does his trick at the wheel.

trident. A three-pronged spear, traditionally carried by Neptune.

trim. *n.* The difference in a boat's draft forward and draft aft in inches. *vb.* 1. A ship or boat may be trimmed by the head or bow or stern which is the same as down by the bow or stern. 2. To trim a sail is to ease or haul in on the sheet or traveler carriage to adjust the angle it makes with the wind.

trimaran. A boat having a central hull with a smaller hull attached to each side. A multihull now popular as a pleasure boat.

trim tabs. Flat and movable surfaces on the stern of a planing boat to control the planing attitude of the boat. Also a trailing edge flap on a fin keel or rudder.

trip. 1. To trip an anchor is to break it out off the bottom by means of a special line. **2.** To swing a mast or yard up or to an upright position prior to lowering. **3.** A strength member bent or strained out of shape is said to be tripped. **4.** To trip something is to let it go, usually by means of a slip or pelican hook.

triradial. Describes the cut of a modern, all-purpose spinnaker in which the threadline is aligned in the direction of stress.

Triton. A one-design keel sloop. LOA 28½', beam 8', draft 4'. Designer: Carl Alberg.

troll, trolling. A method of fishing in which several lures or bait are towed or trolled astern of a boat, several lines to a boat, some on outriggers.

trolling plate. A metal plate lowered abaft a powerboat's propeller to slow the boat to good trolling speed while permitting the engine to run at an efficient speed.

tropic. A circle or parallel of latitude, 23° 27' either north (Tropic of Cancer) or south (Tropic of Capricorn) of the Equator, marking the limit of the tropics where the sun is directly overhead.

tropic tide. Common to the tropics, a diurnal or one-a-day tide that occurs during the period of the moon's greatest declination.

truck. A fitting at the top of a flagstaff or mast, particularly the highest mast. It may include a halyard block and a light. Also called cap.

trunk. Aboard ship an enclosure, casing, enclosed passage, or crawl space.

trunk buoy. A cylindrical mooring buoy with a central trunk through which the end of the mooring pendant is brought up.

trunk cabin. *See* cabin top.

trysail. In modern sailboats a small, strong sail used in heavy weather and often called a storm trysail. On powerboats a sail sometimes set to steady the boat and reduce rolling, particularly while fishing.

tsunami. Japanese word for tidal wave. It is similarly used to mean a seismic sea wave.

Tsushima current. *See* Kuroshio.

tuck. The part of a boat where the after ends of the hull planking meet at the transom at the tuck rail or tuck timber. British word for reef and for making a reef or splice.

Tufnol. A plastic now often used in making blocks.

tugboat. A relatively small, sturdy, high-powered, often very seaworthy vessel used for towing and pushing, salvage, fighting fires, and berthing large ships.

tumblehome. The inward inclination of a vessel's side, a convex curve in a hull; opposite of flare.

tuna. A member of the mackerel family that includes albacore, bonito, yellowtail, skipjack, and the great bluefin tuna or horse mackerel that grow over 1000 pounds. Tuna are fast, pelagic, excellent food and game fish that are heavily fished and declining in numbers. Also called tunny.

tuna clipper. A long range U.S. tuna fisherman that now fishes in all waters.

tuna tower. A lightweight elevated structure built on a fishing and pleasure boat to obtain better visibility.

turkshead. An ornamental collar of small line or white cord braided around a deck stanchion, boat tiller, boat hook, etc.

turn. A sailor turns in to his bunk or turns to when he starts work. A sailor may take a turn around a cleat with a line. A boat that capsizes turns turtle.

Turnabout. A one-design centerboard catboat. LOA 10′, beam 5¼′. Designer: H.R. Turner.

turnbuckle. A mechanical device, a link that can be lengthened or shortened by turning a moving threaded part in the center; used for tightening or setting up shrouds and other gear. Also called a rigging screw and by the British a bottlescrew. The ends of a turn-buckle may be fitted with either an eye or a shackle (clevis). If both ends have shackles it is a jaw-and-jaw turnbuckle; with both ends eyes it is an eye-and-eye turnbuckle, and if mixed it is a jaw-and-eye turnbuckle.

turning block. One used to change the direction of upper spinnaker and jib sheets.

turn of the bilge. *See* bilge.

turtle. A special container that holds the folded spinnaker on deck prior to hoisting. Also called a spinnaker bag and by the British a spinnaker chute.

turtle, sea. *See* sea turtle.

turtleback. The convex curved shape of the deck where the center is higher than the scuppers. Also described as turtledeck or whale-back.

tweaker. A line made fast to a sheet and used for fine adjustment of tension.

tweaker block. A single block on a tag line that is led to a block at the rail amidships and used for a spinnaker guy.

Twelve meter. A racing sloop rated at 12 meters. LOA 68′, beam 12′, draft 9′. Popular for international racing.

twiddling line. A small line used to steady the wheel or tiller. Also called a twigging line.

twingline. Relatively short light line used, when attached to a sail or a sheet, to adjust and improve the trim of a sail, particularly the spinnaker.

twilight. The period after sunset and before sunrise when the navigator can see both stars and the horizon. Civil twilight is that period beginning or ending with the sun 6° below the horizon. Observational twilight is 8°, nautical twilight 12°, and astronomical twilight is defined in terms of the sun being 18° below the horizon.

twin keels. A pair of fins on the bilges of a sailboat.

twin-sheet lead block. One designed to hold two sheets together close to the deck, usually the genoa and staysail sheets.

twin running sails. A pair of identical headsails, used without the mainsail and poled out on opposite sides for long down-wind passages.

two-blocked. Said of a tackle in which the blocks have been brought together block-and-block or chock-a-block.

Two Ten (210). A one-design keel sloop. LOA 30′, beam 6′, draft 4′. Designer: C.R. Hunt.

typhon. A sound signaling device that uses compressed air to sound a warning to ships in low visibility.

typhoon. A very violent tropical storm of the western Pacific and Indian ocean with winds over 64 knots. Same as hurricane, cyclone, and baguio.

U

UHF. *See* ultra high frequency.

ULCC. Ultra Large Crude Carrier, a supertanker larger than a VLCC, now over 500,000 tons and going up.

ultimate wave. *See* rogue wave.

Ultra High Frequency (UHF). 300–3000 megaHertz (MHz), wavelength 10–100 centimeters; used by some radars.

umiak. *See* kayak.

una-rig. *See* cat-rig.

unbend. To untie.

unbitt. To remove the turns of a line around a bitt.

under bowing. Sailing close to the wind with the set of the current against the lee bow, thus almost sailing directly into the wind.

underhauled. Describes a boat at anchor lying at an angle to its normal heading as a result of a subsurface current.

underrun. 1. To haul a boat or float under and along a hawser, cable chain, or trawl for examination, repair, or in the case of the trawl, to remove fish. 2. To underrun a tackle is to separate its parts so that it is ready for use.

under-stand. *See* under-stood.

under-stood. If the skipper in a sailboat beating up to a mark tacks too soon and thus must tack twice again, he has under-stood the mark. If he tacks too late and thus wastes time, he has over-stood the mark.

under the lee. Sheltered from the wind.

under the weather. Describes a ship affected, impeded, or damaged by weather. Now used to mean mildly sick when describing a person.

undertow. The brief downward thrust of a collapsing wave as it breaks on a beach. It can drive a swimmer down and underwater for a few seconds, but a rip current can carry a swimmer out to sea for a moderate distance. The two forces should not be confused.

underway. According to the Rules of the Road a vessel is underway when she is not at anchor, made fast to the shore or aground.

union. The emblem on a national flag or ensign signifying the union of two or more sovereignties, located in the upper inside corner. In the U.S. flag it is the stars representing the states. A flag flown with the union down is a sign of distress.

union jack. A flag consisting of the union or canton alone of the national flag if there is one; otherwise it is a small national flag. It is flown at a jackstaff in the bow of a vessel at anchor or moored.

universal time. As a refinement of mean time, Coordinated Universal Time (UTC) is established by the International Time Bureau using the atomic vibrations of cesium beam oscillators. This is the time broadcast as radio time signals.

unship. To remove from stowage, as a rudder is unshipped, or to take apart.

uphaul. A line on the mast of a windsurfer that pulls the sail up.

upset shackle. One in which the curved end or bow is fixed as in a block or at the lower end of a shroud.

upwelling. The rise of cold sea water from the depths of the ocean bringing up important nutrients.

urchin, sea. *See* sea urchin.

U.S. Coast and Geodetic Survey. Now known as the National Ocean Survey, part of the National Oceanic and Atmospheric Administration.

U.S. Navy Hydrographic Office. Now known as the Hydrographic Center of the Defense Mapping Agency.

US-1. A one-design centerboard catboat. LOA 15½', beam 4½'. Designer: Ralph Kupersmith.

U.S. Power Squadron. A nonprofit organization of powerboat owners devoted to promoting the interests of boat owners, boat safety, and the teaching of navigation and seamanship.

USYRU. The U.S. Yacht Racing Union. *See* NAYRU.

UTC. *See* universal time.

V

Vanguard. A one-design keel sloop. LOA 32½', beam 9¼', draft 4½'. Designer: P.L. Rhodes.

vane. A device made of metal or cloth that is free to rotate on a masthead in order to indicate the relative wind direction.

vane steering gear. *See* wind vane.

vang. A rope or wire used to support or hold in place a spar, boom, or derrick. In a cargo ship it holds the cargo boom in place; if rigged with a block it is a vang purchase. In a sailboat it is the tackle used to keep the boom from lifting and is called a boom vang, boom jack, kicking strap, kicker or martingale. In some sailboats it may be a steel rod whose length can be changed by a screw device; others may use a pivoting vang, a lever vang or a bull-ring vang. The latter has one end made fast to the boom and the other to a traveler carriage that moves on a semicircular track under the boom.

variable pitch propeller. One whose blades can rotate to change pitch.

variation. The angle between the bearing of the magnetic north pole and the actual north pole, measured east or west. It changes with the geographical position of the ship and with time and is indicated on most charts. Sometimes inaccurately called magnetic declination. Together with deviation (errors associated with the ship) it forms the magnetic compass error.

vary luff. *See* jerk string.

vee-bottom hull. Describes the hull of a powerboat that is relatively beamy with hard (straight) chines from bow to transom and has a v-shaped bottom. This hull, given enough power, is faster than a displacement hull because it can plane. There are also modified vee bottoms and deep vee bottoms. *See* displacement hull, hull, hydroplane.

V drive. An arrangement of motor and propeller in a boat in which the engine is placed farther aft than usual, and drives the propeller shaft through a gearbox forward.

veer. 1. To pay out or slack off, as the anchor rode is veered to gain a greater scope. 2. Most lines are veered but sheets are slacked or checked. Sometimes used as a synonym for haul in describing a clockwise shift of wind direction. *See* back.

vendaval. A strong southwest wind off Gibralter in winter.

Verity skiff. A small clinker-built work and fishing boat developed on the southwest shore of Long Island.

vertex. That part of a great circle of a sphere that is closest to a pole of that sphere. *See* composite sailing.

vertical cut. Describes a sail in which the cloths or pieces sewn together lie parallel to the leech.

very high frequency (VHF). 30–300 megaHertz (MHz), wave length 1–10 meters, used for communications, TV and FM.

Very pistol. A hand-held device for firing pyrotechnic distress signals such as parachute flares. Spoken: veery.

vessel. According to the International Rules of the Road, vessel "includes every description of water craft, including non-displacement craft such as surface effect ships and seaplanes, used, or capable of being used, as a means of transportation on water." A power-driven vessel is one propelled by machinery; a sailing vessel is one propelled by sail alone. *See* give-way vessel, not-under-command, stand-on vessel.

Vessel Traffic System (VTS). A system of ship control operated by the Coast Guard in congested waters such as Puget Sound and San Francisco Bay, using radar and voice radio.

VHF. *See* very high frequency.

vigia. Once used on most charts to indicate a possible reef or pinnacle, now replaced for the most part by PD—position doubtful, or ED—existence doubtful.

visibility. Degrees of visibility are indicated in the following generally accepted scale: 0—dense fog, objects not seen at 50 yds. 1—thick fog, objects not seen at 200 yds. 2—fog, objects not seen at 500 yds. 3—moderate fog, objects not seen at one-half mile. 4—thin fog, not seen at 1 mile. 5—poor visibility, not seen at 2 miles. 6—moderate visibility, not seen at 5 miles. 7—good visibility, not seen at 10 miles. 8—very good visibility, not seen at 30 miles. 9—excellent visibility, objects seen over 50 miles away.

Vixen. A one-design sloop-rigged fiberglass centerboard dinghy. LOA 10′, beam 4½′. Designed and built by Greene and Co.

V-jam. A type of jam cleat used in sailboats.

VLCC. Very Large Crude Carrier, up to about 200,000 tons. *See* ULCC.

vmg. The component of a sailboat's speed made good, in the direction of the true wind while sailing to windward.

volt. A measure of pressure behind the flow of electricity.

Voss drogue. A patented folding cone-shaped drogue fitted with cross bars to maintain its shape when open.

voyage. A journey by sea that includes both outward and homebound passages.

VTS. Vessel Traffic System.

W

waist. The central or middle part of a ship, between poop and forecastle above the main deck.

wake. The disturbed water astern and alongside of a moving boat. Because of skin friction the water nearest the hull is pulled along creating a wake current in which the propeller turns and which affects the efficiency of the propeller.

wakesurfing. Riding the wake waves of a boat on a surfboard.

walk back. A turnbuckle may walk back or loosen due to vibration.

walk out. A ship's anchor is walked out, meaning eased out slowly, before letting go in deep water. Also called backing out.

wall knot. One made at the end of a rope by back-splicing the ends, thus forming a knob.

wallow. Describes a boat that rolls heavily in a seaway.

wardrobe. All the sets or suits of sails of a sailboat.

warp. *n.* A rope or hawser used in shifting a vessel from one berth to another or in making fast to a pier. In the latter case it would more often be called a mooring line. Boatmen often call their anchor rode a warp. *vb.* To warp a vessel is to move it by means of warping lines or warps.

warping bollard. *See* checking bollard.

wash. *n.* 1. Disturbed, agitated water caused by, for example, moving propellers, oars, paddles, or breaking waves on rocks. Also called swash. 2. The sound of agitated water. 3. A flat area in a bay or inlet that is sometimes exposed, or a marshy place. *vb.* A man may be washed overboard. *See* swash.

washboard. A strake of thin planking above the gunwales of an open boat to keep out spray and water. Also called a wash strake.

weatherboard, splashboard or waste board. Any removable board or barrier that keeps out water such as the one across a companionway.

washover. A small delta built up by sediment washing over a bar into a lagoon, perhaps by storm waves. Also called a wave delta.

wash strake. *See* washboard.

waste board. *See* washboard.

watch. *n.* Most duties at sea are done in watches of different lengths depending on the number and skill of the men available. A team of men on watch at the same time is a watch. *vb.* To watch, in reference to a floating object, is to be visible as the anchor buoy is reported as watching.

watch buoy. A marker buoy moored near a lightship, for example, so that an anchored position may be verified.

watch cap. The blue knitted cap often worn by seamen.

watch coat. A heavy dark blue or black knee-length coat or reefer worn at sea in cold weather.

water deck iron. An iron collar or flange to keep water out where the stovepipe enters a boat.

water gall. *See* wind dog.

waterjet. A propulsion system for boats in which the propeller is replaced by a pump-driven stream of water expelled aft at high velocity. Also called jet drive.

water marks. The numerals on a ship's stern and her stem indicating draft. Also the numerals on a tide gauge.

waterspout. A local, violent rotary wind storm over water, similar to a tornado ashore, marked by a funnel-shaped cloud that picks up a mass of water where it touches down. This water is called a bush and can be dangerous to boats.

watt. A measure of power, the ability of electricity to do work. Volts times amperes equals watts in direct current.

wave. A moving ridge or swell of water caused usually by wind and moving at about half the wind's speed. The particles of water in each wave move vertically in a rough circle and thus remain stationary except for the tops of breaking waves. *See* blind rollers, ground wave, sea state, seismic sea wave, surf, swell, tidal wave.

wave, bow. That formed by the pressure of the advancing bow of a boat.

wave delta. *See* washover.

wave direction. Direction from which the wave comes.

wave height. Vertical distance in feet between the trough and the crest of a wave. Significant height is the average of the highest one-third of the waves measured. *See* rogue wave, sea state.

wavelength. The distance between crests of adjacent waves. Also the distance traveled by a radio wave during one cycle, in centimeters and meters.

wave refraction. The change in direction of a wave train caused by the reduced speed in shallow water.

wave, rogue. *See* rogue wave.

wave, standing. A stationary wave in which the surface of the water oscillates vertically without moving forward.

wave train. A series of waves, a wave system, all moving together in the same direction.

way. Motion through the water; a ship is legally underway, although she may have no way on, when she is not attached to the shore, at anchor or moored. A boat has headway when going forward and sternway when going astern.

way enough. A command by the coxswain of a pulling boat to his oarsmen to stop pulling.

Wayfarer. A one-design centerboard sloop. LOA 16′, beam 6′. Designer: Ian Proctor.

ways. Short for slipway, ground way or launching way.

wear, wearing. Same as jibe, although the latter may be accidental while a sailboat wears deliberately.

weather. *n.* 1. The side facing the wind, opposite to the lee side, is the weather side. 2. To make heavy weather is to struggle and suffer stress in bad weather; also used to describe a sailor ashore under the influence. *vb.* 1. To weather a cape is to pass it safely. To weather bitt a line is to take an extra turn around it.

weather board. *See* washboard.

weather cloth. A piece of canvas rigged to protect someone or something from the elements. Also called a dodger.

weathercocks. Said of a boat that comes up into the wind easily.

weather deck. Topside, any uncovered deck.

weather gauge. Position to windward of another ship; eagerly sought by racing sailors.

weather glass. A barometer.

weatherly. Describes a sailboat that sails with minimum heel in a strong breeze and thus can sail close to the wind.

weather ship. A ship assigned to a particular ocean area where it reports, for example, pressure, temperature, wind and sea state. Also called an ocean station ship.

wedge cleat. *See* cleat.

weep. A slight leak, as from a cask or along a seam.

weigh. To raise or lift, particularly an anchor.

weir. A sort of fence set at right angle to the shore to catch fish. Often lighted at night if in navigable waters. Also the dam near a lock in a canal or river.

well-found. Describes a boat that is well-equipped and in good material condition.

Western Ocean. The ancient name for the Atlantic, still used by some European mariners.

Western Rivers Rules. *See* Inland Rules of the Road.

West Wight Potter. A one-design centerboard sloop. LOA 14', beam 5½'. Designer: HMS Marine Inc.

West Wind Drift. Same as the Antarctic Circumpolar Current.

wet dock. Part of a port or harbor, a basin enclosed by gates in order to maintain an adequate level of water when there is considerable tidal range. *See* dock. Also called a wet basin.

wet suit. A close-fitting flexible foam rubber suit that permits some water next to the wearer's skin, but provides an insulating barrier. Worn by divers, surfers, water skiers, and others.

whale. A sea-going, air-breathing mammal whose tail is horizontal rather than vertical like that of a fish. There are toothed whales such as porpoise, and sperm whales and the baleen whales such as the blue and the gray. Whales are friendly, highly intelligent creatures, and, for the most part, are being killed to extinction.

whaleback. *See* turtleback.

whaleboat. Originally a double-ended, seaworthy pulling boat, now usually fitted with a diesel engine.

wharf. A structure parallel to the shore to which ships moor for loading and unloading and for minor repairs. Sometimes called a dock or quay but the latter is usually a solid structure whereas a wharf is built on pilings. *See* dock, pier.

wharfage. The charge made for the use of a wharf or pier.

wheelhouse. *See* pilothouse.

whelps. The ribs or ridges on the drum of a capstan, winch, or windlass that provide friction for the rope being hauled. Those on a wildcat fit the links of the anchor chain.

wherry. A light pulling boat with a transom stern.

whip. A rope or wire used as part of a tackle. To whip a rope's end is to wrap it with small stuff to prevent fagging.

whisker pole. A spar used to hold out the clew of a jib when sailing before the wind.

whisker stays. Shrouds providing lateral support to the bowsprit.

whitecaps. The broken water at the top of a wave that is breaking because of wind pressure. They generally start to form when the wind reaches 12 knots. Also called white horses and Neptune's sheep.

white horses. Same as whitecaps.

whiteout. An optical phenomenon encountered in low visibility in polar regions when clouds, shadows, and the horizon are not visible, resulting in severe disorientation.

whoodings. The planks in a wooden boat that fit into the stem.

Wianno Jr. A one-design centerboard sloop. LOA 16½', beam 6'.

Wianno Sr. A one-design keel and centerboard sloop. LOA 25', beam 8', draft 2½'. Designer of the Wiannos: H.M. Crosby.

Widgeon. A one-design centerboard sloop. LOA 12½', beam 5'. Designer: Robert Baker.

wildcat. The chain grab or cable holder drum on an anchor windlass that is fitted with whelps shaped to engage the links of the chain.

Wilderness 21. A one-design keel sloop designed for class racing as well as family use. LOA 21', beam 7', draft 4'. Designer: Chuck Burns.

williwaw. A sudden, violent wind blowing off a mountainous coast, particularly in the Aleutians and in the Straits of Magellan.

willy-willy. Australian word for a tropical storm (cyclone) with winds over 64 knots.

winch. A powered mechanical device used to haul in rope and wire for fishing, cargo handling, etc. Ship winches have horizontal drums and are sometimes called capstans or windlasses, although the latter are normally used to haul in anchors and are known as anchor windlasses. In sailboats winches are usually man-powered, geared, multispeed, and expensive and are used to handle sail quickly when racing. Slang term is coffee grinder or grinder.

wind. Air movement across the earth's surface, largely the result of differences in atmospheric pressure in adjacent air masses. Wind is identified by the direction from which it blows and by local names. Winds may be semipermanent (trade winds), seasonal (monsoon), daily (solar winds), sometimes very violent (typhoons), or irregular due to the movement of high and low pressure atmospheric systems. For wind shift definitions *see* back.

Windmill. A one-design centerboard sloop. LOA 15½', beam 5'. Designer: Clark Mills.

wind dog. A broken or partial rainbow that is supposed to predict wind. Also called a wind gall or watergall.

Windex. An arrow at the top of a mast that indicates the direction of the apparent wind.

windfinder. Another name for a ghoster or drifter.

wind gall. Same as wind dog.

Windigo. *See* jibe.

windjammer. A sailing ship, traditionally a square-rigger. Also the sailor who manned such a ship. Now any sailboat without auxilliary power.

windlass. A mechanical device on the forecastle used to haul in the anchor and to handle lines such as mooring lines. The anchor chain feeds over a revolving steel drum called a wildcat. One or two horizontal drums or heads are used to handle lines and are known as gipsy or warping heads, warping ends or whipping drums.

wind-rode. Said of a boat at anchor lying bow to wind, as opposed to lying bow to tide or tide-rode.

windrose. A diagram, usually on a pilot chart, showing the strength and direction of the prevailing winds in a certain area at a certain time of year.

windsail. A canvas tube with an open mouth rigged to send fresh air below decks. Also called a galley staysail.

windseeker. A sailor's word for any headsail he may use to improve his speed in very light airs. *See* drifter.

windscoop. A portable metal scoop fitted into a porthole to divert ventilating air.

wind sock. A tubular cloth wind direction indicator, usually on a flagstaff.

windsurfing. The sport of sailing a specially designed surfboard by standing on the board while holding a sail rigged on a fully articulated mast. Called boardsailing outside of the U.S. and also called surfsailing, it has become immensely popular worldwide.

Windsurfer. A one-design daggerboard catboat. LOA 12′, beam 2′. Designer: Hoyle Schweitzer.

windtuft. *See* telltale.

windward. The direction from which the wind blows, opposite to leeward.

windward staysail. A small staysail used in going to windward with a double-headed rig.

wind vane. A self-steering device for sailboats that is connected to the rudder and is actuated by wind pressure on the vane. Also called vane steering gear.

wing and wing. Describes a sailboat running before the wind with sails rigged out on both sides.

wing mast. One shaped like an airfoil to reduce turbulence and drag.

wing tanks. Tanks that are the farthest outboard.

wire drag. To establish with certainty a safe depth of water by dragging a weighted wire between two boats at a fixed depth.

wire rope. Rope made from steel wire galvanized, uncoated, or stainless, either wound around a fiber core to ensure flexibility or solid.

wishbone. A sail rig for sailboats that has a double gaff in the approximate shape of a wishbone.

witching. A procedure in sailing to windward through a narrow cut or canal by using bank cushion to reduce leeway.

woodlock. A close-fitting piece of hard wood fitted and secured below a rudder pintle to prevent the rudder from unshipping.

Wood Pussy. A one-design centerboard catboat. LOA 13½′, beam 6′. Designer: P.L. Rhodes.

World Port Index. DMAHC publication 150, a companion volume to the new Sailing Directions, giving detailed information about the ports of the world.

working sails. *See* sails.

worm, parcel, and serve. To worm a rope is to fill the grooves between strands with tarred small stuff. Parceling is wrapping with strips of canvas, and then the rope is wrapped or served with tight turns of marline.

worm shoe. A protective piece at the bottom of the keel of a wooden boat.

wrack. Seaweed cast ashore and collected for fertilizer.

wrecking block. A very large strong block used for salvage work and heavy lifts.

wring. To bend or twist a spar out of line when stays are set too tight.

wrister. A woolen wrist and arm covering used by fishermen when working at sea in cold wind and water.

wye. A metal band around a mast or spar on which one or more eyes are welded.

Y

yacht. Any vessel used for pleasure. Lloyds classifies any pleasure boat over 30′ long as a yacht. The owner is a yachtsman who may keep his boat at a yacht club when not yachting. The word connotes a certain pretension and an owner never refers to his boat as a yacht unless he is a landlubber.

yacht ensign. A flag adopted by the U.S. Congress for yachts only. It shows only 13 stars in the union, together with a fouled anchor.

yachtsman's anchor. Same as old-fashioned anchor.

yankee. A high-cut jib, similar to a genoa but with less overlap, used by sailboats in moderate weather.

yard. A large round spar, tapering towards the ends, used for supporting and extending sails.

yard-arm. Either extremity of a yard that is rigged perpendicular to a mast.

yarn. One of the fiber threads which when twisted together form a strand.

yaw. A temporary change from a boat's course, usually caused by a following sea. A boat is said to yaw when it rotates around a vertical axis. *See* ship motion.

yawl. A two-masted fore-and-aft rigged sailboat with the smaller mizzenmast or jigger mast located abaft the waterline aft, usually abaft the rudder post or tiller. *See* ketch. Also a small double-ended pulling boat.

yawl boat. A small powerboat used to tow a vessel.

Y-flyer. A one-design centerboard sloop. LOA 18′, beam 6′. Designer: A.M. Youngquist.

Yngling. A one-design keel sloop. LOA 21′, beam 6′, draft 3½′. Designer: Jan Linge.

yoke. As commonly found in a boat, a crosspiece fitted to the rudderhead from which wires or chains lead to the steering gear.

Z

Z drive. Same as stern drive.

zenith. The point in the celestial sphere directly overhead.

Zenith. A one-design centerboard sloop. LOA 14½′, beam 6′. Designer: Ian Proctor.

zinc. A piece of zinc fastened near the propeller or other brass or bronze fitting to absorb the corrosive effect of galvanic action in sea water in a boat with a steel hull.

zone description (zd). The correction, plus or minus 1 to 12 to be applied to local time to obtain Greenwich Mean Time.

zone time (zt). An international system of relating local time to Greenwich Mean Time and thus relating different local times to each other. The world is divided into zones 15° wide over which the sun passes in 1 hour. The zones start at longitude zero, Greenwich, with 7.5° on each side, and are numbered plus and minus 1 to 12 with plus being west longitude. A ship at longitude 50° W, for example, will keep +3 time.

zulu time. Another term for Greenwich Mean Time since when the latter is used in rapid communications it is followed by z to show that it is GMT and not local time.

Ref.
GV775
.N58

Noel

The boating dictionary